SPEECH ACTS IN E

Speech acts, those actions carried out mainly by means of language, are used in English in a range of complex ways. However, they have rarely been covered in English as a foreign language (EFL) materials and textbooks. Bringing together current theories from pragmatics and cognitive linguistics, this book addresses this gap by providing a comprehensive model of directive speech acts and showing how to teach them to learners of English. It provides a review of the strengths and weaknesses of current theories of illocution and a critical assessment of existing EFL textbooks. Descriptions of the meaning and form of directive speech act constructions are given in the cognitive pedagogical grammar of directive speech acts (included), which offers a wealth of examples to make the information accessible to non-specialist readers. The book also provides a wide range of practical activities, showing how research on illocutionary acts can be implemented in practice.

LORENA PÉREZ-HERNÁNDEZ is a tenured associate professor of linguistics at the University of Rioja. Her recent publications include *Illocution and Cognition*. She is a member of the editorial board of the *Review of Cognitive Linguistics*, the *Human Cognitive Processing Series*, and the *International Journal of Marketing Semiotics and Discourse Studies*.

STUDIES IN ENGLISH LANGUAGE

General editor
Merja Kytö (Uppsala University)

Editorial Board
Bas Aarts (University College London)
John Algeo (University of Georgia)
Susan Fitzmaurice (University of Sheffield)
Christian Mair (University of Freiburg)
Charles F. Meyer (University of Massachusetts)

The aim of this series is to provide a framework for original studies of English, both present-day and past. All books are based securely on empirical research, and represent theoretical and descriptive contributions to our knowledge of national and international varieties of English, both written and spoken. The series covers a broad range of topics and approaches, including syntax, phonology, grammar, vocabulary, discourse, pragmatics and sociolinguistics, and is aimed at an international readership.

Already published in this series:

Haruko Momma: *From Philology to English Studies: Language and Culture in the Nineteenth Century*
Raymond Hickey (ed.): *Standards of English: Codified Varieties around the World*
Benedikt Szmrecsanyi: *Grammatical Variation in British English Dialects: A Study in Corpus-Based Dialectometry*
Daniel Schreier and Marianne Hundt (eds.): *English as a Contact Language*
Bas Aarts, Joanne Close, Geoffrey Leech and Sean Wallis (eds.): *The Verb Phrase in English: Investigating Recent Language Change with Corpora*
Martin Hilpert: *Constructional Change in English: Developments in Allomorphy, Word Formation, and Syntax*
Jakob R. E. Leimgruber: *Singapore English: Structure, Variation, and Usage*
Christoph Rühlemann: *Narrative in English Conversation: A Corpus Analysis of Storytelling*
Dagmar Deuber: *English in the Caribbean: Variation, Style and Standards in Jamaica and Trinidad*
Eva Berlage: *Noun Phrase Complexity in English*
Nicole Dehé: *Parentheticals in Spoken English: The Syntax-Prosody Relation*
Jock O. Wong: *The Culture of Singapore English*
Marianne Hundt (ed.): *Late Modern English Syntax*
Irma Taavitsainen, Merja Kytö, Claudia Claridge and Jeremy Smith (eds.): *Developments in English: Expanding Electronic Evidence*
Arne Lohmann: *English Coordinate Constructions: A Processing Perspective on Constituent Order*

Nuria Yáñez-Bouza: *Grammar, Rhetoric and Usage in English: Preposition Placement 1500–1900*
Anita Auer, Daniel Schreier and Richard J. Watts (eds.): *Letter Writing and Language Change*
John Flowerdew and Richard W. Forest: *Signalling Nouns in English: A Corpus-Based Discourse Approach*
Jeffrey P. Williams, Edgar W. Schneider, Peter Trudgill and Daniel Schreier (eds.): *Further Studies in the Lesser-Known Varieties of English*
Jack Grieve: *Regional Variation in Written American English*
Douglas Biber and Bethany Gray: *Grammatical Complexity in Academic English: Linguistics Change in Writing*
Gjertrud Flermoen Stenbrenden: *Long-Vowel Shifts in English, c. 1050–1700: Evidence from Spelling*
Zoya G. Proshina and Anna A. Eddy (eds.): *Russian English: History, Functions, and Features*
Raymond Hickey (ed.): *Listening to the Past: Audio Records of Accents of English*
Phillip Wallage: *Negation in Early English: Grammatical and Functional Change*
Marianne Hundt, Sandra Mollin and Simone E. Pfenninger (eds.): *The Changing English Language: Psycholinguistic Perspectives*
Joanna Kopaczyk and Hans Sauer (eds.): *Binomials in the History of English: Fixed and Flexible*
Alexander Haselow: *Spontaneous Spoken English: An Integrated Approach to the Emergent Grammar of Speech*
Christina Sanchez-Stockhammer: *English Compounds and Their Spelling*
David West Brown: *English and Empire: Language History, Dialect, and the Digital Archive*
Paula Rodríguez-Puente: *The English Phrasal Verb, 1650-present: History, Stylistic Drifts, and Lexicalisation*
Erik. R. Thomas (ed.): *Mexican American English: Substrate Influence and the Birth of an Ethnolect*
Thomas Hoffmann: *English Comparative Correlatives: Diachronic and Synchronic Variation at the Lexicon-Syntax Interface*
Nuria Yáñez-Bouza, Emma Moore, Linda van Bergen and Willem B. Hollmann (eds.): *Categories, Constructions, and Change in English Syntax*
Raymond Hickey (ed.): *English in the German-speaking World*
Axel Bohmann: *Variation in English World-wide: Registers and Global Varieties*
Raymond Hickey (ed.): *English in Multilingual South Africa: The Linguistics of Contact and Change*
Jeremy J. Smith: *Transforming Early English: The Reinvention of Early English and Older Scots*
Tobias Bernaisch: *Gender in World Englishes*

Earlier titles not listed are also available

SPEECH ACTS IN ENGLISH

From Research to Instruction and Textbook Development

LORENA PÉREZ-HERNÁNDEZ
University of Rioja, Spain

CAMBRIDGE
UNIVERSITY PRESS

CAMBRIDGE UNIVERSITY PRESS

Shaftesbury Road, Cambridge CB2 8EA, United Kingdom

One Liberty Plaza, 20th Floor, New York, NY 10006, USA

477 Williamstown Road, Port Melbourne, VIC 3207, Australia

314–321, 3rd Floor, Plot 3, Splendor Forum, Jasola District Centre, New Delhi – 110025, India

103 Penang Road, #05–06/07, Visioncrest Commercial, Singapore 238467

Cambridge University Press is part of Cambridge University Press & Assessment, a department of the University of Cambridge.

We share the University's mission to contribute to society through the pursuit of education, learning and research at the highest international levels of excellence.

www.cambridge.org
Information on this title: www.cambridge.org/9781108700207
DOI: 10.1017/9781108677073

© Lorena Pérez-Hernández 2021

This publication is in copyright. Subject to statutory exception and to the provisions of relevant collective licensing agreements, no reproduction of any part may take place without the written permission of Cambridge University Press & Assessment.

First published 2021
First paperback edition 2023

A catalogue record for this publication is available from the British Library

Library of Congress Cataloging-in-Publication data
NAMES: Pérez-Hernández, Lorena, 1972- author.
TITLE: Speech acts in English : from research to instruction and textbook development / Lorena Pérez-Hernández.
DESCRIPTION: New York : Cambridge University Press, 2020. | Series: Studies in English language | Includes bibliographical references and index.
IDENTIFIERS: LCCN 2020020666 (print) | LCCN 2020020667 (ebook) | ISBN 9781108476324 (hardback) | ISBN 9781108700207 (paperback) | ISBN 9781108677073 (ebook)
SUBJECTS: LCSH: Speech acts (Linguistics) | English language–Study and teaching–Foreign speakers.
CLASSIFICATION: LCC P95.55 .P46 2020 (print) | LCC P95.55 (ebook) | DDC 401/.452–dc23
LC record available at https://lccn.loc.gov/2020020666
LC ebook record available at https://lccn.loc.gov/2020020667

ISBN 978-1-108-47632-4 Hardback
ISBN 978-1-108-70020-7 Paperback

Cambridge University Press & Assessment has no responsibility for the persistence or accuracy of URLs for external or third-party internet websites referred to in this publication and does not guarantee that any content on such websites is, or will remain, accurate or appropriate.

To my mother Aurora, the best one I could have wished for, who waited to see this project through.

To my father Luciano, who worked hard all his life to provide me with what he never had.

To my sister Mila, who has always been a second mother and the best of friends.

To my niece Arsema and my daughters Lucía and Payal, who are three dreams come true, who warm my heart with joy and laughter every day, and who represent the most optimistic of all speech acts:

they are a PROMISE of love, future, and life.

Contents

List of Figures	*page* xii
List of Tables	xiii
Acknowledgements	xv
List of Abbreviations	xvi

1	Introduction	1
	1.1 Teaching Directive Speech Acts: Is There Room for Improvement?	1
	1.2 Objectives	5
	1.3 Methodology	10
	1.4 Chapter Contents	13
2	What Contemporary Research Tells Us about Speech Acts	16
	2.1 Speech Acts: The Player All Linguistic Theories Want in Their Team	16
	2.2 Team 1. Codification-Based Theories and the Over-Grammaticalisation of Speech Acts	18
	2.2.1 Weaknesses of the Literal Force Hypothesis and Ross's Performative Hypothesis	18
	2.2.2 Halliday's Over-Grammaticalisation of Speech Acts	20
	2.3 Team 2. Convention-Based Theories: Indirect Speech Acts	23
	2.3.1 Searle: Inference and Convention in Speech Acts	23
	2.3.2 Morgan's Conventions of Usage and Short-Circuiting Implicatures	26
	2.4 Team 3. Inference-Based Theories: Over-Pragmatisation of Speech Acts	27
	2.4.1 Standard Pragmatics Approach: Bach and Harnish's Speech Act Schemas	28
	2.4.2 Direct Access Approaches I: Leech's Interpersonal Rhetoric	29
	2.4.3 Direct Access Approaches II: Conversational Approaches	32
	2.5 A Cognitive-Constructional Approach to Directive Speech Acts	35
	2.5.1 What Experimental Linguistics Has Revealed about Speech Act Processing	35
	2.5.2 Redefining the Literal Force Hypothesis in terms of Sentence Type/Speech Act Compatibility	39

	2.5.3	Revisiting the Notions of Direct and Indirect Speech Acts	43
	2.5.4	Constraining Inferences via Cognitive Operations: Conceptual Metonymy	48
	2.5.5	Illocutionary Idealised Cognitive Models and (Multiple Source)-in-Target Metonymies	50
	2.5.6	Assembling the Illocutionary Puzzle: Families of Illocutionary Constructions	60

3 Critical Assessment of the Representation of Speech Acts in Advanced EFL Textbooks   69
- 3.1 Analytical Categories and Corpus of Textbooks for Analysis   70
- 3.2 Quantitative Assessment of the Treatment of Directive Speech Acts in Advanced EFL Textbooks   73
- 3.3 Qualitative Assessment of the Treatment of Directive Speech Acts in Advanced EFL Textbooks   77
    - 3.3.1 Inclusion of Semantic/Pragmatic Information about Speech Acts   77
    - 3.3.2 Treatment of the Constructional Nature of Directive Speech Acts   80
    - 3.3.3 Treatment of Conversational Aspects of Directive Speech Acts   82
    - 3.3.4 Treatment of Cross-Cultural and Cross-Linguistic Areas of Discrepancy between L1 and L2   84
- 3.4 Conclusions and Way Forward: Explicit Instruction through a Corpus-Based Cognitive Pedagogical Grammar   85

4 A Cognitive Pedagogical Grammar of Directive Speech Acts I: Know-What and Know-How of Directives   88
- 4.1 Orders   89
    - 4.1.1 The Know-What of Orders   90
    - 4.1.2 The Know-How of Orders   96
- 4.2 Requests   102
    - 4.2.1 The Know-What of Requests   103
    - 4.2.2 The Know-How of Requests   110
- 4.3 Beggings   120
    - 4.3.1 The Know-What of Beggings   123
    - 4.3.2 The Know-How of Beggings   130
- 4.4 Suggestions   136
    - 4.4.1 The Know-What of Suggestions   137
    - 4.4.2 The Know-How of Suggestions   143
- 4.5 Advice Acts   152
    - 4.5.1 The Know-What of Advice Acts   152
    - 4.5.2 The Know-How of Advice Acts   159
- 4.6 Warnings   169
    - 4.6.1 The Know-What of Warnings   170
    - 4.6.2 The Know-How of Warnings   177

5 A Cognitive Pedagogical Grammar of Directive
   Speech Acts II: Activities and Practice Materials   183
   5.1 Teaching the Know-What of Directives   186
   5.2 Teaching the Know-How of Directives   196
   5.3 Teaching Cross-Cultural and Cross-Linguistic Issues
       of Directives   208

6 Conclusions   218

   References   229
   Index   246

Figures

2.1	Cost–benefit and politeness interactions (Leech, 1983: 107)	*page* 31
2.2	Metonymic activation underlying examples (2.17) and (2.18)	53
2.3	Metonymic activation underlying examples (2.19)–(2.22)	55
2.4	(Multiple source)-in-target metonymic operation underlying the request act in example (2.23)	57
2.5	Conceptual motivation underlying the CAN vs. COULD YOU DO X? request constructions in examples (2.24) and (2.25)	58
4.1	Force schema underlying the conceptualisation of orders	90
4.2	Force schema underlying the conceptualisation of requests	103
4.3	Force schema underlying the conceptualisation of beggings	123
4.4	Force schema underlying the conceptualisation of suggestions	137
4.5	Force schema underlying the conceptualisation of advice acts	152
4.6	Force schema underlying the conceptualisation of warnings	169
5.1	Force dynamics of orders: S = speaker; F = force; H = hearer	187
5.2	Force dynamics of requests: S = speaker; F = force; H = hearer	187
5.3	Force dynamics of beggings: S = speaker; F = force; $H_{R/S}$ = hearer as rational/social being; H_A = hearer as agent	188
5.4	Force dynamics of suggestions: S = speaker; F = force; H_R = hearer as rational being; H_A = hearer as agent	189

Tables

2.1	Deep structure versus surface structure in question for information versus request interpretation	*page* 20
2.2	Attributes configuring the ONTOLOGY of directive illocutionary ICMs	51
2.3	Ontology for the illocutionary ICM of the act of requesting	52
2.4	Social variables configuring the STRUCTURE of directive illocutionary ICMs	59
2.5	STRUCTURE of the illocutionary ICM of the act of requesting in terms of interactions between attributes, as well as between attributes and social variables	60
2.6	Realisation procedures for the attributes of the ICM of requesting	65
2.7	Number of occurrences in iWeb for the realisation procedures of the requests in examples (2.27)–(2.31)	66
2.8	Base constructions for the act of requesting	67
2.9	Summary of contemporary theoretical advancements on speech acts	68
3.1	Range and distribution of exercises devoted to the teaching/practice of directive speech acts in advanced EFL textbooks	74
3.2	Analytical categories for the assessment of current EFL textbooks as regards their treatment of directive speech acts	77
4.1	The know-what of orders	96
4.2	Base constructions for the act of ordering in English	97
4.3	Imperative base construction + realisation procedures for orders	99
4.4	Comparison of base constructions for the act of ordering in English and Spanish	101
4.5	The know-what of requests	111
4.6	Base constructions for the act of requesting in English	113
4.7	Imperative base construction + realisation procedures for requests	114

4.8	Comparison of base constructions for the act of requesting in English and Spanish	121
4.9	The know-what of beggings	129
4.10	Base constructions for the act of begging in English	130
4.11	Imperative base construction + realisation procedures for beggings	131
4.12	Comparison of base constructions for the act of begging in English and Spanish	135
4.13	The know-what of suggestions	143
4.14	Base constructions for the act of suggesting in English	144
4.15	Imperative base constructions + realisation procedures for suggestions	145
4.16	Comparison of base constructions for the act of suggesting in English and Spanish	149
4.17	The know-what of advice acts	160
4.18	Base constructions for the act of advising in English	161
4.19	Realisation procedures for the act of advising	162
4.20	Imperative base construction + realisation procedures for the act of advising	164
4.21	Solicited and unsolicited bare imperative advice acts	165
4.22	Comparison of base constructions for the act of advising in English and Spanish	166
4.23	The know-what of warnings	176
4.24	Base constructions for the act of warning in English	178
4.25	Realisation procedures of the act of warning	180
4.26	Comparison of base constructions for the act of warning in English and Spanish	182
5.1	The know-what of suggestions	190
5.2	The know-what of requests (short version)	197
5.3	The know-what of requests (interactions between attributes and variables)	203
5.4	Linguistic realisation procedures for combination with request base constructions	205
5.5	Fieldwork, comparison, and discussion task	209
5.6	Base constructions for requests in English	210
5.7	Base constructions for requests in Spanish	212
5.8	Base constructions for advice acts in English	213
5.9	The know-what of advice acts (interactions with socio-contextual variables)	214
5.10	Discourse-completion task	215
5.11	Repair and comparison task	217

Acknowledgements

I would like to thank the two anonymous referees who read the initial book proposal. They helped me to see the weaknesses in my arguments and provided very good advice on how to improve them. I am also indebted to Dr Merja Kytö, the general editor of the Studies in English Language series, for her comments on the final draft of this book.

I would especially like to acknowledge Helen Barton, the commissioning editor for Linguistics at Cambridge University Press, and her editorial assistant Isabel Collins, who have been the most helpful allies in the process of writing this book, providing constant encouragement, and making every step of the way easy and enjoyable.

There are many people who have provided the necessary life scaffolding for me to be capable of writing this book. My small family, first and foremost, who are always there, generously offering the little time and energy they have to enable me to find the space to write. My friends (Ana, Nuria, Asun, Chelo, Josefina, Guillermo, and the rest of my dear 'Epicúreos', Alejandro, Miguel Ángel Longas, James Wong), those of the past and of the present, who have provided pragmatic and emotional support and the necessary happiness to face the long research hours. And especially in the last few years, the brave women in ASFAM (Pilar, Raquel, María, Silvia y Ester), who have opened up a bright path of hope in the power and possibilities of friendship, shared dreams, altruism, and joint human actions. My friend, Dr Karine Duvignau, who has so many times provided a shelter in Toulouse, one of the most beautiful cities in Europe, for me to write. My dearest friend and mentor Prof. Ruiz de Mendoza, who taught me to investigate language and to pay attention to detail.

All shortcomings are my own.

The investigation supporting the findings reported in this book has been financed by FEDER/Spanish Ministry of Science, Innovation and Universities, State Research Agency, project no. FFI2017-82730-P and by the University of La Rioja (PID Convocatoria 2019/20).

Abbreviations

A1	first starters level of proficiency
A2	second starters level of proficiency
BNC	British National Corpus
CARLA	Centre for Advance Research on Language Acquisition-University of Minnesota
CEFR	Common European Framework of Reference for Languages
CL	cognitive linguistics
CORPES XXI	Corpus del Español del Siglo XXI
CREA	Corpus de Referencia del Español Actual
C1	first advanced level of proficiency
C2	second advanced level of proficiency
EFL	English as a foreign language
F	force
FL	foreign language
H	hearer
H_A	hearer as agent
H_R	hearer as rational being
H_S	hearer as social being
ICM	idealised cognitive model
IFIDs	illocutionary force indicating devices
ISA	indirect speech act
L1	first, or native, language
L2	second/foreign language
S	speaker
TB1–TB10	textbooks 1–10

I

Introduction

1.1 Teaching Directive Speech Acts: Is There Room for Improvement?

Every day of our lives we use language to tell stories, to express feelings, to describe the world, and also, as was lucidly revealed by Austin (1962) in his book *How to Do Things with Words*, to perform actions. There are some things we do physically with our hands or legs, and others we do verbally by means of words. One essential thing we can do and often do primarily by means of language is to try to influence other people into a certain path of action. Thus, we can move them to do something in their benefit (by advising or warning them), in our own benefit (by ordering, requesting, or begging them), or in mutual benefit (i.e. by suggesting a common course of action). Actions of this kind, which we carry out linguistically and which have as their main objective to prompt our interlocutors to do something, are known in the literature as directive speech acts.

Directives are ubiquitous. We start producing them as soon as we learn to speak and, for the rest of our lives, we use them on a daily basis. Directives are useful because they allow us to attain our goals by persuading or pushing other people to act according to our wishes, but they are not free from risks. Using directive acts inappropriately can offend our interlocutors. As a result, the directive act may turn out to be ineffective and our goals may end up unfulfilled. Alternatively, we may succeed in getting the listener to carry out the desired action but at a high social cost. Human interaction is very sensitive to the use of directives, which are a potential source of interpersonal conflict.

Learning to produce directive speech acts correctly in a second or foreign language is a crucial but difficult task. Speech acts are rich, kaleidoscopic concepts, and their use involves juggling with many social, interactional, and contextual variables at once: the relative power of the speakers, their social closeness, the formality of the situation, or the cost–benefit of the action being requested, etc. These are only some of the factors that need to be considered by a speaker if she wants to produce a contextually and socially felicitous speech act that stands a chance to be successful. A request like *If you don't mind, would you please be so kind as to open the window?* functions well in a formal context or in a situation in which the speakers are strangers to each other, or one of them is more powerful than the other (e.g. an employee talking to her boss). However, the same request would most probably sound odd and possibly move the receptor to search for some ulterior hidden meaning (e.g. irony), if used among close friends in an informal setting.

In addition, directive speech acts do not have a unique linguistic form. The system of options offered by language is lavishly exploited in the production of speech acts, each directive displaying a rich array of possible linguistic realisations. Some of them are virtually synonymous (e.g. *If you don't mind, could you please open the window? – If it's not too much trouble, would you mind opening the window?*). Others differ in order to accommodate the directive act to the social/contextual variables at stake (e.g. *Please, could you open the window?* (formal context) versus *Open the window, will you?* (informal context)). As shall be made apparent in Chapter 4, the variety and wealth of forms and linguistic realisations involved in the production of each directive speech act is fascinating and a reflection of the creativeness, flexibility, and communicative power of language.

Their conceptual complexity and formal richness make the learning of directive speech acts a challenging, demanding, and often strenuous task for students of a foreign language. Nevertheless, the ability to perform and interpret speech acts correctly is an essential competence that needs to be acquired to master the use of a second language. Illocution has, therefore, become a pivotal aspect of language pedagogy. Shortly after the inception of speech act theory, textbooks of English as a foreign (or second) language (EFL) started including sections devoted to the teaching of speech acts. Several contemporary studies have made manifest, however, that speech acts are largely underrepresented in current EFL coursebook series (Vellenga, 2004; Ren & Han, 2016; Pérez-Hernández, 2019), and that their teaching presents several problematic issues: poor treatment of pragmatic use of the target language (Cohen & Ishihara, 2013); insufficient contextual information being provided (Harwood, 2014); and pragmatic strategies being unsystematically and stereotypically dealt with (McConachy & Hata, 2013). In addition, Pérez-Hernández (2019) has observed a disconnection between current research advancements on illocution and the extent to which they have found their way into textbooks and teaching materials.

This fissure between theory and practice is manifest in at least three main areas: (1) contrastive studies between first, or native, language (L1) and second/foreign language (L2); (2) cognitive analyses of the mental processes and operations that underlie the production and interpretation of speech acts; and (3) recent accounts on the idiosyncratic nature of illocutionary constructions.

More specifically, current EFL textbooks do not take advantage of contemporary studies on contrastive aspects of the performance of speech acts in native and foreign languages (Luomala, 2010; Neddar, 2012; Pérez-Hernández, 2019). The English directive construction *Can you pass me the salt, please?*, in which a question about the capacity of the listener to perform an action is used as a request for him to actually do the action, is also possible and comprehensible for Spanish speakers (e.g. *¿Me puedes pasar la sal, por favor?*). However, the latter is not a conventional, frequent way of requesting something in Spanish. Interestingly enough, the directive construction that Spanish speakers would use in the same context (e.g. *¿Me pasas la sal, por favor?*) does not have a literal counterpart in English (cf. **Do you pass me the salt, please?*). Coverage of this type of mismatch between L1 and L2 in the performance of speech acts has not reached the textbooks. This may cause EFL students to make mistakes in their production of speech acts in the L2 based on language interferences and faulty literal translations from their L1.

Present-day EFL textbooks also ignore relevant aspects of the cognition of speech acts. For the past three decades, cognitive linguistics has been mounting up evidence about the metonymic basis of speech act production (Gibbs, 1984, 1994; Pérez-Hernández, 1996, 2001, 2012, 2013, 2019; Panther & Thornburg, 1998, 2003, 2005; Pérez-Hernández & Ruiz de Mendoza, 2002, 2011; Ruiz de Mendoza & Baicchi, 2007; Del Campo, 2013; among others). Just as the painter (Picasso) metonymically stands for its work in *I just bought a Picasso*, it is also the case, in the production of a directive act, that asking about one of the preconditions for a successful request may activate the act of requesting as a whole. By way of illustration, the utterance *Have you got a pen, please?* literally asks about one of the preconditions that needs to be fulfilled for a request to be successful (i.e. the fact that the listener is in possession of the object that the speaker needs). However, in the appropriate context, this literal question about one of the preconditions of requests may metonymically stand for the full act of requesting and have a similar illocutionary force to that of an explicit request (e.g. *I request you to lend me a pen*). As shall become apparent in Chapters 2 and 4, awareness of this metonymical basis of speech act performance, as well as of other cognitive mechanisms (i.e. conceptual metaphor, force dynamics) that underlie the production and understanding of indirect directive acts, will prove essential in the design of more powerful and effective materials for their teaching.

Finally, lack of consideration of formal aspects of illocution, such as the existence of speech act constructions, is also flagrant in contemporary EFL textbooks. A reason that explains this may be the fact that illocutionary acts do not generally exhibit fixed form-meaning pairings, at least not in the sense in which form-meaning pairings are understood at other levels of linguistic description (Goldberg, 1995, 2006). Even conventional constructions for the expression of a specific directive can also often be interpreted literally with a different illocutionary meaning. This is the case with CAN YOU DO X? forms (e.g. *Can you pass me the salt?*), which in different situations can be used as either conventional requests or as questions about the listener's ability to physically perform the stated action. For decades, the observation that one linguistic form may have different illocutionary forces (e.g. request versus informative question), depending on the context in which it is used, led to the belief that a constructional treatment of illocution was unattainable. Speech acts were subsequently considered a pragmatic phenomenon dependent on inferential processes to a greater (Bach & Harnish, 1979; Leech, 1983, 2014; Levinson, 1983; Geis, 1995; Sperber & Wilson, 1995) or a lesser extent (Searle, 1969, 1975; Halliday, 1978, 1994; Morgan, 1978; Dik, 1989, 1997). Nevertheless, recent studies of how form and meaning are assembled in the expression of speech acts have revealed that it is, in fact, possible to speak of speech act constructions (Pérez-Hernández, 2001, 2013; Pérez-Hernández & Ruiz de Mendoza, 2002, 2011; Stefanowitsch, 2003; Mauri & Sansò, 2011; Del Campo, 2013; Vassilaki, 2017). As shall be argued in Chapters 2 and 4, illocutionary constructions are necessarily more flexible and more ductile than morphological, lexical, or syntactic constructions, and they exhibit different degrees of codification. Some of them are highly codified and, therefore, allow only for a directive reading. WOULD YOU MIND DOING X? constructions, as in *Would you mind lending me a pen?*, are highly unlikely to be interpreted with an illocutionary force different from that of a directive. Others lack full codification, but still display a certain amount of conventionalisation in the production of directives. I NEED X constructions, as in *I need a pen*, could be interpreted as simple assertions (i.e. *I need a pen. I am going to buy one*), but in the appropriate context they are highly conventionalised formulae for requesting people to do something for us. Their conventional use as directives is reflected in their high frequency of occurrence and in that they are compatible with some linguistic realisations that are typical of polite directives (e.g. requests, suggestions), such as the adverb *please* or question tags (i.e. *I need a pen, please; I need a pen, could you?*). Yet other illocutionary constructions fully hinge on inferential processes for their understanding as directives (e.g. *The pen has run out of ink*). To understand this example as a request, the listener would have to infer that (1) the speaker wants/needs a pen, and (2) that she is asking him to provide her with one. The lack of conventionality for the performance of directive speech acts of expressions of this type makes them less likely to be compatible with the use of politeness markers (i.e. ?*The pen has run out of ink, please*).

Speech act constructions are complex, interactive, and multifaceted. This is only to be expected if they are to adapt themselves to the changing and varied communicative needs of speakers in different contexts. Despite their prismatic nature, contemporary studies of speech acts have revealed that it is possible to build inventories of base constructions for each illocutionary act, together with repositories of additional linguistic realisation procedures that can be used to modulate their degree of explicitness and politeness to adapt them to the users' needs in different contexts (Pérez-Hernández, 2001, 2012, 2013). Once described and formalised, these illocutionary base constructions can be taught to students of an L2 to help them improve their illocutionary performance in the target language.

As argued in this section, there is still ample room for improvement in the treatment of directive speech acts in EFL textbooks. In addition, there exists an important gap between present-day theoretical knowledge on the performance of directives and its implementation in EFL teaching materials. This book fights the current state of the art in the teaching of speech acts and argues that neither the complexity of the illocutionary phenomenon itself, nor the attested disconnection between theoretical advancements and their pedagogical application, should prevent EFL textbooks from offering a richer and more accurate portrayal of directive speech acts in order to facilitate their learning by EFL students. To this aim, it offers a theoretically updated and psychologically valid account of directive speech acts translated into a set of instructions and practice materials for its use by EFL professionals.

1.2 Objectives

The present book identifies those aspects of speech act performance that are still underdeveloped in current EFL textbooks and applies recent research findings in the design of a specific set of instructions and practice materials for its effective teaching. In this regard, it responds to recent calls to implement contemporary research in the fields of applied and cognitive linguistics on the development of more solid textbooks for the teaching of EFL (Ishihara, 2010; Tomlinson, 2013; Achard, 2018).

By merging content and practical proposals to identify and solve present shortcomings in the description, explanation, and teaching of speech acts, this book offers a full-fledged theoretical architecture of the most representative and frequently used directive speech acts (i.e. ordering, requesting, begging, suggesting, advising, and warning), which incorporates contemporary research advancements in pragmatic, cognitive/constructional, and contrastive aspects of illocution. Theoretical contents are presented in the form of a corpus-based cognitive pedagogical grammar of directive speech acts. Practical teaching proposals are the result of exploiting and implementing this pedagogical grammar into a set of innovative exercises and activities that can improve current methods of teaching speech acts to advanced EFL students.

The instructional suggestions and teaching materials included in this book are based on a thorough investigation of the nature and functioning of illocutionary acts that brings together research advancements from diverse but compatible theoretical frameworks. This book represents, therefore, an attempt to find synergies between strong and relevant but so far isolated theoretical approaches to illocution. Pragmatic-functional, cognitive-constructional, and contrastive perspectives on illocutionary production and interpretation are brought together into a comprehensive framework that allows an all-encompassing, fine-grained treatment of illocutionary phenomena. The resulting corpus-based cognitive/constructional account of speech acts is also compatible with the experimental data stemming from current psycholinguistic studies on illocution. Nevertheless, as Achard (2018: 37) remarked in relation to the contribution of linguistic models to EFL practices, 'linguists have seldom made the effort to explicitly spell out the pedagogical ramifications of their theoretical positions, which makes it difficult for instructors to create appropriate activities in the classroom'. In this connection, this books also aims to bridge the existing gap between recent theoretical findings and their implementation in textbooks and teaching materials. Thus, the theoretical account on speech acts presented in Chapter 2 supports the subsequent design of instructions and practice materials for the teaching of speech acts to Spanish advanced EFL students in Chapters 4 and 5. While Chapter 2 contains an in-depth discussion on theoretical aspects of illocution and is, therefore, aimed at a more specialised readership

1.2 Objectives

(speech act and EFL theoreticians, postgraduate students of linguistics), Chapters 4 and 5 are presented in plain, largely jargon-free language to make the information accessible to designers of EFL instructors and textbooks interested in creating new teaching activities and materials for the EFL classroom.

According to the theoretical framework adopted for this investigation, it is argued that teaching how to perform directive speech acts correctly in a foreign language involves at least three main objectives.

1. Teaching the semantic and pragmatic attributes and variables that make up each directive speech act.
2. Teaching the base constructions and related linguistic realisation procedures that the language system offers for the instantiation of the semantic and pragmatic knowledge that characterises each directive speech act.
3. Teaching the areas of discrepancy between L1 and L2 that may result in difficulties to the EFL student.

Objectives (1) and (2) lead to a cognitive, constructional approach to the description of speech act categories as form-meaning pairings.

The knowledge that native speakers have about the meaning of each directive speech act under consideration will be captured in terms of illocutionary idealised cognitive models (ICMs) (Lakoff 1987; Pérez-Hernández, 2001, 2013). Illocutionary ICMs include information such as the communicative purpose for which the act is used (e.g. a request is used to ask the listener to do something in the speaker's benefit, while a piece of advice is used to tell the listener to do something in his own benefit), the social factors that need to be taken into consideration to decide on the most suitable linguistic form for the expression of the speech act in a particular context (i.e. the social distance between speakers, the relative power between them, etc.), the amount of politeness that the speech act requires (i.e. orders make use of social power to overcome politeness needs, while beggings require high amounts of politeness due to the condition of inferiority that affects the speaker), the social cost of performing a particular speech act (i.e. requests and orders are costly for the addressee, while pieces of advice and warnings are not), etc. In other words, illocutionary ICMs are exhaustive collections of the semantic and pragmatic attributes and variables that characterise the meaning and conceptual fabric of each directive speech act. In this manner, readers will be presented with a comprehensive and accessible description of the meaning side of each directive speech act type under consideration. Real language examples will be provided to illustrate the semantic and pragmatic components of each directive speech act and to highlight the differences and similarities between them.

The formal side of directives will be approached by offering the *base constructions* used in English for their expression. Together with the specific base constructions, this book also provides an exhaustive collection of related linguistic realisation procedures corresponding to each of the semantic and pragmatic components that define the speech acts under scrutiny. These linguistic realisation procedures are shown to be useful in further specifying the subtype of directive force of the speech act (i.e. order, request, piece of advice, warning, beg, or suggestion), in modulating the degree of explicitness or politeness of the directive act, and in adapting the illocutionary act to the interactional needs required by each context. Thus, it will be shown how a base construction like the CAN YOU DO X? interrogative question can be modulated into a request or a begging depending on the additional linguistic resources activated by the speaker (e.g. *Can you hold this for a second?* – request versus Please, please, please, *can you hold this?* – begging).

The complex conceptual nature of illocutionary acts makes it virtually impossible for speakers to explicitly verbalise all the semantic and pragmatic components defining a particular directive speech act. Thus, depending on contextual, social, and politeness requirements, a variable and limited number of such components are activated linguistically in an overt manner and, in so doing, they metonymically stand for the whole speech act. Indirect speech acts will be shown to be grounded on this type of metonymic cognitive operations that enable speakers to economically produce illocutions with different degrees of explicitness as required by the different contextual needs.

Objective (3) asks for careful comparison and consideration of the areas of overlap and contrast between a L2 and the learner's L1, as regards both the conceptual (i.e. meaning) and formal (i.e. linguistic realisations) aspects of speech act production included in objectives (1) and (2) above. Recent contrastive analyses show that languages have different constructions and constructional properties that are likely to cause transfer effects and faulty representations in a L2 (Hijazo-Gascón, Cadierno & Ibarretxe-Antuñano, 2016; Ruiz de Mendoza & Agustin, 2016). In fact, according to Holme (2009: 84), one of the main sources of errors for EFL students is their use of L1 forms and meanings when using an L2. This has prompted many voices within the cognitive linguistics paradigm to be raised in support of a greater acknowledgement of the pervasiveness and relevance of constructions in EFL teaching (Römer, O'Donnell & Ellis, 2014; Achard,

2018). Identifying the semantic, pragmatic, and formal mismatches between the two languages can help students to avoid those traps by serving 'the purpose of preparing teaching materials and exploiting these in L2/FL instruction' (De Knop & De Rycker, 2008: 2). Despite the relative youth of construction-based pedagogical approaches, experimental evidence on the psychological reality of constructions for EFL learners and the effectiveness of a pedagogical intervention based on the explicit teaching of form-meaning pairings is mounting up in the literature (Holme, 2010; Baicchi, 2016; Sung & Yang, 2016).

Altogether, objectives (1)–(3) advocate a contrastive, cognitive-constructional approach to the teaching of directive speech acts. One of the central tenets of cognitive linguistics is that language is composed of form-meaning pairings, also known as constructions (Goldberg, 1995, 2006; Langacker, 2008). Linguistic choices are paired with idealised representations of reality that include propositional, pragmatic, contextual, and cultural knowledge. Meaning is, therefore, understood in a broad sense, as the idealised collection of encyclopaedic knowledge that language users have about a topic. This view of language allows cognitive linguistics to explain the motivation of linguistic forms and makes of it a promising theoretical framework to inform EFL teaching practices and to guide the design of EFL didactic materials. As Jacobsen (2018: 669) puts it:

> Using select, carefully adapted for unprepared audiences, and contextualised CL concepts in L2 instruction can reveal the perspective of a native speaker and make form-meaning mappings relatively transparent for L2 learners. Accordingly, the underlying conceptual characteristics of CLs make it a good candidate for the role of providing a comprehensive theory that could successfully support L2 instruction (Achard & Niemeier 2004; Tyler & Evans 2004; Tyler 2012).

So far, as noted in Jacobsen (2012, 2015), there is mounting experimental, quantitative (Chen & Oller, 2008; Valenzuela & Rojo, 2008; Jacobsen, 2018), and qualitative evidence that these cognitive linguistics tenets can successfully be applied to the teaching of diverse aspects of language, such as phrasal verbs (Dirven, 2001; Liu, 2010), metaphorical/idiomatic language (Lindstromberg & Boers, 2005; Littlemore & Low, 2006; Boers & Lindstromberg, 2008; Yasuda, 2010), and grammar (prepositions: Lindstromberg, 1996; Tyler & Evans, 2004; Tyler, Mueller & Ho, 2011; tense and aspect: Niemeier & Reif, 2008). There is a notorious lack, however, of applications of cognitive linguistics to the teaching of higher levels of language description, among which there is the teaching of speech acts. As shall be explained in the next section, this book incorporates a contrastive, cognitive-constructional approach to directive speech acts into the EFL teaching practice and the design of EFL teaching materials based on explicit instruction.

1.3 Methodology

In accordance with the three objectives specified in the previous section, our proposal advocates an explicit instruction approach to the teaching of speech acts, which has already been proved to be more beneficial than implicit L2 teaching (Norris & Ortega, 2000; Ellis, 2001, 2002; Spada & Tomita, 2010), with specific studies providing evidence about its effectiveness on the realm of grammar (Sharwood Smith, 1981; Rutherford, 1987; Ellis, 2001), and, more recently, also of pragmatics (Taguchi, 2015; Tello Rueda, 2016). Explicit instruction is also better adapted to the capacities and needs of advanced students of a L2, who already have the necessary command of that language to understand the explanations in the L2 explicit instruction textbook or class. Teachers and authors of advanced EFL textbooks can profit from their students' linguistic competence to explicitly teach subtle nuances of the L2, which at lower levels have to be necessarily taught in a more implicit fashion.

To facilitate the explicit instruction of directive speech acts, this book takes a cognitive pedagogical grammar approach to their characterisation. Taylor (2008: 38) explains that a pedagogical grammar may be defined 'as a description of a language [or an aspect of a language] which is aimed at the foreign language learner and/or teacher, and whose purpose is to promote insight into, and thereby to facilitate the acquisition of, the foreign language'. Pedagogical grammar differs from descriptive or linguistic grammars, which are written by linguists for linguists, and which are not aimed at meeting the needs of the students and/or teachers of a language (Dirven, 1985, 1990, 2001). Thus, pedagogical grammars make use of accessible terminology and represent concepts in a reader-friendly manner to be able to reach their intended audience. In addition, they place the focus of attention on those aspects of a language that may pose a problem or a difficulty for learners and offer succinct, intuitive, and straightforward explanations of idiosyncratic aspects of the L2 (Taylor, 2008: 38–39).

To comply with the objectives that were set up in Section 1.2, the cognitive pedagogical grammar offered in this book includes contrastive, cognitive, and constructional information about speech acts. A word of caveat is in order. The term 'grammar' should not be understood here in a narrow sense as applying exclusively to morphological and syntactic aspects of language. Cognitive pedagogical grammar inherits the cognitive linguistics conception of grammar as the collection of form-meaning pairings (i.e. constructions) that occur at all levels of linguistic description, including morphology, lexicon, syntax, illocution, and discourse (Goldberg, 1995, 2006; Langacker, 2008; Ruiz de Mendoza & Galera, 2014). Cognitive pedagogical grammar is, therefore, an adequate tool for the description and explanation of the directive illocutions under scrutiny. More specifically, the contrastive, cognitive-constructional pedagogical grammar approach to directive speech acts adopted in this book can help teaching professionals (whether teachers, lecturers, and/or textbook authors) to prepare their teaching sessions and design their didactic materials on this topic, while it may be useful for postgraduate students and new researchers who are looking to gain an understanding of the workings of directive illocutionary acts.[1]

A second relevant methodological decision on which the present proposal hinges is the use of real language data for the analysis of both the semantic and the formal sides of directive illocutionary constructions. At present, corpus-based cognitive pedagogical grammars are scarce. Meunier (2008: 99) points to the relative youth of the fields of corpus linguistics and cognitive pedagogical grammar as the main reason for the lack of availability of this type of materials. One exception is Carter, Hughes, and McCarthy's (2000) *Exploring Grammar in Context*, which does not, however, include the description of speech acts.

As noted in Meunier (2008: 102), whether the use of authentic language in pedagogical grammars and teaching materials is beneficial to the learning process is a matter of controversy. Some authors defend the exclusive use of authentic material (Römer, 2004, 2006) and others argue that learners have more to gain from exposure to prototypical, didactic, and learner-adapted examples (Widdowson, 2003). The cognitive pedagogical grammar of directive speech acts offered in this book takes sides with Valdman's (2003: 61) equidistant position to the effect that it reflects 'the actual speech of target language speakers in authentic communicative situations, and should conform to native speakers' idealised view of their speech use, should conform to expectations of both native speakers and foreign learners concerning the type of behaviour appropriate for foreign learners, and should take into account processing and learning factors'.

---

[1] See De Knop and De Rycker (2008), De Knop and Gilquin (2016), Masuda (2018), Gonzálvez-García (2019), and Ibarretxe-Antuñano and Cheikh-Khamis (2019), among others, for cognitive pedagogical grammar approaches to different linguistic phenomena.

Thus, the description and explanation of the meaning and formal sides of directive speech acts in Chapter 4 stem primarily from the analysis of authentic instances of language taken from the British National and the iWeb corpora for English data, and the CREA and CORPES XXI corpora for Spanish data (see below). Five hundred random instances of each directive category under consideration have been retrieved from the aforementioned corpora for analysis. Whenever possible and as required by the teaching and learning needs, this corpus has also been used to illustrate the theoretical points offered in Chapter 4, as well as in the development of activities and practice materials in Chapter 5. In this the present book follows and acknowledges recent fine proposals on how to effectively use corpus data in the development of classroom materials for teaching EFL pragmatics (Bardovi-Harlig, Mossman & Vellenga, 2014a, 2014b; Bardovi-Harlig & Mossman, 2016; Bardovi-Harlig, Mossman & Su, 2017).

Nevertheless, both illustrative examples of theoretical aspects of speech acts and those illocutionary act samples included in the activities and practice materials need not always exhaustively copy the rough data in the corpora used for analysis. If needed, they have been adapted to meet teaching and learning requirements. The use of adapted data is especially useful when the object of study involves higher level pragmatic concepts, such as directive speech acts. As explained in Section 1.2, the successful use of directive illocutions often involves managing complex amalgams of pragmatic, semantic, and conversational knowledge. For teaching and learning purposes, it is, therefore, clearer to initially present the students with adapted examples that illustrate the workings of just one or two of these variables at a time. Once the different strands of knowledge needed to perform a directive speech act correctly have been mastered, it then seems the right time to present the students with more complex, corpus-based samples and exercises that juggle with several of those variables simultaneously. This book, therefore, adheres to a mixed approach to the use of corpus data. While the theoretical proposals on the nature of speech acts are based on the analysis of real language examples, the use of the latter for illustration or in the design of teaching materials is conditioned to the teaching needs. Therefore, both adapted and corpus-based examples are used as required by instructional purposes.

For the English data, the analysis makes use of the British National Corpus (BNC) and the more recent iWeb corpus, which allows specific searches for the different varieties of English. Together, these corpora offer over fourteen billion words, including both written and spoken data, for analysis.

For the Spanish data, the Corpus de Referencia del Español Actual (CREA) has been chosen, because it has a good balance of written and spoken sources; together with the Corpus del Español del Siglo XXI (CORPES XXI), which is yearly updated with twenty-five million extra forms. Both the CREA and the CORPES XXI allow specific searches on the Castilian variety of Spanish.

Given the kaleidoscopic and often non-conventional nature of speech acts, however, the use of corpora may sometimes run short of providing an exhaustive picture of the semantic and formal characterisation of speech acts. Therefore, a mixed method has been implemented in order to find the most exhaustive collection of linguistic realisations for each speech act type: (1) a corpus-based search has been performed in order to find indirect speech acts which are introduced by reporting performatives (e.g. *He requested: 'Could you help me out with this mess?'*) in the BNC, iWeb, CREA, and CORPES XXI corpora described above. In this way, it has been possible to take advantage of the categorisation made by native speakers of the speech acts they are reporting; (2) the initial corpus-based list has been enriched with other directive configurations taken from a thorough revision of the literature on speech acts and additional research resources, such as the CARLA (Centre for Advance Research on Language Acquisition-University of Minnesota) website; and (3) the final collection of speech acts for analysis has been completed with instances of directive acts that the author has come across in her everyday life interaction with English native speakers or arising from her own native speaker's intuition in the case of the Spanish language. Before including the linguistic configurations stemming from (2) and (3) in the final list of linguistic realisations for speech acts, an additional search of those configurations in rich computerised corpora (i.e. iWeb, Web Corp Live) has been conducted to assess their productiveness and to confirm that they are in actual use. Given the indirect nature of speech acts, this combined method guarantees the necessary degree of exhaustiveness in the final collection of linguistic configurations.

1.4 Chapter Contents

The contents of the book have been organised as follows.

Chapter 2, What Contemporary Research Tells Us about Speech Acts, provides an accessible and reader-friendly outlook on contemporary theoretical research on speech acts, explaining and illustrating the latest pragmatic, functional, conversational, and cognitive/constructional contributions to the understanding of illocutionary phenomena.

The chapter advocates a contrastive, cognitive/constructional theory of speech acts, showing how this approach is capable of integrating pragmatic, semantic, and syntactic aspects of speech acts into a unified and comprehensive account that is compatible with current psycholinguistic knowledge on the production and understanding of speech acts. This chapter also sets the theoretical foundations for Chapters 4 and 5, offering a full-fledged theoretical proposal on the semantic and formal features of directive illocutionary acts in terms of illocutionary constructions and metonymic operations. The semantic side of the constructions is captured in the form of illocutionary ICMs, and the formal side takes the form of inventories of base constructions and linguistic realisation procedures. It is further argued that speakers can modulate the explicitness of their directive speech acts through (multiple source)-in-target metonymic operations.

At the end of Chapter 2 and stemming from the previous overview of contemporary theories of illocution, the reader is presented with a relevant list of theoretical aspects about the meaning and form of speech acts, which have been found to be essential in their production and understanding, and which are, therefore, expected to be included in textbooks and instructional materials in order to guarantee their correct learning. This inventory of relevant theoretical aspects that need to be taken into account in the description of directive speech acts will serve as a guide to the critical assessment of their representation in current EFL textbooks in Chapter 3.

Chapter 3, Critical Assessment of the Representation of Speech Acts in Advanced EFL Textbooks, reports the results of a study which looks into a collection of textbooks for advanced EFL students in order to assess their treatment of directive speech acts. This chapter considers aspects related to (1) the quantitative representation of directive speech acts in the textbooks (i.e. determining if there is a balanced portrayal of the most frequent categories of directive speech acts) and (2) the qualitative treatment of directive speech acts (i.e. assessing if the depiction of directive speech acts in EFL textbooks has incorporated the main research advancements described in Chapter 2).

Chapter 4, A Cognitive Pedagogical Grammar of Directive Speech Acts I: Know-What and Know-How of Directives, applies the cognitive-constructional approach to speech acts presented in Chapter 2 to the task of providing an exhaustive description of the meaning and form of the six directive speech acts under consideration (i.e. orders, requests, beggings, suggestions, advice acts, and warnings), including contrastive considerations about the realisation of these illocutionary acts in Spanish (L1) and English (L2). The description of the constructional nature of the aforementioned directive speech acts takes the form of a cognitive pedagogical grammar. Information is, thus, presented in an accessible, largely jargon-free manner, so that it can be used by teachers and textbook developers for the explicit teaching of the workings of directive illocutions to advanced Spanish EFL students. For each directive category, this chapter offers relevant information about its semantics (i.e. know-what) and its formal configurations (i.e. know-how).

Chapter 5, A Cognitive Pedagogical Grammar of Directive Speech Acts II: Activities and Practice Materials, draws on the description of the meaning and form of directive speech acts reported in Chapter 4 in order to offer a collection of practical activities for their teaching. Activities are grouped attending to the semantic, formal, or contrastive aspects that need to be taught. Some of them are designed to improve the students' recognition and production of those illocutionary constructions and linguistic realisation procedures which allow the communication of the different illocutionary forces. Others are specifically devoted to help teachers and textbook developers show students (1) the motivation of the form of directive speech acts in their underlying semantics and force dynamics, (2) the role of conceptual metonymy in the production of directive speech acts, and (3) the existence of families of speech act base constructions whose illocutionary force can be further modulated by means of linguistic realisation procedures.

The final chapter, Conclusions, summarises the main contributions of the previous chapters and offers suggestions for future research.

2

What Contemporary Research Tells Us about Speech Acts

2.1 Speech Acts: The Player All Linguistic Theories Want in Their Team

The story of theoretical studies of speech acts is one of appropriation: three all-star teams of linguists, representing largely opposing theoretical positions about the nature of language, wanting so badly to sign speech acts for their club that they do not hesitate to simplify their true nature in order to secure them for their crew.

Team 1 represents those theories which support the belief that language allows speakers to fully codify what we want to say. Full codification leads to unambiguous, risk-free linguistic interactions, but it denies two of the most central and valuable characteristics of language: its creativity and its flexibility to adapt to diverse communicative needs. Adopting a full codification view of language, however attractive this position may seem in terms of cognitive economy and the prevention of misunderstandings, leads linguists to overlook pivotal aspects of human communication, such as the indirect uses of language that underlie ironic, figurative, or polite expressions, among others.

At the opposite end of the spectrum of linguistic theories, supporters of Team 3 envision speakers of a language as a sort of intelligent, fast-processing, walking computer that manages to swiftly calculate, on the spot, the meaning of each expression they hear in their daily lives. This theoretical stance is capable of accommodating the creativity and flexibility of so-called indirect forms of language, but it does so at a high cognitive cost. Granted human brains are powerful devices, however, having to calculate the meaning of each and every single utterance that we come across in our daily interactions appears at first sight as a cognitively costly and time-consuming approach to language. Even computers make use of rules, patterns, and scripts to automatise frequent and recurrent tasks. Why would the human mind function differently?

2.1 Speech Acts in Linguistic Theories

Team 2 holds an intermediate position, allowing for the existence of at least some conventional means of expressing our thoughts and wishes and, therefore, for more creative, but also safer, and more cognitively efficient ways of communicating our thoughts than those proposed by Teams 1 and 3, respectively. As shall be shown in Section 2.3, Team 2 also has deficits to its game: its advocates defend an all-or-nothing view of conventionality. Thus, they claim that a speech act is either conventional or not. CAN YOU DO X? forms, for instance, would be considered conventional expressions of requests by followers of this team. Section 2.5 provides evidence that this is often an oversimplification of how the production of speech acts works. Conventionality is shown to be itself a blurry theoretical category, which can be modulated linguistically to produce speech acts with a higher or lower conventional meaning, which thus gradually approach either the codification or the inferential ends of the illocutionary continuum proposed by Teams 1 and 3.

For decades, linguists have attempted to confine speech acts into the limits of radical conceptions of language, in which either codification, convention, or inferential processes, represented by our three imaginary teams of linguists above, took pride of place in the explanation of the illocutionary component of language. This chapter unveils these attempts and argues in favour of a wide-ranging, comprehensive approach to speech acts that highlights their polychromatic, ductile, and adaptable nature. In so doing, it will be argued that the story of speech acts is also the story of a highly fluid player who can perform equally well for these three teams as required by contextual and interactional needs, and who resists permanent affiliation.

What motivates the existence of these three codification-, convention-, and inference-based theories of speech acts is their adherence, or lack of, to the Literal Force Hypothesis (Levinson, 1983). This hypothesis assumes that each sentence has an illocutionary force of its own built into it. In other words, that the speech act conveyed by a sentence derives from its form. This can be done in two different ways.

i. Using an explicit performative verb that names the speech act that wants to be communicated, such as *beg* in *No, my lord, I **beg** you keep this thing secret* (BNC).
ii. Or, alternatively, using one of the three major sentence types in English (i.e. imperative, interrogative, and declarative), which have the forces traditionally associated with them (i.e. ordering (or requesting), questioning, and stating, respectively). According to this, an interrogative sentence like *Can you hear me?* (BNC), for example, would have a questioning illocutionary force.

Sections 2.2–2.4 below analyse the virtues and flaws of the Literal Force Hypothesis and explain how either acceptance or rejection of its premises derives in membership to one of the aforementioned three views of speech acts. Different theories within each 'team' are revised, their weaknesses exposed, and their strengths pick out, later, to be integrated into our own theoretical proposal on how speech acts are produced and interpreted (Section 2.5). The resulting proposal advocates a modified, weaker version of the Literal Force Hypothesis (Risselada, 1993; Alston, 2000; Kissine, 2011, 2012, 2014) that sets up the possibility of integrating the three existing antagonistic approaches to illocution into a single, all-encompassing framework for the study of speech acts and its ensuing application to language teaching.

2.2 Team 1. Codification-Based Theories and the Over-Grammaticalisation of Speech Acts

2.2.1 Weaknesses of the Literal Force Hypothesis and Ross's Performative Hypothesis

Accepting the Literal Force Hypothesis leads to a rather limited and rigid view of speech acts. Fully codified, unambiguous linguistic acts are restricted to those three (i.e. stating, questioning, and ordering/requesting) that can be expressed by means of the corresponding three universal sentence types (i.e. affirmative, interrogative, and imperative) or by means of explicit performatives.

A quick search in the BNC, however, reveals that explicit performatives are rare in real life communicative exchanges. Simple searches of performative sentences like *I order you to …, I request you to …, I beg you to …, I advise you to / that …, I warn you to / that …,* or *I suggest that you …* yield less than twenty results each on average in a hundred-million-word corpus like the BNC. Speakers of English do not often use explicit performatives to order, request, beg, advise, warn, or suggest other people to do something. This is only to be expected since fully explicit, lexicalised acts such as these do not easily adapt themselves to the varied communicative needs of different social settings. By way of illustration, in a situation in which a large social distance or an asymmetrical power relationship between the speakers asks for a polite request, a performative directive like *I request you to repeat it* does not seem to be the best possible choice to make the act as polite as required by the context. An indirect, conventional request such as *Can you repeat it, please?* (BNC), on the contrary, would come through as more natural. In fact, request constructions of the CAN YOU DO X (please)? form have a higher frequency of occurrence in the same corpus with one hundred fifty-nine occurrences.

This latter example reveals yet another weakness of a theory of speech acts based on the acceptance of the Literal Force Hypothesis. The allegedly literal force of the three basic sentence types can be interpreted, and it is, in fact, often interpreted with a secondary illocutionary force. *Can you repeat it, please?* displays an interrogative sentence type. According to the Literal Force Hypothesis, interrogatives are associated with the speech act force of questioning. Nevertheless, if we consider the context in which this specific instance of the CAN YOU DO X (please)? construction was uttered, it is clear, by the addressee's reaction, that the interrogative sentence was not primarily understood as a question but rather as a request for him to do something:

> he carefully folded the paper and put it in the desk on top of the blotter. (laugh) I remember / **Can you repeat it please?** / Yes. When he had finished reading, he carefully folded the paper and put it in the desk on top of the blotter. (BNC)

In fact, even explicit performative sentences can be used to perform speech acts different from the one named by their performative verbs. Thus, an act of ordering realised by means of an explicit performative, *I order you to keep this information hidden*, can easily be transformed into a different speech act, such as that of threatening or coercing, just by adding a disjunctive clause stating a potentially harmful action aimed at the addressee: *I order you to keep this information hidden or I'll put you in prison for life*.

The fact that both explicit performatives and the three basic sentence types can be used with a secondary illocutionary force, different from the one named by the performative verb or the one traditionally associated with their sentence form, gave rise to the notion of *indirect speech act* (ISA).

There have been attempts to explain the existence and workings of ISAs without rejecting the Literal Force Hypothesis. Among them, there are some theories developed as far back as the 1970s, such as Ross' (1970) Performative Hypothesis and Sadock's (1974) Idiom Theory of Indirect Speech Acts. These authors take advantage of the, at the time, mainstream Chomskyan distinction between surface and deep

Table 2.1 *Deep structure versus surface structure in question for information versus request interpretation*

Deep structure	Surface structure
I *ask* you whether you are able to repeat it I *request* you to repeat it	Can you repeat it?

structure to explain the fact that ISAs have a primary and a secondary illocutionary force.[1]

An utterance like *Can you repeat it?* would, according to these accounts, have two different deep structures, the first one corresponding to its primary force of a question about the listener's ability to physically carry out the stated action, and the second one matching its secondary illocutionary force of requesting the listener to do the action (see Table 2.1). This solution was not without problems. The most obvious one stemming from the fact that these theories did not explain how speakers chose the correct deep structure in a specific communicative setting. Gordon and Lakoff (1975), who also accepted the premise of the existence of different explicit performatives in the deep structures of ISAs, resorted to inference in order to offer a plausible explanation to how this was done. These theories, however, have long been abandoned due to the mounting evidence countering them over the past four decades (see Kaufmann (2012), Leech (1983), and Levinson (1983), among others, for detailed arguments revealing the inadequacy of the performative hypothesis accounts on ISAs).

2.2.2 *Halliday's Over-Grammaticalisation of Speech Acts*

A more recent attempt to account for speech acts as non-inferential, fully codified messages has been put forward within the framework of Systemic-Functional Grammar (Halliday, 1973, 1978, 1994).

The systemic-functional approach takes an original stance as regards the identification of the basic types of speech acts. Traditionally, these had been equated with the three universal sentence types (i.e. affirmative-assertions, interrogative-questions, and imperative-orders) as captured in the Literal

---

[1] The notions of *deep* and *surface* structure stem from the generative linguistic tradition (Chomsky, 1964, 1965). Deep structures are theoretical constructs that unify different but related surface structures. Thus, *I hit the table* and *The table was hit by me* would represent two surface structures that have a roughly similar deep structure, since the agent, patient, and type of action are the same in both sentences.

2.2 Team 1. Codification-Based Theories

Force Hypothesis. Halliday (1994) shifts from a formal to a semantic/functional criterion for the classification of speech acts. Thus, he looks into the functions for which they are used. More specifically, he makes use of two semantic oppositions. The first considers the type of commodity that is exchanged in a social transaction (i.e. whether the speech act involves a transfer of information or goods/services). The second assesses the role of the speaker in the exchange (i.e. whether he is giving or demanding the commodity). These semantic/functional criteria yield four basic speech act types: *offers* (giving + goods/services), *commands* (demanding + goods/services), *statements* (giving + information), and *questions* (demanding + information).

The resulting classification of speech act functions is no longer compatible with the Literal Force Hypothesis, since offers do not have a specific sentence type associated with them, as *commands, statements,* and *questions* do. Does this asymmetry mean that offers, and all those speech acts that do not have a specific sentence form associated with them (i.e. begs, suggestions, pieces of advice, warnings, promises, etc.), cannot be accounted for within grammar? The systemic-functional model believes that it is, in fact, possible to treat all speech act types grammatically, without having to resort to inferential processes belonging to the realm of pragmatics. This is so, according to Thibault and Van Leeuwen (1996), thanks to the idiosyncratic conceptions of language and grammar held by systemic-functional linguists. In this tradition, language is understood as a network of interlocking options for the creation of social meaning (Halliday, 1994: 14). In turn, grammar is defined as a resource for creating meaning by means of a semantically motivated careful choice of lexico-grammatical elements within the system of language (Halliday & Matthiessen, 1999: 3).

Derived from these conceptions of language and grammar, the systemic-functional tradition contributes two pivotal notions to the study of speech acts. First, it makes it manifest that speech acts are social constructs that are used by members of a society. Therefore, their use needs to consider social aspects (e.g. power, social distance relationships) and also conform to the needs of social interactions (e.g. politeness, effectiveness of communication). In this, the systemic-functional approach is close to pragmatic and cognitive proposals such as those of Leech (1983, 2014), Panther and Thornburg (1998, 2003), or Pérez-Hernández (2001, 2012, 2013), as will be made apparent in Sections 2.4 and 2.5. Second, the system of options represented by language offers speakers the potentiality to produce speech acts unambiguously and in a fairly economical manner, without needing to resort to costly inferential processes. The following example illustrates how this can be done. Let us imagine that a person wants to request a pair of scissors from someone sitting next to him in an arts and crafts seminar. He has considered the social factors that affect the type of request he needs to produce in the context in which the interaction takes place. Since there is no familiarity between the speakers (i.e. they do not know each other), the request needs to be polite. Nevertheless, the politeness requirements are not too high because their social status is similar, and the context is informal and relaxed. Once the social setting in which the request is to be uttered has been assessed, the speaker turns to the lexico-grammatical options that the language system offers him to produce an effective speech act, which could resemble the following example: *I need a pair of scissors. You have one, don't you? Can you share them, please?* The resulting request makes use of several linguistic resources to codify and convey the meaning of the act of requesting: it states the speaker's need and expresses the fact that the listener is in possession of the required object (declarative sentences); it also communicates politeness directly, through the use of the adverb *please*, and indirectly, through the optionality inherent in the interrogative sentence asking about the capacity of the listener to share the scissors with him. As pointed out by Pérez-Hernández (2001: 37):

> If the systemic-functional proposals are correct, them most of our illocutionary activity would be linguistically coded by means of delicate co-patternings of selections on the lexico-grammatical system, which would result in a higher level of explicitation and, therefore, in an important economy of effort in cognitive processing.

In fact, since it is rather unlikely that, in the context under consideration, the previous example would be interpreted as anything other than a request, it can be concluded that it is possible to fully codify linguistic acts, and that inference is not necessary in the production of speech acts. However attractive this view of illocution may be, the systemic-functional proposals have often been criticised for over-grammaticalising linguistic phenomena whose nature could also fit into a pragmatic/inferential description. Thus, the fact that the language system allows the speaker in our previous example to express his request in a highly codified manner does not necessarily mean that a less explicit request would have been unsuccessful. The speaker could have managed to get the pair of scissors by using more implicit expressions like *I need the scissors, (please / could you?)*, or *Can / Could you lend me your scissors for a sec?* In fact, most requests in our corpus are of this second type, as will be shown in Chapter 4. A sound description of illocutionary performance should be able to accommodate not only fully explicit speech acts, but also those that hinge on inferential calculations to a larger or a lesser extent. The systemic-functional proposals run short of offering this type of all-encompassing description of speech acts.[2]

2.3 Team 2. Convention-Based Theories: Indirect Speech Acts

For those linguists who, unlike the systemic-functional followers, still accepted the validity of the Literal Force Hypothesis, there remained a different problem, namely that of accounting for those instances of speech acts in which the literal force expressed by the sentence form or the explicit performative was not the one intended by the speaker. Example (2.1) illustrates this puzzle:

(2.1) Albini thinks of Big Black and says, 'We were a pretty good live band.' To anyone in a band now, he **advised**, 'Develop your aesthetic and execute it, you will find your audience, your audience will find you.' (BNC)

Develop your aesthetic and execute it is an imperative sentence, which, as predicted by the Literal Force Hypothesis, has the literal force of an order. Nevertheless, in this conversation, the utterance is clearly being used with the additional indirect illocutionary force of advising, as indicated by the narrator himself. It becomes, therefore, necessary to explain how this indirect illocutionary force relates to and is derived from the literal one.

2.3.1 Searle: Inference and Convention in Speech Acts

An initial attempt to offer an explanation came from one of the founding fathers of speech act theory. In his 1975 influential paper, 'Indirect speech

---

[2] Another functional attempt to offer an account of illocution within grammar (i.e. based on codification) was carried out by Dik (1989, 1997). This author put forward the notion of *grammatical illocutionary conversion* (i.e. the process whereby the literal force of a sentence can be turned into a derived illocutionary force). This could be done by means of *illocutionary conversors*. In *Please give me the scalpel* the adverb *please* functions as a conversor that turns an imperative sentence into a request (Dik, 1997: 243–244). Consequently, Dik argues that the three basic speech act types associated with the basic sentence forms, together with those illocutionary acts for which a language provides illocutionary conversors would be dealt with within grammar. All other speech acts would belong to the realm of pragmatics. In his analysis of English, Dik was only capable of identifying seven types of derived illocutionary forces. In practice, this meant that, despite Dik's attempts to account for speech acts in terms of codification, the vast majority of speech acts resisted this treatment and had to be accounted for inferentially within a pragmatic theory of language.

acts', Searle couched his account of indirect speech acts in terms of inference triggers, a theory of the conditions of satisfaction for the production of speech acts, general principles of co-operative conversation (Grice, 1975), and human inferential abilities. Making use of these theoretical and processing tools, Searle (1975: 74) argued that the first step in understanding example (2.1) as a piece of advice is realising that the literal force associated with the imperative sentence is not the one intended by the speaker. He further explained that there is usually a trigger that signals the need to find an alternative indirect illocutionary force matching the speaker's actual communicative intention. In example (2.1) this trigger is represented by the two juxtaposed affirmative sentences following the imperative: *you will find your audience; your audience will find you.* These sentences refer to the benefit that may come from complying with the action expressed by the imperative: *Develop your aesthetic and execute it.* The benefit is not for the speaker but for the listener, who will get an audience. This clashes with the illocutionary purpose of the literal force of the imperative, since orders typically result in a benefit for the speaker. The inference trigger sets off an inferential process that leads the listener to calculate the advising force of the utterance, taking as a point of departure the initial literal force of order associated with the imperative sentence form. In this he makes use of his knowledge of the conditions of satisfaction for the speech act of advising, such as for instance the fact that the listener is to be the agent of the proposed action, that the proponent of the action should have superior knowledge on the topic than the receiver, and that the proposed action should bring about a benefit for the listener. The speaker in example (2.1) has the necessary experience and knowledge superiority to issue a piece of advice because he is the leader of a band himself. The action is proposed for the listener to be carried out, and it is meant to be beneficial to him. Therefore, if the speaker is being co-operative, as the Gricean principle of co-operation leads us to expect, the utterance can be interpreted as a piece of advice.[3]

Searle was aware, however, that there are instances of speech acts which are much less dependent on inference. As opposed to example (2.1), whose

[3] For a more exhaustive description of the steps proposed by Searle to derive the indirect illocutionary force from the literal one, see Searle (1975: 73–74). For analyses exposing the weaknesses of Searle's approach to illocution, see Burkhardt (1990), Katz (1990), Rofl (1990), Escandell (1993), Holdcroft (1994), and Pérez-Hernández (2001).

advising force needs to be calculated as explained, the following examples are more straightforwardly interpreted as pieces of advice:

(2.2) 'You ought to wrap up more,' he **advised**. 'Now that it's winter. You've a terrible cough.' (BNC)
(2.3) 'The best thing you can do is go home and tuck yourself up with a hot-water bottle,' she **advised**, pulling on her coat. (BNC)
(2.4) 'I'd take Mother Benedicta if I were you,' **advised** Amsterdam, trying to dispel the sting of the marquis's response. (BNC).

Searle (1975: 76) reaches the conclusion that some linguistic forms are more efficient than others in communicating an indirect force different from the one codified by its sentence form. He observes this phenomenon in relation to the act of requesting, where forms like *Can you open the door?* are more easily recognised as requests than synonymous realisations like *Are you able to open the door?* This was so despite the fact that both sentences questioned the same preparatory condition (i.e. the capacity of the listener to carry out the requested action). Searle (1975: 76) concluded that some linguistic forms have become conventional expressions for conveying certain illocutionary forces. He does not explain, however, the reasons why they have reached such conventional status for the expression of indirect speech acts.

Searle starts off from a semantic stance, close to that of linguists in Team 1 (see Section 2.2), according to which there are several illocutionary forces that are linguistically codified in the sentence forms (i.e. orders, questions, and assertions). It is precisely his acceptance of the Literal Force Hypothesis that leads him to put forward an additional inferential theory of interpretation for those speech acts which are not linguistically codified (i.e. indirect speech acts). In this he approaches the postulates of Team 3 (see Section 2.4). This inferential theory, however, is incapable of accounting for the existence of conventional instances of illocutions. As pointed out by Geis (1995), one of the reasons why Searle's account cannot deal with conventionality is that it focuses on transactional aspects of speech acts and overlooks their interactional side. In fact, some conventional forms of requests with modal verbs in the past tense (e.g. *Could / Would you open the door?*) are motivated by the interactional need of acting politely. This weakness is a direct consequence of Searle's assumption that speech acts are essentially linguistic and his failure to realise their social dimension. As argued by Halliday (1978, 1994), Marcondes (1984), and Geis (1995), among others, warnings, requests, orders, and other communicative acts are social constructs that can also be realised by non-linguistic means (i.e. gestures).

The social nature of speech acts and the interactional factors that affect their performance will be extensively dealt with by inference-based theories (see Section 2.4).

Searle, however, can be credited for bringing to the fore the existence of the especial category of conventional speech acts, which not being fully codified, are more readily understood than fully inferred/calculated speech acts. The literature shows several attempts to account for them.

2.3.2 Morgan's Conventions of Usage and Short-Circuiting Implicatures

Morgan (1978) was one of the first to take on the challenge of explaining the functioning of conventional speech acts. In order to do so, he distinguished between *conventions of language* (i.e. those that account for the literal, arbitrary meaning of sentences) and *conventions of usage* (i.e. those based on cultural conventions that govern the use of a sentence with a fixed literal force for the performance of a different act in a particular culture). Language users have knowledge of conventions of language that account for the fact that an interrogative sentence (e.g. *Can you hold the book?*) has the literal meaning of a question, as predicted by the Literal Force Hypothesis. Additionally, they are also aware of the convention of usage that justifies that the same sentence can also be used as a request. In order to understand why there is a convention of usage by virtue of which a sentence like *Can you hold the book?* can be interpreted as a request, it should be possible to reconstruct the inferential steps leading from its literal force of a question to its indirect interpretation as a request. This could be done using the same theoretical apparatus proposed by Searle. Thus, CAN YOU DO X? forms question one of the preparatory conditions for the performance of requests. However, it is arguable whether speakers do actually calculate the requestive value of the sentence in such a burdensome fashion. On the contrary, they seem to straightforwardly jump to the request interpretation. Morgan (Morgan, 1978: 274, 263) referred to this phenomenon as *short-circuiting implicatures*:

> The expression *Can you ...* is not an idiom but has only the obvious literal meaning of a question about the hearer's abilities. One can readily see how the expression could have, via Grice's maxims, the implicature of a request. In fact, it has become conventional to use the expression in this way. Thus, speakers know not only that *Can you ...?* has a literal meaning (a convention of language): they know also that using *Can you...* is a standard way of indirectly making a request (a convention of usage). Both are involved in

a full understanding by the hearer of what is intended in the use of the expression.

> ... although *Can you pass the salt?* is indeed CALCULABLE, it is not in fact calculated: rather, one gets the point more or less directly, without any inferential processing.

Thus, thanks to the existence of conventions of usage, speakers can avoid tiresome calculations and short-circuit the inferential process that would lead to the interpretation of CAN YOU DO X? forms as requests. Morgan's proposal allow us to understand the different functioning of near synonym constructions, such as CAN YOU DO X? and ARE YOU ABLE TO DO X?, in terms of degree of conventionalisation. According to his view, only in the case of CAN YOU DO X? interrogative sentences is there a convention of usage that explains their interpretation as requests. No explanation is given, however, about the reasons why these conventions of usage are established for some linguistic forms and not for others that are close synonyms. The explanatory power of Morgan's conventions of usage and short-circuiting implicatures is not capable either of motivating the existence of a varied range of slightly different linguistic forms of the same speech act. *Will / Would you hold the book?*, *Can / Could you hold the book?*, *Hold the book, can / will / could / would you?*, *Would you mind holding the book?*, etc. are all possible instances of conventional requests. What prompts speakers to use one or the other is often related to politeness and interactional factors. Just like Searle, Morgan's view of speech acts overlooks their social side, thus offering a limited portrayal of illocution.

2.4 Team 3. Inference-Based Theories: Over-Pragmatisation of Speech Acts

In Sections 2.2 and 2.3 it has been shown how the different attempts to explain speech acts as either fully codified or conventional acts, respectively, are not without problems: some of them are not flexible enough to account for the creativity, flexibility, and economy of language (e.g. Halliday's systemic-functional proposal), some fall short of explaining the vast range of linguistic realisations available for the expression of a speech act (e.g. Searle's and Morgan's accounts), and most of them cannot provide a full picture of illocutionary performance, since many speech acts, in fact, escape codification and conventionalisation, requiring inferential processes to a larger or lesser extent for their full understanding. This section looks into those proposals that give pride of place to inference in the understanding of speech acts.

2.4.1 Standard Pragmatics Approach: Bach and Harnish's Speech Act Schemas

Bach and Harnish (1979) were among the first linguists to question the validity of the Literal Force Hypothesis and, consequently, of the role of codification in speech acts (Dobrovie-Sorin, 1985; Recanati, 1987, 1994; Dascal, 1989; Bertolet, 1994). Their contribution is relevant, because it paved the way for some mainstream theories of illocutionary performance in the last decades, including conversational approaches (e.g. Levinson, 1983; Geis, 1995), pragmatic accounts (e.g. Leech, 1983, 2014), and relevance-theoretical proposals (e.g. Sperber & Wilson, 1995).

Bach and Harnish (1979: 17) approached speech acts from an extreme inferentialist viewpoint, according to which their performance is thought to involve 'the speaker's having a special sort of intention (an intention that the hearer make a certain sort of inference) and the hearer's actually making that inference'. Let us consider example (2.1) again, reproduced here as (2.5) for convenience:

(2.5) Albini thinks of Big Black and says, 'We were a pretty good live band.' To anyone in a band now, he **advised**, 'Develop your aesthetic and execute it, you will find your audience, your audience will find you.' (BNC)

Linguists in Team 2 (e.g. Searle, Morgan), who accepted the Literal Force Hypothesis, would claim that the imperative sentence *Develop your aesthetic and execute it* has both a literal force of order (i.e. the one associated with its imperative sentence form) and an indirect force of advising, which is reached through several inferential steps (see Section 2.3). In their account, the literal force is codified in the linguistic form, the indirect force is inferentially calculated. In addition, it is argued that speakers only bother to calculate the indirect force when a trigger makes them realise that the literal force does not fit the context. In contrast to this, the extreme inferentialists in Team 3 reject the Literal Force Hypothesis and widen the scope of the inferential processes involved in speech act interpretation to the effect that both literal and indirect speech acts need to be calculated (Bach & Harnish, 1979: 132). The inferential speech act schemas put forward by Bach and Harnish do not assume that the imperative in example (2.5) is directly linked to the illocutionary force of order. On the contrary, these schemas make use of mutual contextual knowledge and general principles about the nature, stage, and direction of the talk exchange (i.e. conversational presumption) to infer whether the imperative sentence is, in fact, intended as an order.

If the contextual information and the conversational presumptions validate this interpretation, the inferential process would come to an end. However, since this is not the case in the example under consideration, the listener needs to continue with her inferential calculations until she reaches the advising interpretation intended by the speaker.[4]

Surprisingly enough, when faced with conventional instances of speech acts, like examples (2.2)–(2.4) above, Bach and Harnish adopt a position close to that of Morgan. Bach and Harnish (1979: 198) refer to conventional speech acts, such as *If I were you, I would do X* pieces of advice or *Can you do X?* request forms as *standardised*. They further argue that in these cases the inferential route is short-circuited, and the hearer identifies the speaker's advising or requestive intent without having to grasp the literal intent of questioning associated with the interrogative sentence type (see also Bach, 1998).

2.4.2 Direct Access Approaches I: Leech's Interpersonal Rhetoric

Following the inference-based path to the analysis of speech acts opened by Bach and Harnish, other linguists have attempted to investigate the factors that guide and motivate the inferential interpretation of the intended force of speech acts. Among them, special attention should be paid to pragmatic proposals that not only provide a principle-based account of the inferential mechanisms involved but do so by acknowledging the social and conversational nature of speech acts.

Undoubtedly, a prominent representative of this trend is Leech's (1983, 2014) account of speech acts in terms of interpersonal rhetoric. In relation to the codification/conventionalisation vs. inference dichotomy, Leech (1983: 17) states the following:

> There are important issues which cannot be pursued here, particularly the question of how far the relation of questions and mands to the illocutions they typically perform (viz. askings and impositives) is conventional, rather

---

[4] For a detailed description and critical analysis of Bach and Harnish's (1979) Speech Act Schemas, see Pérez-Hernández (2001: 41–45). Sperber and Wilson's (1995) relevance-theoretic account follows Bach and Harnish in their assumption that even the literal meaning of an utterance needs to be inferred. They propose their own schema of interpretation based on the *Principle of Relevance*: first assessing the literal interpretation, then assessing its relevance, and, if it does not fit the contextual needs, deriving the non-literal interpretation. Bach and Harnish's and Sperber and Wilson's approaches are known as Standard Pragmatics models, which differ from the so-called Direct Access models (represented by Leech's contributions and those of the conversational theories of illocution) in that the latter make use of contextual information to derive the intended meaning of a speech act directly, without needing to assess the validity of the literal force of the utterance in the first place.

than determined by Interpersonal Rhetoric. Kempson (1975: 147) opts for a conventional mapping of one on to the other set of categories, whereas I prefer to go the whole pragmatic hog, and attempt an explanation entirely in terms of Interpersonal Rhetoric.

In other words, Leech takes on an extreme inferentialist approach to the analysis of speech acts, according to which the distinction between literal and indirect speech acts becomes irrelevant, and it is necessary to calculate the meaning of all speech acts. Contrary to Bach and Harnish, Leech does not consider it necessary to calculate the literal meaning first and then, if shown that it does not fit the context, to continue with the calculation of the indirect force. In Leech's account, speakers make use of contextual and social information to directly calculate the intended meaning.[5] In fact, what makes his proposal stand out from previous inferential accounts is its focus on the social dimension of illocution. More specifically, Leech states that the need to be polite in our social interactions is one of the essential motivations underlying and guiding the production and interpretation of illocutionary acts.[6] For different reasons, on many occasions in our daily lives we are forced to carry out linguistic acts that may put our social relations at risk: acts that involve asking our interlocutors to do something that is costly to them in terms of time, resources, etc. (e.g. requests, beggings), acts that may be felt as impositions on their freedom (e.g. orders, threats), acts that may clash with our listeners' plans (e.g. suggestions), etc. To minimise or prevent the social conflicts that may arise from acts like these, speakers make use of their knowledge of interpersonal rhetoric, a keystone of which is the Politeness Principle: 'minimise the expression of impolite beliefs, and maximise the expression of polite beliefs' (Leech, 1983: 81). In the case of directive speech acts, being polite involves, among other things, trying to minimise the cost of the action that is requested from the hearer (tact maxim). In order to calculate the cost of the act and the corresponding degree of politeness needed to compensate for it and to keep interaction

---

[5] This Direct Access model of speech act interpretation has been followed by other authors such as Gibbs (1994, 2002).

[6] Considerations of politeness as motivating factors of speech act performance were also explored by other contemporary authors like Brown and Levinson (1987). Brown and Levinson's proposal in terms of the notion of *face* (i.e. social image of a person) leads to a binary conception of politeness, whereby speech acts are either polite (when they maintain people's face) or impolite (when they do not). Leech's pragmatic scales, on the contrary, allow for a scaled gradation in the assessment of the politeness requirements of particular instances of speech acts, which reflects the needs of actual social interaction more closely. Leech's proposals have been chosen for this study due to their encompassing and detailed nature. For a comparison of Brown and Levison's and Leech's politeness theories, see Pérez-Hernández (1999, 2001).

2.4 Team 3. Inference-Based Theories

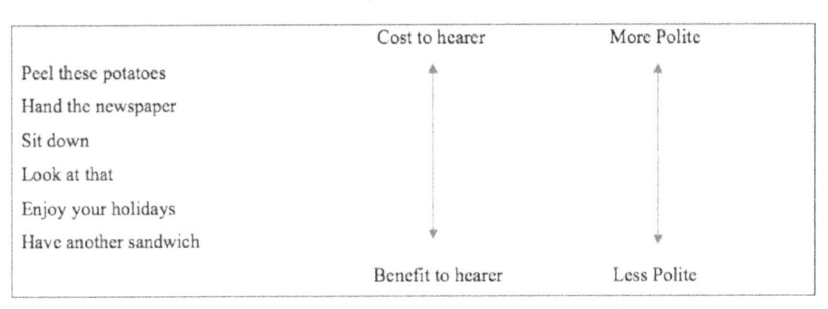

	Cost to hearer	More Polite
Peel these potatoes	▲	▲
Hand the newspaper		
Sit down		
Look at that		
Enjoy your holidays		
Have another sandwich	▼	▼
	Benefit to hearer	Less Polite

Figure 2.1 Cost–benefit and politeness interactions (Leech, 1983: 107)

running smoothly, Leech (1983, 2014) puts forward a *scale of cost–benefit* or *weightiness of the transaction*. Figure 2.1 illustrates how different directive speech acts can be ordered along a scale depending on how costly they are and how the need for politeness increases with the cost.

A costly action, such as peeling the potatoes, would require a more polite linguistic realisation than the offer *Have another sandwich*, which is beneficial to the hearer.

Directive speech acts are very sensitive to social factors, and their cost is not the only variable that affects their potentiality for causing social disruption. As pointed out by Leech (2014: 11), power asymmetries between speakers (i.e. scale of vertical distance) or the existence of a large social distance between them (i.e. scale of horizontal distance) may also call for higher doses of politeness. In asking someone to do something, we may get by using a simple imperative like *Peel the potatoes* when talking to a sibling or a friend, because they are close to us and hold a similar power status. However, if we wanted a stranger to comply with a costly request, we would preferably make use of a more polite realisation (e.g. *If you don't mind, will you peel the potatoes, please?*).

Additionally, the degree of politeness of a directive speech act can be modulated by varying the optionality offered to the hearer to comply with the action (i.e. scale of optionality) or the indirectness of the act (i.e. the length of the inferential path linking the illocutionary act to its communicative goal, scale of indirectness). Requests expressed by means of interrogative sentences display a higher degree of optionality by default. By way of illustration, an utterance like *Can you peel the potatoes, please?* leaves a door open for the hearer to express non-compliance. On the contrary, imperatives present the action as unavoidable: *Peel the potatoes!* Thus, leaving the hearer without a chance to say 'no' is felt as impositive and, therefore, less polite. Likewise, the more indirect a request is, the more its politeness increases, since it is easier for the hearer to deny understanding of the intended meaning and hence to avoid compliance without losing face. A highly explicit request expressed by a performative (e.g. *I request you to peel the potatoes*) leaves little option to the hearer but to comply with it. Explicitness reduces optionality and, hence, the politeness of the act. A highly implicit request like *Has someone peeled the potatoes yet?*, on the contrary, allows the hearer to overlook the requestive interpretation and answer to the question force of the utterance with a simple 'yes', 'no', or 'I don't know'.

Scales, like those of cost–benefit, optionality, indirectness, social power, and social distance, allow speakers to assess the politeness needed in a particular interaction and to act accordingly, thus keeping their social interactions largely free from the conflict inherent to costly speech acts like directives. In his more recent revision of the politeness of speech acts, Leech (2014: 14) further argues that pragmalinguistics should be additionally concerned with the task of revealing the 'lexico-grammatical resources of language, their meanings [...], and how they are deployed as linguistic strategies of politeness'. In this, Leech paves the way for a constructional account of illocution such as the one we shall propose in Section 2.5. His model, however, runs short of explaining the conceptual operations that work on illocutionary constructions and which are responsible for their flexibility and adaptability to different contexts and interactional needs (i.e. conceptual metonymy). These issues will be addressed in our proposal.

Leech's scales are also useful in distinguishing between different subtypes of directives. Thus, orders, requests, and beggings involve a cost to the hearer, while pieces of advice and warnings are beneficial to them. Requests and suggestions are characterised by their high optionality, as opposed to orders or threats. Orders are typically associated with powerful speakers, while requests and beggings are not. In Chapter 4, we shall make extensive use of Leech's scales in our description of the semantic side of illocutionary constructions.

2.4.3 *Direct Access Approaches II: Conversational Approaches*

Conversational approaches represent a mainstream group of speech act accounts that, along with others in Team 3, reject the Literal Force Hypothesis and place inference at the centre of speech act performance (e.g. Schegloff, 1979, 2007; Levinson, 1983; Mey, 1993; Geis, 1995; Kasper, 2006). These accounts focus on suprasentential aspects of illocutionary acts in terms of pre-sequences, adjacency pairs, and preferred/dispreferred responses. Levinson's (1983: 361) well-known example of a request for cigarettes illustrates these notions:

(2.6) A: Do you have Marlboros? (T1)
       B: Yeah, hard or soft? (T2)
       A: Soft, please. (T3)
       B: Okay. (T4)

For a request to be successful it is necessary that the addressee possesses the object that the speakers wants. Thus, it could be argued that, in example (2.6), T1 is a simple question about possession, and the actual request is formulated in T3 (i.e. *Soft, please*). Levinson points out that the recurrent occurrence of conversational exchanges like the one in example (2.6) eventually leads speakers to recognise *pre-sequences* like T1 as full requests by dropping the second and third turns of the conversational sequences.

Example (2.6) also illustrates the notions of *adjacency pairs* and *preferred/ dispreferred response*. The notion of adjacency pair constitutes a relevant contribution of conversational approaches to the study of illocution. Locastro (2012) explains that it is usually the case that speech acts require an answer by the addressee in the form of a confirmation, ratification, or rejection. Questions, for instance, form adjacency pairs with positive or negative answers. Requests can be followed by the act of compliance or by a declination to comply, the first one being the preferred option. Example (2.6) is formed by two adjacency pairs (i.e. question–answer; request–answer). In addition, preference organisation (Glaser, 2009; Carroll, 2011) explains that some of those answers are conversationally preferred (i.e. those that agree with the position of the speaker taking the first action), and others are dispreferred (i.e. those that show disagreement, refusal, or rejection). Preferred turns are usually unmarked; and therefore, they are not preceded by silence or produced with delays or mitigation, as is the case with dispreferred turns. In the request adjacency pair in example (2.6), speaker B has chosen the preferred response (i.e. compliance), which fits the social expectation that one should help others if possible.

As illustrated by the analysis of example (2.6), conversational linguists believe that illocutionary meaning is not static and dependent on the speaker's intention, as proposed by pragmatists and speech act theorists, but that it is rather built through interaction. A consequence of this is the emphasis they place on the analysis of large corpora of real data and their attention to suprasentential aspects of speech act performance. In this, the conversational analysis approach to illocution also differs from previous studies carried out within traditional speech act theory, which focus their attention on invented examples, most of them restricted to the limits of the sentence level. Conversational analysis transcends these boundaries and offers a more realistic account of speech acts. The advantages of considering conversational issues in the correct performance of speech acts have been amply dealt with in the literature, and this is, in fact, one of the few research advancements that has already made its way into current EFL textbooks (see Pérez-Hernández, 2019).

Leaving aside the ground-breaking contributions to the study of the interactional, social, and conversational aspects of illocution reviewed in Sections 2.4.2 and 2.4.3, inference-based accounts of illocution in Team 3, as a whole, are characterised by their rejection of the Literal Force Hypothesis. This allows extreme inferentialists to provide a unified account of how speech acts are understood in terms of inferential calculations. The account, however, is inconsistent with typological evidence supporting the fact that most languages display three universal sentence types (e.g. imperative, affirmative, interrogative). It seems counter-intuitive that these three linguistic forms would not be somehow linked to three salient meanings or functions that are equally pivotal in most cultures. Section 2.5 reveals how a weaker version of the Literal Force Hypothesis may reconcile the typological evidence about the existence of three universal sentence types with their use in the expression of different illocutionary acts beyond the three basic ones of ordering, asserting, and questioning.

An extreme inferentialist stance on speech acts also fails to acknowledge the fact that some linguistic expressions are more frequently and extensively used than others for communicating a speech act force (e.g. CAN YOU DO X? forms are more widely used for expressing a request than the synonymous ARE YOU ABLE TO DO X? linguistic realisations). The conventional status of some speech acts, as revealed by those linguists in Team 2, is a reality that cannot be overlooked. In fact, some linguists in Team 3 have restated their views on this issue. Leech (2014: 14), for instance, has recently acknowledged the fact that some expressions may become highly conventionalised for the performance of some speech acts. He refers to this process as *pragmaticalisation* and further argues that *pragmalinguistics* should be concerned with the lexico-grammatical resources of language and with how their frequency of use leads to their conventionalisation/pragmaticalisation. In Section 2.5, we shall argue that a sound and exhaustive account of speech acts should also aim at explaining the motivations underlying the wider use of conventional forms.

2.5 A Cognitive-Constructional Approach to Directive Speech Acts

The revision of previous theoretical accounts of speech acts in Sections 2.2–2.4 reveals that the portrayals of illocutionary performance are diverse and often even contradictory. If we thought of those portraits as jigsaw puzzles, some of them would have relevant gaps. Thus, social considerations are not taken into account in Searle's and Morgan's accounts, the role of inference is overlooked in Halliday's functional-systemic approach, the possibility of full codification is not considered by Bach and Harnish or Leech, and the motivations of conventionality are not clear in most of them. These are just some of the missing pieces that render traditional accounts of illocution somehow incomplete.

While the need to understand speech acts as social constructs (Leech, 2014), rather than as exclusively linguistic in nature (Searle, 1975), or the advantages of considering the conversational dimension of speech acts (Levinson, 1983; Geis, 1995; Schegloff, 2007) have gradually been accepted in the literature; other issues, like the compatibility of the existing typological evidence supporting the Literal Force Hypothesis, on the one hand, with the role played by codification, conventionalisation, and inference in the performance of speech acts, on the other, are still open to debate. In fact, these three pivotal pieces concerning the relative weight of linguistic form, convention, and inference in the performance of speech acts have not yet found their exact place in the puzzle. So far, as shown in Sections 2.2–2.4, theoretical efforts have, in most cases, been devoted to justifying the predominance of one of them to the exclusion of the others.

2.5.1 What Experimental Linguistics Has Revealed about Speech Act Processing

In this connection, experimental studies aimed at assessing the psychological reality of those competing models have been scarce and often contradictory. Back in the 1970s, Clark and Lucy's (1975) experiments suggested that the interpretation of indirect speech acts took longer than that of literal speech acts, which was taken as proof that the Literal Force Hypothesis is valid, and that it is necessary to recognise the direct force of an utterance prior to the understanding of the indirect meaning intended by the speaker. More recently, eye tracking experiments have yielded similar results (Yin & Kuo, 2013). In this view, both codification and inference seem to play a role in speech act processing, and the longer response times in the interpretation of indirect speech acts suggest that speakers need to decodify the literal meaning before calculating the indirect one, as predicted by the Standard Pragmatics Approaches (e.g. Searle, 1969, 1975; Bach & Harnish, 1979; Sperber & Wilson, 1995).

As shown in previous sections, indirect speech acts are not, however, a homogenous category. Some indirect speech acts have become conventional (Searle, 1969, 1975; Morgan, 1978) or standardised (Bach & Harnish, 1979) for the performance of specific acts (e.g. CAN YOU DO X? requests), while others rely exclusively on inferential calculations (i.e. non-conventional indirect speech acts). Experimental studies have also attempted to assess the psychological reality of this distinction. Clark (1979) carried out an experiment based on question–answer pairs, which showed that the use of conventional forms made it less likely for the listener to retrieve the literal meaning. Both Clark's (1979) and Abbeduto, Furman, and Davies' (1989) similar experiments provided evidence supporting a model of likelihood estimates, in which increasingly specialised linguistic forms for the expression of a given speech act could decrease the need to access the literal meaning of the sentence in order to reach the intended interpretation. This set of experiments seems to corroborate the distinct nature of conventional forms of speech acts and the prototypical nature of the notion of conventionality itself (i.e. different instances of speech acts can display different degrees of conventionality). In much the same vein, Holtgraves' (1994) experimental comparison about processing differences between conventional and non-conventional speech acts shows that the latter require additional processing time. In these studies, the psychological reality of conventional speech acts seems to be experimentally corroborated: speakers do rely on the linguistic form of an expression for its interpretation.

A subsequent collection of experiments carried out by Gibbs (1979, 1984, 1994, 2002), Ervin-Tripp et al. (1987), and Gibbs and Gerrig (1989) gathered evidence supporting the opposing view, namely, that the intended illocutionary force is straightforwardly calculated through inferential processes based on contextual and mutual information, rather than on the linguistic form of the utterance. The response time tests performed by these psycholinguists suggested that, when enough contextual information is available, indirect speech acts do not take longer to be understood than literal expressions. More recent experiments based on electroencephalography (EEG) data about neural activity (Coulson & Lovett, 2010) yield similar response time results. As predicted by proponents of the Direct Access Approaches (Leech and the conversational approaches

2.5 A Cognitive-Constructional Approach

to illocution, among others), these experiments seemed to highlight the role of inference and contextual information in speech act performance to the detriment of linguistics cues. Ruytenbeek (2017: 15) points out, however, that most of these experiments provide rich contextual information to guide the speaker's interpretation of the speech act. It would be 'interesting to see whether any differences in response times would be found when more neutral contexts precede the target utterances, i.e. when the request meaning is not primed by the contexts'.

In sum, experimental data as to whether speakers take longer in interpreting direct or indirect (either conventional or non-conventional) speech acts is inconclusive, and this is probably due to the fact that different experiments present a bias as to providing a higher or lesser amount of linguistic versus contextual information in their design.

What most contemporary experimental studies do conclude is that there exist differences in the way direct and indirect speech acts are processed. Coulson and Lovett's (2010) measurements of electrical brain activity reveal a higher amount of memory retrieval in the case of indirect speech acts. Van Ackeren et al.'s (2012) and Gisladottir, Chwilla, and Levinson's (2015) experiments reported an extra activation of the Theory of Mind areas (medial pre-frontal cortex and temporo-parietal junction) in the interpretation of indirect speech acts. Pupillometry tests (Tromp, Hagoort & Meyer, 2016) showed that indirect speech acts have a higher processing cost which correlates with larger pupil diameters. These studies refer exclusively to differences between direct versus non-conventional indirect speech acts. Nevertheless, it should be remembered that previous research had already revealed response time differences between conventional and non-conventional indirect speech acts (Clark, 1979; Abbeduto, Furman & Davies, 1989; Holtgraves, 1994).

All in all, contemporary experimental findings do point to differences in processing between direct (codified) and indirect (conventional and non-conventional or fully inferred) speech acts. As pointed out by Trott (2016) and Ruytenbeek (2017), however, the psycholinguistic and neuroscience studies carried out to date do not offer detailed explanations for the cognitive mechanisms involved in the processing of those three types of speech acts. They do not answer the question of how direct and indirect (conventional and non-conventional) speech acts are performed. To overcome this void, the approach to speech acts that will be spelled out in the next sections seeks to be compatible with current knowledge on the type of cognitive operations involved in language processing, as described within the cognitive linguistics framework. The resulting proposal also attempts to integrate the relevant pieces of the illocutionary puzzle that have been identified in our previous discussion of contemporary theoretical accounts of speech acts, and the existing experimental evidence on their performance. In particular, our approach will endeavour to be consistent with the following.

- Typological evidence pointing to the universal existence of three major sentence types.
- Psycholinguistic and neuroscientific evidence about the differences in processing and response times among direct (fully codified) and indirect speech acts (conventional and non-conventional or fully inferred), accounting for the lower response times needed when either (1) contextual information or (2) the linguistic form provide cues about the speech act involved.
- The mainstream theoretical observation that some linguistic forms display a conventional status and are more frequently used than others in the communicative realisation of different speech act types.
- Current psycholinguistic evidence that conventional speech acts are not a homogeneous category, and that their conventionality may be modulated using linguistic forms with a higher or lower degree of specialisation for the expression of a speech act.
- The need to transcend the linguistic nature of speech acts and regard them as social constructs, hence considering interactional (i.e. politeness, social power, and distance, formality) and transactional (i.e. cost–benefit) variables in their description.
- The advantages of considering speech acts as a non-static phenomenon based in interaction and, hence, of adopting a suprasentential and conversational perspective in their depiction.

In sum, we shall argue that the final speech acts puzzle, in order to be complete, should include pieces pertaining to the social nature of illocutionary categories and also to one of their potential realisations (i.e. by means of language). Since linguistic communication is kaleidoscopic, and speakers can make use of different mechanisms (i.e. codification, conventionalisation, and/or inference) in conveying their messages, the resulting theoretical speech act puzzle should make room for these three essential aspects of human communication and explain how speakers resort to one or another mechanism in a principle-based manner and as required by the context in which the communicative act takes place. In order to accomplish these objectives, the ensuing theoretical proposal on speech act performance will take advantage of the current knowledge about

2.5 A Cognitive-Constructional Approach

the cognitive operations that underlie human reasoning and inferential abilities, as described within the cognitive linguistics framework.

2.5.2 Redefining the Literal Force Hypothesis in terms of Sentence Type/Speech Act Compatibility

Most languages distinguish three sentence types (i.e. affirmative, imperative, and interrogative) and the Literal Force Hypothesis states that each of them matches a basic communicative function or speech act (i.e. assertion, order, and question). Nevertheless, it is an observable fact that these three sentence types do not match those three basic speech acts univocally. We can use affirmative sentences to ask for information (e.g. *I would like to know if you are coming*) and to give orders (e.g. *Please, I want you to stop!*), interrogatives to express orders (e.g. *Can you stop, NOW!!!?*), imperatives to formulate questions (e.g. *Let me know who's coming*), etc. In addition, each of the three basic sentence types can also be used to perform a wider range of speech acts different from the three basic ones.

As shown in previous sections, all speech act instances in which a sentence type is used with a force that is different from the one originally associated with it are considered indirect speech acts. If it were really necessary to decodify the direct meaning before calculating the indirect one, this should yield longer response times for indirect speech acts. As reported in Section 2.5.1, however, experimental evidence as to whether direct or indirect speech acts take longer to be interpreted is inconclusive. The Literal Force Hypothesis, as it stands, is not clearly supported by the data. What the experiments do tell us is that there are clear differences between the processing mechanisms involved in the interpretation of these two groups of speech acts (i.e. direct versus indirect), as well as between conventional and non-conventional illocutions. In other words, we interpret direct and indirect (conventional and non-conventional) speech acts in different ways, but this does not necessarily mean that some of them are most costly or time-consuming than the others.

Models of illocutionary performance should be consistent with the aforementioned experimental findings and should also acknowledge the typological fact that most languages have three sentence types. In order to satisfy these two conditions, it is necessary to reformulate the Literal Force Hypothesis in such a way that it does not force a two-step interpretation pattern of indirect speech acts, according to which speakers first access their direct force and only at a later stage derive the indirect one. This original formulation of the Literal Force Hypothesis is straightforwardly linked to higher processing times in the case of indirect speech acts, a fact that experimental studies have not been able to confirm.

In this connection, some linguists have posed the question of whether it is actually necessary to posit a strong Literal Force Hypothesis in which sentence types correspond to specific speech act forces. Granted that all languages distinguish three sentential forms, Risselada (1993) has argued that these do not need to be straightforwardly associated with the three basic functions of ordering, asserting, and questioning. She proposes a weaker version of the Literal Force Hypothesis which ascribes less specified illocutionary forces to the three universal sentence types (Risselada, 1993: 71):

- affirmative sentences: those which present a proposition
- interrogative sentences: those which present a proposition as (partially) open
- imperative sentences: those which present the content of a proposition for realisation.

According to Risselada, therefore, the relationship between sentence type and speech act force is no longer one of univocal association but rather one of compatibility: each sentence form is compatible with a range of illocutionary acts.[7] Affirmative sentences display the highest standards of compatibility. Since affirmative sentences simply 'present a proposition', they can be used to express virtually any type of speech act (e.g. representative acts, like asserting: *This car is blue*; commissive acts, like promises: *I will buy you the bike of your dreams*; and a large collection of directive acts like requests (e.g. *I would like you to read my book*), questions for information (e.g. *I would like you to tell me more about yourself*), pieces of advice (e.g. *If I were you, I would consider moving to a bigger apartment*), and threats (e.g. *You are going to raise your hands if you don't want me to shoot you in the head*), etc.). Imperatives 'present the content of a proposition for realisation', which leads to a lower degree of compatibility. In fact, they are only compatible with those speech acts that involve a future action by

---

[7] This idea is in line with Alston's (2000: 186) suggestion to take as the meaning of a sentence its potential to perform illocutionary acts: 'A sentence's having a certain meaning consists in its being usable to perform illocutionary acts of a certain type'. Kissine (2011, 2012, 2014: 4) and Kissine and Jary (2014: ch. 2) also provide a case against the univocal association of illocutionary forces to sentence types. In line with Risselada, these authors define imperatives as those sentence types 'presenting their propositional content as potential', which makes them particularly suited for the performance of directive speech acts but not incompatible with other non-directive illocutionary forces (e.g. questions for information, offers, etc.).

someone different from the speaker. They can be used to perform directive acts like orders (e.g. *Finish your report by tomorrow*), requests (e.g. *Finish your report by tomorrow, please / will you? / can you?*), advice acts (e.g. *Study more if you want to pass your exams*), warnings (e.g. *Don't cross that road if you want to be alive*), suggestions (e.g. *Let's go to the cinema this evening, shall we?*), threats (e.g. *Raise your hands or I'll shoot you*), and even questions for information (e.g. *Let me know your address, please*), among others. Nevertheless, imperatives do not allow the expression of commissive acts (e.g. promises, refusals) or representative acts (e.g. asserting, concluding, remarking, etc.). Finally, interrogative sentences, which 'present a proposition as (partially) open', are compatible with some directive forces that allow optionality of choice for the addressee to comply (e.g. requests: *Will you help me with this?*; beggings: *Please, please, please, can you help me with this?*; etc.) but prototypically not as much with other directives that presume the addressee's compliance (e.g. warning, ordering); and they are blatantly incompatible with the expression of representative (e.g. asserting, concluding, etc.) and commissive acts (e.g. promises, refusals, pledges, etc.).

The redefinition of the Literal Force Hypothesis in terms of compatibility wires the speakers' interpretation processes towards a default set of meanings, thus restricting the potential set of targets to those compatible with each sentence type. It does not, however, assign a particular illocutionary force to each sentence type, thus making unnecessary the two-step interpretation process (i.e. first direct, then indirect force) that derived from the original formulation of the Literal Force Hypothesis and that was not supported by experimental findings. If this weak version of the Literal Force Hypothesis is accepted, then it is only necessary to further specify the intended illocutionary force of an utterance so that the listener can choose from those initially compatible with the sentence form. This can be done linguistically, by making use of lexico-grammatical resources that further clarify the illocutionary force of the message, or contextually, when the situational setting itself provides enough clues to reach the intended interpretation. By way of illustration, consider example (2.7):

(2.7) Turn down the volume

According to the traditional version of the Literal Force Hypothesis, this utterance displays an imperative sentence form, and it should, therefore, be associated with the speech act force of orders. Any other illocutionary force that could be expressed by this utterance in specific contexts (e.g. requesting, advising, warning, etc.) would have to be calculated after verifying that the order interpretation does not suit the context at hand.

By contrast, if the weaker version of the Literal Force Hypothesis is applied to the interpretation of this utterance, then its imperative sentence form will simply be taken as an indicator of the range of potential illocutionary forces that it may express: mostly directive speech acts like orders, commands, requests, beggings, suggestions, warnings, pieces of advice, threats, offers, invitations, etc. As it stands, the bare imperative in example (2.7) is largely underspecified as its exact illocutionary meaning. If no other contextual or linguistic information is provided, the speaker will be largely at a loss in its interpretation. Luckily this is rarely the case. Speakers often provide additional linguistic information that guides the interpretation of the message; and when they do not, it is usually the case that this information can be directly retrieved from the context. Let us see each mechanism in turn. The exact illocutionary force could be further specified through linguistics means, as illustrated by the following elaborations of example (2.7).

(2.8) Turn down the volume, will you? / please / if you don't mind
(2.9) Turn down the volume, if you don't want to become deaf
(2.10) Turn down the volume, or I'll punish you
(2.11) Please, please, please, turn down the volume

Each of the examples above activates a key attribute of a specific directive speech act, thus cutting down or straightforwardly restricting the interpretation of the illocutionary force of the initial imperative to that of a particular directive speech act. In example (2.8), the adverb *please*, the question tag, or the conditional phrase explicitly conveys the fact that the addressee has the freedom to decide whether to do the action or not. This element of optionality is not compatible with directives like orders and threats, but it is central to the act of requesting, which turns out to be the most likely interpretation of this example. The utterance in (2.9) makes use of a conditional phrase that states the negative consequences that the action of hearing the radio at a high volume may have for the listener. Helping others avoid costs or harms is central to the nature of the act of warning, and the imperative is thus very likely to be interpreted as such. In example (2.10) the juxtaposed phrase communicates the action that the speaker will carry out against the listener if he does not comply. Stating negative actions against the addressee in the case of non-compliance is a pivotal trait of threats, which is the most predictable reading of this imperative. Finally, the iterative use of politeness markers (e.g. *please, please, please*) in example (2.11) reflects an insistence which stems from the lack of power of the speaker and the intensity of his wanting, both of which define the act of begging. In all examples above the use of additional linguistic resources has explicitly activated items of the semantics of different directive categories, thus guiding the listener to the most likely interpretations.

The clues leading to a final interpretation of the initial imperative in example (2.7) need not be linguistic, they can also stem from the context in which the utterance has been produced. Thus, imagine that example (2.7) is uttered by a boy sharing his room with one of his friends. In this context in which the social distance between participants is small, it is already manifest to both speaker and listener that the latter has the freedom to choose whether or not to do the action. The optionality feature that characterises the act of requesting is already active and its knowledge mutually shared by both interactants. This makes it unnecessary to use additional linguistic resources to make it explicit (e.g. *please, if you don't mind*, etc.). This mutually shared knowledge of the listener's optionality makes the order, threat, or begging readings easily discarded and leads to a request interpretation.

Relying on contextual information is clearly riskier. Speakers may assume that there is mutual knowledge of the necessary pieces of information for the interpretation of an illocutionary act, but this may not be the case. However, all things being equal, it can be entertained, as a theoretical hypothesis, that the interpretation of sentence (2.7) as a request can be reached as fast when the optionality variable is activated by the context as when it is activated by linguistic resources. In fact, this theoretical proposal fits the experimental data available to date. As shown in Section 2.5.1, those experiments which were rich in providing contextual information retrieved fast response times for so-called indirect speech acts (see Section 2.5.1 on Gibbs', Ervin-Tripp et al.'s and Gibbs & Gerrig's experiments). It was also the case that an increase in the linguistic specification of the force of the act also yielded lower response times for conventional speech acts (see Section 2.5.1 on Clark's, Holtgraves', and Abbeduto, Furman & Davies' experimental findings). Those seemingly contradictory results stemming for experimental studies of speech acts find an explanation in this theoretical proposal that advocates a weaker form of the Literal Force Hypothesis in terms of sentence type-speech act compatibility.

2.5.3 *Revisiting the Notions of Direct and Indirect Speech Acts*

Accepting the revised weaker version of the Literal Force Hypothesis put forward in Section 2.5.2 naturally leads to a redefinition of the concepts of *direct* and *indirect* speech acts. It can be concluded that a speech act is *direct* when the addressee has enough available information to be able to recognise its illocutionary force. This information can be provided linguistically or contextually, as shown in the previous section. Either way, if there is enough information at the addressee's disposal, the interpretation of the illocutionary force of an utterance will be reached easily and unproblematically. On the contrary, a speech act is *indirect* if the information available is not so rich. Lack of information, either contextual or linguistic, necessary implies a higher cognitive cost, as well as a higher risk of misinterpreting the intended force of the utterance.

It is important, in this respect, to distinguish clearly between the notions of indirectness and implicitness. Whether a speech act is explicit or implicit is a linguistic issue dependent on the degree to which its conceptual nature has been linguistically revealed. Whether a speech act is direct or indirect, on the contrary, depends on how much information the speaker has at her disposal about the conceptual nature of the act, regardless of whether that information is provided by contextual or linguistic means. Thus, as argued in Section 2.5.2, a bare imperative, like the one in example (2.7), is implicit (i.e. the lack of explicitness of its linguistic form does not provide enough information to determine its illocutionary force) but not necessarily indirect. If the context provides the addressee with the relevant information, the illocutionary interpretation of the imperative will be straightforward (i.e. direct). It should be borne in mind that, since our revised version of the Literal Force Hypothesis does not assign specific speech act forces to the sentence types, 'indirectness' does not involve a two-step process in which the literal force needs to be reinterpreted according to the context, but rather just a higher amount of inferential calculations to determine which of the illocutionary forces compatible with that sentence form is the one intended by the speaker.

The notions of indirectness and implicitness have often been merged in traditional theories of speech acts. The weaker version of the Literal Force Hypothesis assumed in this piece of research allows us to draw a clear distinction between them. In addition, it may offer a plausible solution to the experimental puzzle, reported in Section 2.5.1, regarding the fact that the process of interpretation of indirect speech acts yielded different response times in different experiments depending on the degree of contextual cues available to the addressee. Under the present redefinition of the notions of indirectness and implicitness, it is to be expected that those speech acts that are not only implicit (i.e. linguistically underdetermined) but also indirect (i.e. lacking relevant information, either linguistic or contextual about their semantics) will show higher response times than those which are implicit

2.5 A Cognitive-Constructional Approach

but not indirect (i.e. those for which the context provides relevant cues, thus making up for the underdetermination of the linguistic form).

Interestingly enough, the newly re-defined notions of direct and indirect speech acts are capable of showing prototypicality effects. The indirectness of a speech act may vary depending on the amount of information provided by the context, through linguistic means, or through a combination of both. Consider the following examples of requests.

(2.12) Open the door
(2.13) Can you open the door?
(2.14) If you don't mind, can you open the door?
(2.15) If you don't mind, can you open the door, please?
(2.16) If you don't mind, could you open the door, please?

Let us assume a situation between two strangers in which the context does not provide any relevant information that may help the listener identify the illocutionary forces of these utterances. In this situation, example (2.12) would come through as a rather implicit and indirect speech act, which would probably leave the listener wondering if he is being ordered, suggested, or requested to carry out the action. The lack of contextual information, together with the linguistic underspecification of the utterance (i.e. a simple imperative sentence presenting a proposition for its realisation) does not ease the interpretation process. Example (2.13), which makes use of an interrogative sentence type, presents the proposition as partially open. This is compatible with the illocutionary force of questioning but also with that of requests (which are characterised by their optionality, see Chapter 4). The optionality feature, implicitly activated by the use of the interrogative sentence type, also makes the utterance incompatible with other illocutionary forces that do not present their content as open but rather as compulsory (e.g. orders, commands, threats, etc.). Consequently, the range of potential interpretations of example (2.13) has been reduced, and its indirectness has decreased. Examples (2.14)–(2.16) activate the attribute of optionality more explicitly, not only by means of the openness of the interrogative sentence, but also through the use of the phrase *if you don't mind*, which clearly leaves the decision of carrying out the action in the hands of the listener. In addition, examples (2.15) and (2.16) also activate linguistically the attribute of politeness (*please*, use of past modal *could*), which is a characteristic of requests but not compatible with questions for information. As the explicitness of the linguistic forms increases, the indirectness of the utterances gradually decreases to the point that examples (2.15) and (2.16) could hardly be interpreted as anything other than requests.

The previous explanation of examples (2.12)–(2.16) assumes a neutral context, which does not provide speakers with relevant information that can guide them in the interpretation process. The latter, therefore, relies exclusively on linguistic cues. Under those circumstances, example (2.12) is fully implicit and indirect, while examples (2.13)–(2.16) gradually increase their degree of explicitness and directness thanks to the addition of linguistic cues that guide the interpretation process.

Does this mean that simple imperatives like that in example (2.12) are always indirect requests simply because they are linguistically underspecified? Under the present proposal, the answer is no. Let us imagine a rich context in which the speakers have a similar social status and in which it is clear that neither of them can impose his will on the other (e.g. siblings). In this context, it is mutually known by both speakers that politeness requirements are low or inexistent, and that optionality is taken for granted (i.e. one does not generally feel under an obligation to act as told by their equals if one does not want to). The context itself activates the optionality and politeness attributes characteristic of requests and fills in the necessary information for the listener to interpret (2.12) as a request and not as an order. In this context, the simple imperative is as direct and straightforward an example of request as example (2.16) was shown to be in the neutral, uninformative context above. Indirectness would only arise in those cases in which both the context and the linguistic expression fail to provide the necessary information to identify the intended illocutionary force of an utterance.

This model also fits well with one piece of experimental evidence about speech act processing that has puzzled linguists to date: the fact that examples like (2.12), which have traditionally been considered indirect speech acts, seem to involve a higher amount of memory retrieval (Coulson & Lovett, 2010). Going back to our explanation of examples (2.12)–(2.16) in the presence versus the absence of contextual and/or linguistic information, it is easy to see in which way the interpretation processes differ, and the memory retrieval requirements increase significantly in relation to example (2.12).

In the presence of linguistic information, the listener needs only retrieve his knowledge of the semantic attributes characterising the different speech acts compatible with the sentence type, and then see which one matches those attributes that are activated linguistically. Thus, example (2.16) activates the attributes of politeness and optionality that prototypically define requests. The listener only needs to confirm this matching, by retrieving from his memory the semantics of this particular speech act type.

When the information derives from the context and not from linguistic cues, the process of interpretation is not as straightforward. In the case of the simple imperative in example (2.12), the context tells us that the speakers, being siblings, are equals as regards their power status and close to each other in terms of social distance, but it does not activate explicitly the attributes of optionality and politeness as the linguistic cues do in example (2.16). These semantic attributes of requests are reached inferentially and through a process that involves memory retrieval not only of the speech act categories compatible with the sentence type, but also of other relevant principles and maxims of social interaction. Thus, the Politeness Principle and the social distance scale, for instance, inform the listener that politeness is not as necessary in interactions between people who are socially close to each other, thus making unnecessary the use of a polite request; the optionality scale tells him that the closer two people are in the social distance dimension, the less one can impose on the other, thus ruling out the potential imposing flavour of the bare imperative. Since optionality is presumed in this context, many speech acts types are discarded from the interpretation (i.e. orders, threats, commands). Additionally, since politeness is not necessary, other directives are ruled out (i.e. beggings, which require of politeness even when carried out between socially closed speakers). As a result of these context-based inferences, the request interpretation is reached.

As explained in the previous paragraphs, our theoretical model is capable of offering an explanation for the higher memory retrieval requirements of those speech acts whose interpretation relies exclusively on contextual information. By way of summarising, linguistic information can directly activate semantic attributes of speech act categories. Contextual information can only activate social variables (i.e. social power, social distance, formality), and then the speaker needs to further retrieve her knowledge (1) of the semantics of the different speech act categories that are compatible with the sentence form of the utterance, and (2) of the principles and scales of social interaction that act on the semantics of speech act categories, helping listeners to infer which speech act categories are compatible both with the sentence type of the utterance and with those social scenarios. The higher memory retrieval requirements of non-conventional indirect speech acts, as attested in experimental studies, therefore, find a plausible explanation within this model of illocution.

2.5.4 Constraining Inferences via Cognitive Operations: Conceptual Metonymy

As illustrated in Section 2.5.3, the interpretation of speech acts involves a process in which the listener identifies the illocutionary force intended by the speaker, among those that are compatible with the sentence type used for its expression. This process is guided and enabled by cues provided either contextually or linguistically. Such cues have been shown to reflect one or more of the characteristic attributes of the speech act type involved (e.g. optionality, politeness, etc.). If all the attributes of an illocutionary category were made explicit, the listener would not have any difficulty in interpreting such an explicit instance of speech act. For different reasons, however, the fact is that fully explicit illocutions are scarce. One obvious reason is that speech acts are polyhedral, kaleidoscopic phenomena whose semantics comprises varied information regarding interactional, transactional, and social features. To give just one example, the meaning of requests includes the following:

- the knowledge of who is expected to perform the requested action (i.e. addressee)
- who is the beneficiary of the action (i.e. speaker)
- the cost of the action and the person upon whom it falls (i.e. addressee)
- the degree of freedom that the addressee has to decide as to whether to perform the requested action or not (i.e. optionality)
- the politeness requirements of the act of requesting (i.e. requests are expected to be polite)
- the knowledge of how the cost of the requested action, the social distance and power relationships between the speaker and the addressee, and the formality of the context may affect the politeness requirements of the act, etc.

Making all these semantic ingredients of requests explicit in their linguistic expression would turn communication into a cumbersome exchange of long-winded utterances. Often this is also unnecessary, because part of that semantic information is provided by the context. And many times, it is not even desirable, because by not making all the semantic items explicit, the speaker can regulate the indirectness of her illocutionary acts, thus increasing the optionality granted to the addressee, decreasing the imposing feeling of her speech acts, and eventually increasing their politeness. In other words, lack of explicitness can be exploited as a means of producing speech acts that do not threaten social conviviality.

2.5 A Cognitive-Constructional Approach

Granted that full explicit rendering of all the features defining an illocutionary category is often not an option, the question that arises is how it is possible for the addressee to identify the speech act category intended by the speaker on the basis of the linguistic expression of just a few of the semantic attributes that define it. Cognitive linguists have provided an answer to this question based on the interaction of two cognitive models: a non-dynamic model of propositional knowledge organisation (whose nature may vary slightly in different approaches and may be referred to as *illocutionary frame, propositional cognitive model*, or *scenario*) and a dynamic cognitive model that operates on the former (e.g. *conceptual metonymy*).[8]

The first attempt to explain the interpretation of speech acts in these terms was put forward by Panther and Thornburg (1998: 759). These authors coined the term *illocutionary scenario* to refer to the collection of semantic attributes defining each illocutionary category that speakers have stored in their long-term memories. The request scenario was said to consist of the following elements.

a. Before component
   The hearer (H) can do the action (A).
   The speaker (S) wants H to do A.
b. Core component
   S puts H under a (more or less) obligation to do A.
   H is under an obligation to do A (H must / should / ought to do A).
c. After component
   H will do A.
   S has emotional response.

Speakers do not make explicit all the knowledge they have about requests when they want to perform this speech act. Panther and Thornburg's proposal elaborates on Gibbs' (1994: 352) insight that 'speaking and understanding indirect speech acts involves a kind of metonymic reasoning, where people infer wholes (a series of actions) from a part'. Thus, Panther and Thornburg argue that, in order to produce a request, speakers explicitly activate one of the components of the scenario (e.g. *I would like / want a coke, Can you hold on a sec?* – Before component) to evoke the whole illocutionary act. In this way, metonymic projections on illocutionary scenarios provide natural inferential schemata for the performance of speech acts.

---

[8] The distinction between dynamic and non-dynamic cognitive models stems from Ruiz de Mendoza and Galera Masegosa's (2014) work on cognitive modelling.

Panther and Thornburg's model of illocutionary scenarios reflects the transactional and dynamic nature of speech acts by focusing on the temporal sequence of events characterising them (i.e. before, core, after components). Nevertheless, it largely overlooks the social and interactional side of illocutions. Together with the illocutionary scenario components, knowledge about the act of requesting also comprises facts about the politeness needed to make it successful and about how social aspects like the degree of intimacy or power between the speakers, the cost of the requested action, or the formality of the context affect the politeness requirements of the act (Pérez-Hernández, 2001; Huddleston & Pullum, 2002; Pérez-Hernández & Ruiz de Mendoza, 2002; Mauri & Sansò, 2011; Takahashi, 2012). Formalising all this rich transactional and interactional information about speech act categories exceeds the potentiality of illocutionary scenarios and asks for a more comprehensive model of knowledge organisation, as well as for more specific types of metonymic projections. Section 2.5.5 deals with these issues in detail and lays out a constructional model of illocution that attempts to explain how speech act performance is operationalised.

2.5.5 *Illocutionary Idealised Cognitive Models and (Multiple Source)-in-Target Metonymies*

In the light of the above observations, a more granular conceptual characterisation of illocutionary categories is required to account for all the possible metonymic manifestations of a particular speech act such as the request instances analysed in the previous examples. In this connection, different authors such as Pérez-Hernández (2001, 2013), Huddleston and Pullum (2002), Mauri and Sansò (2011), and Takahashi (2012) have argued that additional parameters like those of power, cost, benefit, optionality, and politeness, among others, would be essential for a comprehensive, solid conceptual characterisation of directive speech acts. As shown above, the inclusion of this type of attributes exceeds the limits of a scenario approach and requires of a more comprehensive model of knowledge organisation for their formalisation.

Pérez-Hernández (2001, 2013) has offered corpus-based evidence about the potentiality of illocutionary ICMs for this task. Illocutionary ICMs consist of an *ontology* and a *structure* (Lakoff, 1987: 285). In relation to illocutionary acts, the *ontology* would comprise the values taken by the attributes conforming to the semantics of each speech act category (e.g. addressee's capability, speaker's need, cost–benefit, optionality, politeness, etc.). In turn, the *structure* would capture the interplays between the

2.5 A Cognitive-Constructional Approach

Table 2.2 *Attributes configuring the ONTOLOGY of directive illocutionary ICMs*

Agent: person who is expected to perform the proposed action (i.e. speaker, addressee, both of them).
Beneficiary of the action: person who benefits from the action (i.e. speaker, addressee, or both of them).
Agent's capability: assessment of the agent's capability to perform the proposed action.
Speaker's willingness: assessment of the speaker's desire that the proposed action is carried out.
Addressee's willingness: assessment of the addressee's desire to perform the proposed action.
Possession of the requested object: assessment of possession of the requested object by the speaker or the addressee.
Speaker's need: assessment of the speaker's need that the proposed action is carried out.
Cost–benefit: assessment of the cost/benefit of the proposed action.
Optionality: assessment of the degree of freedom granted to the agent to carry out the proposed action or to opt out.
Mitigation: assessment of the degree to which the cost of the proposed action is mitigated.
Politeness: assessment of the politeness requirements of the illocutionary act.

---

different attributes (e.g. how the cost of the requested action affects the politeness requirements of the act), as well as between those attributes and certain extralinguistic variables that may affect their assessment (e.g. how the power relationship between the speakers determines the optionality of the addressee to decide about his course of action). Since our description of directive illocutions in Chapter 4 will be based on these theoretical constructs, let us look in more detail into the nature of the ontology and the structure of directive speech acts in turn.

The ontology of directive illocutionary ICMs comprises the attributes listed in Table 2.2 (elaboration of the initial proposal in Pérez-Hernández (2013: 133–134) based on the new corpus data in this study).

As revealed in previous sections, the description of the semantic side of illocutionary acts should include considerations about participants (e.g. agent's capability, speaker's needs, etc.), dimensions of social interaction (e.g. politeness, optionality, etc.), and aspects of the transactions involved (e.g. cost–benefit, possession of the requested object). By way of illustration, Table 2.3 displays the specific ontology of the illocutionary ICM of requesting, which captures the prototypical parametrisation of the attributes conforming to this illocutionary act.

As shall be made apparent in the remainder of this section, the exhaustive description of the semantic attributes that define the act of

Table 2.3 *Ontology for the illocutionary ICM of the act of requesting*

Agent: addressee.
Beneficiary: speaker.
Agent's capability: the agent needs to be capable of performing the requested action.
Speaker's willingness: the speaker wants the requested action to be carried out.
Addressee's willingness: the addressee's willingness to carry out the action is required.
Requested object: the requested object should be in the possession of the agent or be accessible to him.
Speaker's need: the speaker needs the requested action to be carried out.
Cost–benefit: the requested action is typically costly.
Optionality: the addressee is typically free to decide upon his course of action in relation to the request.
Mitigation: the cost of the requested action is mitigated/minimised.
Politeness: requests are polite speech acts.

requesting in the form of an illocutionary ICM enhances the scope of its metonymic exploitation. Additionally, it increases the explanatory power of a metonymic account of illocution, overcoming some of the limitations of the illocutionary scenario approach, at least in four different respects.

1. *Illocutionary ICMs allow speakers to distinguish different speech act categories.* According to the illocutionary scenario approach, in examples (2.17) and (2.18) the core component of the request scenario is activated by means of the imperative sentence, which puts the hearer under the obligation to hold the book for the speaker. If they both activate the same component, it would logically follow that they realise the same act of requesting. However, while the adverb of immediateness *now* prompts an order interpretation, the conditional clause *if you don't mind* favours a request reading. The explanatory power of the scenario approach is not capable of distinguishing specific illocutionary acts (e.g. orders, requests, warnings, etc.) within the broader category of directive speech acts.

    (2.17)   Hold this book now! (Web Corp Live, accessed August 5th, 2012)
    (2.18)   Hold this book, if you don't mind (Web Corp Live, accessed August 5th, 2012)

    By contrast, illocutionary ICMs include the necessary information to allow speakers to distinguish between subtypes of directives like those in examples (2.17) and (2.18). Thus, both *now* and *if you don't mind* are

2.5 A Cognitive-Constructional Approach

Hold this book now! – Order construction / Hold this book, if you don't mind – Request construction

ICM OF ORDERING → Agent: addressee, Beneficiary, Agent's capability, Speaker's willingnes, Addressee's willingness, Possession of requested object, Speaker's need, Cost-benefit, Optionality [low], Mitigation, Politeness

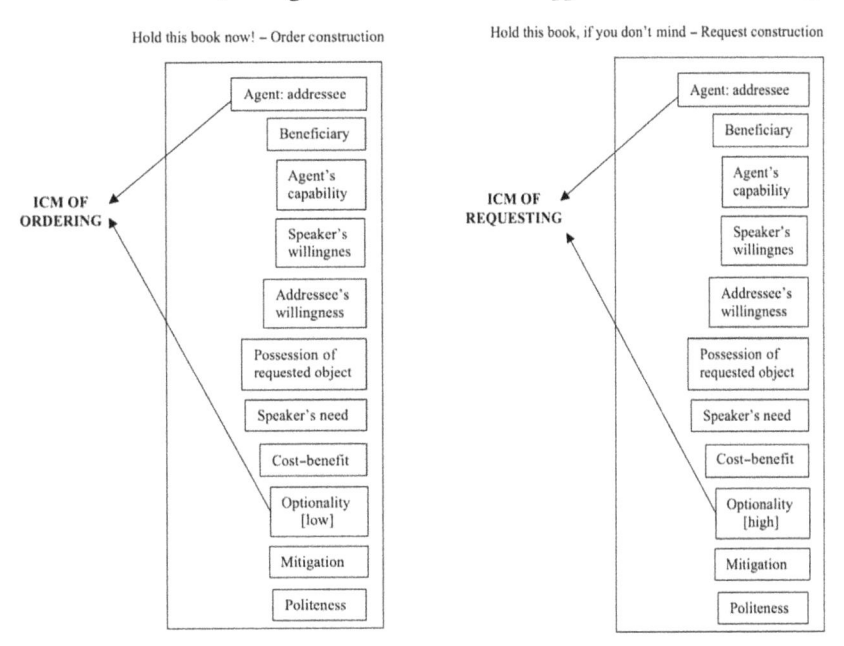

ICM OF REQUESTING → Agent: addressee, Beneficiary, Agent's capability, Speaker's willingnes, Addressee's willingness, Possession of requested object, Speaker's need, Cost-benefit, Optionality [high], Mitigation, Politeness

Figure 2.2 Metonymic activation underlying examples (2.17) and (2.18)

linguistic resources that help modulate the *optionality* granted by the speaker to the addressee to carry out the requested action. Different directive acts are characterised by allowing diverse amounts of freedom to the addressee to comply with the speaker's wishes. Orders, being prototypically imposing acts, display lower levels of optionality. By contrast, requests typically exhibit high doses of optionality, offering the addressee the freedom to refuse to do as solicited. By linguistically activating the different values of the optionality attribute that characterise orders or requests, the utterances in examples (2.17), and (2.18) metonymically activate the corresponding speech act, as shown in Figure 2.2.

2. *Illocutionary ICMs provide motivation for a higher number of speech act constructions, thus enhancing the scope of their metonymic exploitation.* As pointed out by Pérez-Hernández (2013: 132), illocutionary scenarios, focusing mainly on sequential aspects of illocutionary performance, do not provide an explanation for many of the speech act expressions used in our everyday life interactions. While metonymic exploitation of Panther and Thornburg's illocutionary scenario of requesting accounts for instances of requests based on the before (e.g. *Can you*

pass me the book?, *I want a book*), core (*Pass me the book*), and after components (*Will you pass me the book?*), respectively, it is incapable of accommodating the following examples of requests, since they do not metonymically activate any of the components of the scenario.

(2.19)   I need a little more information (Web Corp Live, accessed August 5th, 2012)

(2.20)   Have you got a pen? (Web Corp Live, accessed August 5th, 2012)

(2.21)   Would you mind washing the car for me? (Web Corp Live, accessed August 5th, 2012)

(2.22)   Would it be too much trouble for you to cook me dinner tonight? (Web Corp Live, accessed August 5th, 2012)

By contrast, in the illocutionary ICMs approach, example (2.19) metonymically activates the requesting illocutionary ICM by making explicit the *speaker's need* and *optionality* attributes. Example (2.20) does so through the *possession of the requested object* and *optionality* attributes. In example (2.21), the request reading is metonymically cued by the *agent, beneficiary, optionality,* and *politeness* attributes. Finally, the utterance in example (2.22) also makes use of the *cost–benefit* attribute, thorough the use of a question aimed at assessing the cost of the requested action (i.e. Would it be *too much trouble ...?*).[9] Figure 2.3 illustrates the metonymic operations at work in the interpretation of each the above utterances as requests:

3. *The metonymic exploitation of illocutionary ICMs accounts for variations in the degree of explicitness of speech acts.* If examples (2.19)–(2.22) are observed closely, it becomes apparent that not all instances of requests metonymically instantiate the same number of attributes of the corresponding illocutionary ICM. Examples (2.19) and (2.20) only instantiate two attributes, while examples (2.21) and (2.22) activate four and five attributes, respectively. This type of metonymic operation, in which not just one but several source subdomains are mapped onto the same target domain, has been labelled *(multiple source)-in-target metonymy* and has been found to allow for a continuum of degrees of explicitness in the performance of speech acts (Pérez-Hernández,

---

[9] In examples (2.19)–(2.22) the optionality variable is indirectly activated by the use of declarative and interrogative sentence types, which as opposed to imperatives, offer the hearer the possibility of refusing to carry out the proposed action without blatantly losing face. In example (2.20), for instance, the hearer can simply answer negatively to the question for information (i.e. *I haven't got one*), and thus avoid compliance with the request without coming through as impolite.

2.5 A Cognitive-Constructional Approach 55

I need X – Request construction

ICM OF REQUESTING
- Agent: addressee
- Beneficiary
- Agent's capability
- Speaker's willingnes
- Addressee's willingness
- Possession of requested object
- Speaker's need
- Cost-benefit
- Optionality
- Mitigation
- Politeness

Have you got X? – Request construction

ICM OF REQUESTING
- Agent: addressee
- Beneficiary
- Agent's capability
- Speaker's willingnes
- Addressee's willingness
- Possession of requested object
- Speaker's need
- Cost-benefit
- Optionality
- Mitigation
- Politeness

Would you mind doing X for me? – Request construction

ICM OF REQUESTING
- Agent: addressee
- Beneficiary
- Agent's capability
- Speaker's willingnes
- Addressee's willingness
- Possession of requested object
- Speaker's need
- Cost-benefit
- Optionality
- Mitigation
- Politeness

Would it be too much trouble for you to do X for me? – Request construction

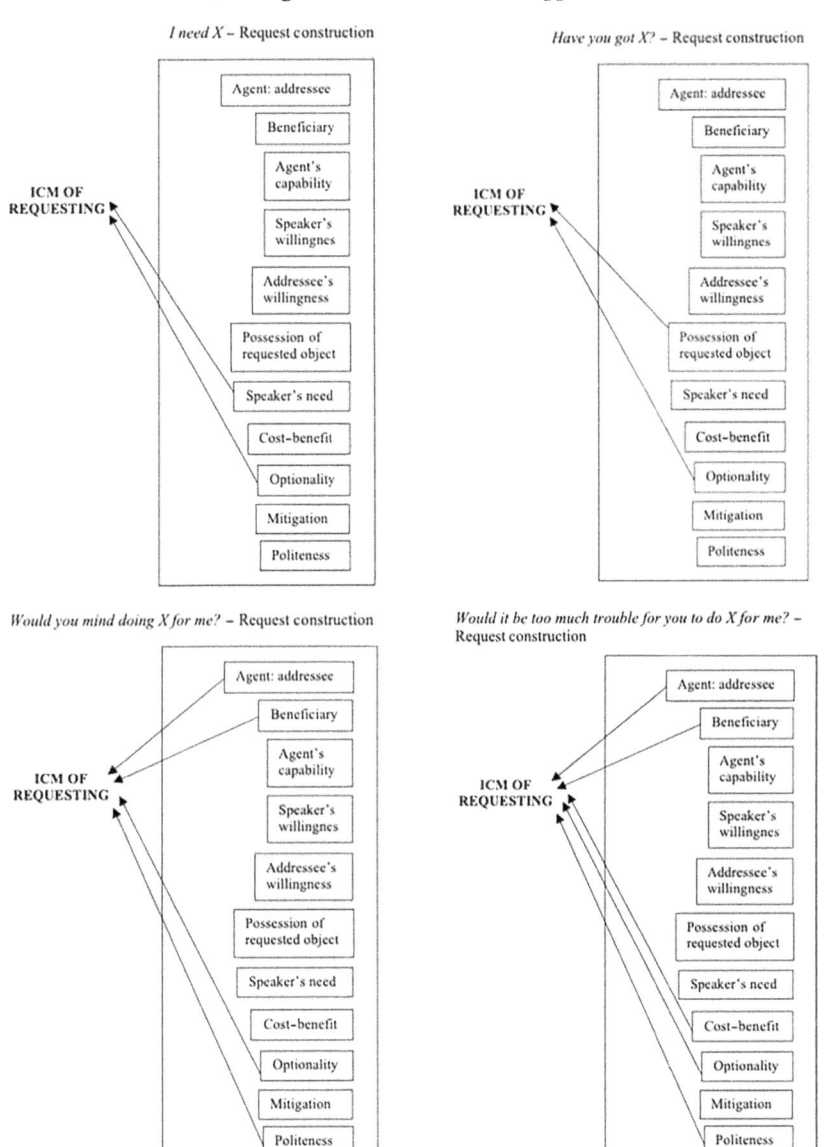

ICM OF REQUESTING
- Agent: addressee
- Beneficiary
- Agent's capability
- Speaker's willingnes
- Addressee's willingness
- Possession of requested object
- Speaker's need
- Cost-benefit
- Optionality
- Mitigation
- Politeness

Figure 2.3 Metonymic activation underlying examples (2.19)–(2.22)

2013). Thus, the higher the number of attributes that are made explicit linguistically and, in turn, metonymically projected onto a particular illocutionary target domain, the higher the codification of the act is and the lower the need for inferential mechanisms will be in its interpretation.[10] Example (2.23) illustrates a highly explicit instance of request which metonymically instantiates seven attributes of this illocutionary category.

(2.23) If you don't mind, could you please give me a little jump start in finding some of these names and their sources? (iWeb).

Figure 2.4 displays the multiple attributes of the illocutionary ICM of requesting that are projected to render a request interpretation: addressee as the agent of the action (*you*), speaker as the beneficiary of the action (*me*), optionality granted to the addressee to choose whether or not to do the action (*if you don't mind*), and politeness (*please*, oblique modal *could*). The costly nature of the action is indirectly activated through the instantiation of the mitigation attribute (*a little*). If compared to previous examples like I NEED X OR HAVE YOU GOT X? (Figure 2.3), example (2.23) illustrates an extreme case of linguistic explicitation of the act of requesting. The fact that so many attributes have been instantiated linguistically renders its interpretation as a different speech act highly unlikely.

4. *Illocutionary ICMs account for subtle differences between similar illocutionary expressions.* Previous proposals based on illocutionary scenarios also run short of capturing the necessary knowledge about requests to explain the differences between similar instances of speech acts like the two CAN YOU DO X? interrogative requests in examples (2.24) and (2.25). Both utterances metonymically activate the same before component (i.e. the ability of the addressee to carry out the requested action). Nevertheless, they differ as to their meaning implications.

(2.24) **Can** you convince him a deal's already in place? (iWeb)
(2.25) **Could** you convince him a deal's already in place?

As shown in Pérez-Hernández (1996), the choice of the oblique modal in example (2.25) is tied to considerations of politeness that exceed the

---

[10] Pending experimental confirmation, this model of illocutionary performance can at least entertain the hypothesis of a lower cognitive cost in terms of reaction times in the interpretation of those speech act expressions offering access to a higher number of subdomains of a particular illocutionary act.

2.5 A Cognitive-Constructional Approach

If you don't mind, could you please give me a little jump start in finding some of these names and their sources? – Request construction

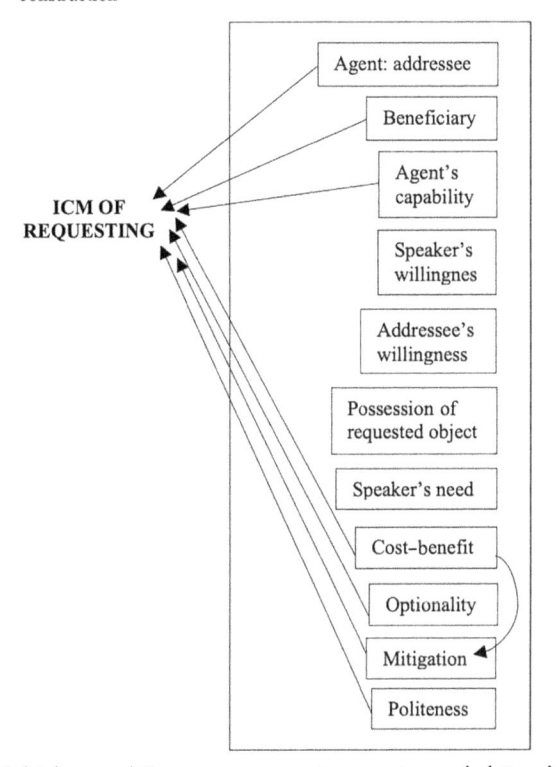

ICM OF REQUESTING
- Agent: addressee
- Beneficiary
- Agent's capability
- Speaker's willingnes
- Addressee's willingness
- Possession of requested object
- Speaker's need
- Cost–benefit
- Optionality
- Mitigation
- Politeness

Figure 2.4 (Multiple source)-in-target metonymic operation underlying the request act in example (2.23)

information provided by illocutionary scenarios. Common knowledge about requests also includes the fact that they are inherently polite acts. This feature distinguishes requests from prototypical orders, threats, and other directives. The explicit linguistic activation of this central attribute of the illocutionary category of requests favours its interpretation as such. The illocutionary ICM model accommodates this distinction through the additional projection of the politeness attribute. See Figure 2.5 for a visual representation of the subtle but relevant differences in the conceptual motivation of examples (2.24) and (2.25).

As shown so far, the ontology of each illocutionary ICM captures the attributes that define the prototypical instances of a particular

58 What Contemporary Research Tells Us about Speech Acts

Can you convince him a deal's already in place? –
Request construction

Could you convince him a deal's already in place? –
Request construction

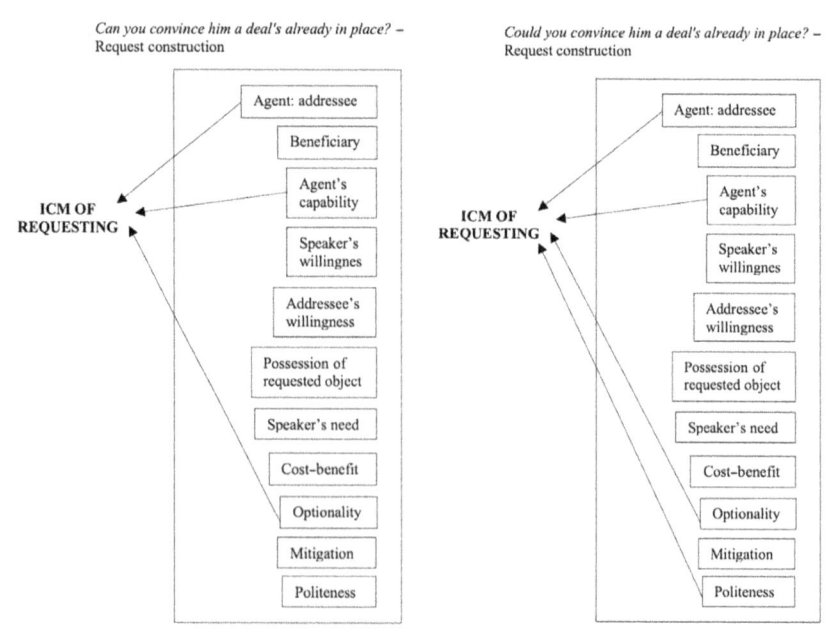

ICM OF REQUESTING

- Agent: addressee
- Beneficiary
- Agent's capability
- Speaker's willingnes
- Addressee's willingness
- Possession of requested object
- Speaker's need
- Cost-benefit
- Optionality
- Mitigation
- Politeness

ICM OF REQUESTING

- Agent: addressee
- Beneficiary
- Agent's capability
- Speaker's willingnes
- Addressee's willingness
- Possession of requested object
- Speaker's need
- Cost-benefit
- Optionality
- Mitigation
- Politeness

Figure 2.5 Conceptual motivation underlying the CAN vs. COULD YOU DO X? request constructions in examples (2.24) and (2.25)

speech act category and serves as basis for the metonymic activation of the corresponding illocutionary constructions. Some of the attributes are scalar in nature and may take different values in different contexts (e.g. the cost of the requested action may vary, the speaker's need or desire that the action is carried out may also change from one situation to another, etc.). More importantly, the values taken by one attribute may affect those of others. To give just one example of the potential interactions between attributes, if the cost of the requested action increases (i.e. if the speaker is asking for something that has a high cost in time or effort for the addressee), then the need to mitigate the cost of the act and the politeness requirements to secure compliance with the request will also tend to increase.

Additionally, the values taken by the attributes conforming to the ontology of the illocutionary ICM may also be affected by some social variables, such as the power relationship between the participants, the social distance between them, and the formality of the context in which the interaction is taking place. Thus, if the social power of the addressee is markedly higher than that of the speaker, the latter will feel a need to increase the

2.5 A Cognitive-Constructional Approach

Table 2.4 *Social variables configuring the STRUCTURE of directive illocutionary ICMs*

Power: power relationship holding between the speakers. The vertical asymmetries of power between speakers can stem from their social status as members of different social classes, professional categories, institutional ranks, or knowledge groups.
Social distance: social distance existing between the speakers. This is a horizontal dimension pertaining to familiarity or friendship relationships (i.e. friends, strangers, relatives).
Formality: the formality of the context in terms of its politeness requirements.

optionality, the politeness, and/or the mitigation of his act to guarantee its success. This is so because speakers are aware of the workings of social interaction and have learned through experience that imposing their wishes on someone who is socially more powerful requires some tact.

These interplays between the attributes of an illocutionary ICM or between one of these attributes and one or more social variables (social power, social distance, formality) need to be formalised to reach a proper understanding of the functioning of speech acts. In this book, such interplays are included in the so-called *structure* of each illocutionary ICM. The social variables conforming to such structure are defined in Table 2.4.

These social, extralinguistic variables interact with four of the ontological attributes (i.e. cost–benefit, optionality, mitigation, and politeness) and force their reassessment. The specific structure for each illocutionary ICM will comprise these interactions together with those holding between the ontological attributes themselves. Thus, by way of illustration, in relation to the illocutionary act of requesting, some of the interactions conforming to the structure of its illocutionary ICM are captured in Table 2.5.

These interplays are specific of each illocutionary act category, and they guide and constrain the speakers' choice of realisation procedures for the performance of their speech acts. Thus, even though prototypical requests are characterised by their politeness, speakers know that in a context of social familiarity (e.g. mum–son relationship), optionality increases, and that this, in turn, makes politeness requirements decrease. Thus, in such a context, an apparently non-polite formula (e.g. a simple imperative like *Mum, pass the salt*) will be unproblematically understood as a request.

Before ending this section devoted to the semantics of illocutionary categories, it is necessary to bring to the front a relevant theoretical postulate offered as far back as the 1980s by Givon (1989). As this cognitive-functional linguist remarked, it is essential to approach the study of the

Table 2.5 *STRUCTURE of the illocutionary ICM of the act of requesting in terms of interactions between attributes, as well as between attributes and social variables*

Power–optionality: the relative power of the speakers affects the optionality of the addressee to perform the action. Thus, the more powerful the speaker, the lower the addressee's freedom to decide upon his course of action and vice versa.
Social distance–optionality: the closer the speakers are in the social distance axis (i.e. the higher their degree of intimacy), the higher the optionality that the addressee has to choose upon his course of action and vice versa.
Optionality–politeness: the lower the amount of optionality granted to the speaker to decide upon her course of action, the lower the politeness of the speech act and vice versa.
Cost/benefit–politeness: the higher the cost of the requested action, the higher the politeness needs will be in order to secure the addressee's compliance and vice versa.

semantic fabric of speech acts from a typological perspective. Cross-cultural studies of illocution will reveal that societies often differ as to the politeness requirements needed and/or expected for the performance of a particular speech act, as well as to the degree to which social variables (power, social distance, formality) affect the realisation of illocutionary acts. Explicit instruction of these subtle cultural differences in the semantics of speech acts is pivotal for the correct learning of the illocutionary component of a second language.

2.5.6 Assembling the Illocutionary Puzzle: Families of Illocutionary Constructions

The constructional treatment of speech acts is an old longing of linguists from all traditions. The Literal Force Hypothesis itself was an attempt to pair linguistic forms (sentence types) with particular illocutionary forces. Since the very beginning of speech act theory, linguists have tried to identify fixed form-meaning pairings for the expression of speech acts. Communication would be all the more straightforward and unproblematic if speakers had at their disposal clear linguistic formulae with which to communicate their wishes unequivocally. Following this path of thinking, Searle (1969) put forward the notion of *illocutionary force indicating devices* (*IFIDs*), which were expressions that were thought to be activators of a certain illocutionary category. He observed that I'LL DO X formulae, such as *I'll buy you a bike,* are conventionally understood as promises, and CAN YOU DO X? expressions activate the illocutionary force of requesting. Dik (1989, 1997) introduced the notion of *illocutionary conversors*. These

2.5 A Cognitive-Constructional Approach

are certain linguistic items that can change the illocutionary force of an utterance, such as the tag question *Will you?* or the adverb *please*, which can turn an imperative, usually associated with orders, into a request (e.g. *Turn off the radio, will you? / please*). These and similar attempts have not withheld the test of use, since all the examples corresponding to Searle's IFIDs, as well as those stemming from the application of Dik's (1989) illocutionary conversors, can ultimately express other illocutionary forces in alternative contexts (e.g. *I'll buy you a bike tomorrow*, for example, need not be a promise but just a statement of intention).

As explained in Pérez-Hernández (2013: 140), some years later, Stefanowitsch (2003) has made a strong case in support of the constructional nature of some speech act expressions. He argues that some request constructions display a number of semantic and formal properties that cannot be predicted from their component parts or from previous constructions. Thus, the CAN YOU DO X? request construction, according to Stefanowitsch (2003: 16), displays an agentive subject and allows preverbal request markers (e.g. *please, kindly*), alternation of present and conditional forms (e.g. *CAN / COULD YOU DO X?*), and co-occurrence with a preposed subordinate clause explaining the speaker's reason for making the request (e.g. *Since you are stronger than me, can / could you please hold this?*). This view is largely shared by most contemporary constructional accounts of illocution (Panther & Thornburg, 2005; Ruiz de Mendoza & Baicchi, 2007; Brdar-Szabó, 2009; Del Campo, 2013).

However, this proposal does not account for the fact that an expression like *Can you hold this for me?*, which contains no request marker and no preposed subordinate clause, is still unequivocally understood as a request. Contemporary constructional accounts of illocution also fail to explain the different degrees of explicitation of request expressions. As shown in Section 2.5.5, illocutionary constructions can be made more explicit as a higher number of attributes of an illocutionary ICM are linguistically realised: *Can you hold this? > Can you hold this for me? > Can you please hold this for me? > Could you please hold this for me? > If you don't mind / If it's not too much trouble, could you please hold this for me for just a sec?*, etc.

Pairing full linguistic forms with illocutionary meanings has long failed as an attempt to describe illocutionary constructions. As was made apparent in Section 2.5.5 in our description of illocutionary ICMs, the conceptual nature of speech acts is too complex and dynamic to be confined into a fixed form. As argued before, it is also often the case that speakers do not want or need to make all the conceptual material of a speech act explicit, either because it is not necessary (the context fills in the missing information), or because it is interactionally desirable to highlight some aspects of the semantic fabric of the act over others: if a request is costly, speakers may appeal to this issue and try to minimise the cost (e.g. *Can you step aside for a sec?*), if the addressee's co-operation is not clear, they may target his willingness as a strategy to gain his compliance (e.g. ***If you will**, could you step aside?*), if there is a large power asymmetry between speakers, a more polite realisation may be preferred (e.g. student to headmaster: ***Could** you step aside **please**?*), while that same politeness will become unnecessary if the social distance between them is small (e.g. son to his mother: ***Can** you step aside?*), etc.

Does this intrinsic variability make a constructional account of speech acts unfeasible? This book argues that it is, in fact, possible to offer a constructional treatment of illocution, as long as the notion of construction is redefined and adapted to the dynamic, multidimensional nature of speech acts. Goldberg (1995, 2006) defined constructions as non-compositional learned pairings of forms and semantic and/or discourse functions in which one or more of their properties are not predictable from knowledge of other constructions in the language. Constructions vary in size, complexity, and generality and include words and idioms, as well as phrasal linguistic patterns (Goldberg & Suttle, 2010: 469). The orthodox notion of construction, as defined by Goldberg (1995, 2006) within cognitive linguistics, was originally designed to account for argument-structure configurations. This linguistic phenomenon, however, does not need to accommodate the rich social, transactional, and interactional variability that characterises higher levels of linguistic description (pragmatics, discourse/conversation), and that affects so straightforwardly the performance of speech acts. Hence the need to adapt the original notion of construction for this purpose.

As pointed out by Goldberg and Suttle (2010: 469–470), 'it is clear that we need to posit a construction when there is something non-compositional that needs to be learned [... as well as when usage yields a] highly frequent form-meaning pairing. [...] both the items and the generalisations are represented within the interrelated network of constructions: the "construct-i-con"'. As the description of directive speech acts in Chapter 4 will show in detail, this is certainly the case with speech acts. On some occasions, illocutionary constructions can be highly idiomatic, while in most cases they are non-compositional form-meaning pairings motivated by a variable number of the semantic attributes of illocutionary ICMs. Thus, expressions like WOULD YOU MIND DOING X? are idiomatically used as requests as attested by the over 7,000 instances of this construction found in the iWeb corpus. In turn, CAN YOU DO X? expressions constitute

2.5 A Cognitive-Constructional Approach

highly frequent, non-compositional constructions with varying degrees of conventionality and explicitation. This latter type of illocutionary constructions, to which we shall refer as *fluid illocutionary constructions*, do not exhibit fully fixed idiomatic formulae, but rather they are capable of adapting themselves to the variable needs of interpersonal communication, modulating their degree of explicitness and their semantic focus as needed in a particular situation. Fluid illocutionary constructions consist of a fixed *base construction,* which metonymically activates one attribute of the corresponding speech act category, plus a variable number of optional *realisation procedures*, which instantiate other attributes of the same speech act as needed in each concrete interaction. Consider the following instances of requests.

(2.26) **Can you** add a mildewcide to paint at the time of purchase? (iWeb)
(2.27) **Can you** give *me* a sample of a recommendation letter? (iWeb)
(2.28) **Can you** *please* take a look at the one linked below? (iWeb)
(2.29) **Can you** describe *a bit* more the problem with combat controls? (iWeb)
(2.30) *If possible*, **can you** post the solution in the comments? (iWeb)
(2.31) Horace *if it's not too much trouble* **can you** post the locations of the events here? (iWeb)

All of the examples (2.26)–(2.31) share the same base construction, which consists in an interrogative sentence of the CAN YOU DO X? type. This base construction metonymically activates two attributes of the ICM of requests: the addressee's capability to perform an action, by means of the use of the modal verb *can*, and the optionality attribute through the use of the interrogative sentence type, which presents an event for its potential realisation but also leaves open the possibility for the event not taking place at all. The constructional nature of this base construction for the expression of requests is attested by its high frequency of occurrence in the iWeb corpus, in contrast to similar expressions, such as the ARE YOU ABLE TO DO X? construction, which activates the same attributes but which has specialised as a question for information. Thus, a random search of 5,000 instances of the CAN YOU DO X? construction shows that 4,304 instances correspond to requests and only 696 to questions for information. Those CAN YOU DO X? instances that function as questions for information display perception or understanding verbs (e.g. hear, see, understand, etc.), which unlike action verbs (e.g. give, read, sing, etc.), cannot have the speaker as their beneficiary and, therefore, do not comply with one of the central attributes of the ICM of requesting. On the contrary, a similar search for the ARE YOU ABLE TO DO X? structure reveals that this construction is used mainly as a question for information in 4,987 of the cases (e.g. *Are you able to state positively whether or not that indentation was present before the shooting?*) and as a request in just thirteen occurrences, all of which include the politeness marker *please* (e.g. Are you able to *please* provide us some more details regarding your hire?). Experimental studies have argued (Ruytenbeek, Ostashchenko, & Kissine, 2017) that ARE YOU ABLE TO DO X? expressions are understood as requests as easily as CAN YOU DO X? constructions. This is only to be expected, since both expressions activate the same attributes of the ICM of requesting. However, the fact that both of them could be understood as requests does not mean that speakers use them interchangeably. The aforementioned corpus-based evidence shows a high degree of conventionalisation of the CAN YOU DO X? base construction for the expression of requests. In fact, its specialisation for the expression of this illocutionary force becomes manifest in examples like *If you are able, can you check what his current overall ranking is now?* (iWeb), where the division of work between these two constructions becomes transparent. It has also been argued in the literature that CAN YOU DO X? forms may also be used to perform other directive acts, like orders or begs. For example, in a context in which the speaker is socially more powerful than the addressee, CAN YOU DO X? may be used to express a polite order. Again, although possible in very specific contexts, corpus data indicates that this is not the prototypical use of this construction. The random sample of 5,000 CAN YOU DO X? instances yields no occurrences in which this construction is used to express an order. These findings show that previous studies were mistaking the theoretical potential of the construction with its actual use. The CAN YOU DO X? formula is rarely found instantiating any other speech act type than a request in actual usage, and when it does, it corresponds to non-prototypical instances of other illocutionary categories such as the aforementioned polite order.

In addition, the CAN YOU DO X? base construction can be further specified linguistically for the instantiation of requests, so that its directive flavour is highlighted, and its interpretation as a question for information is totally ruled out. Let us consider once more examples (2.27)–(2.31), reproduced here for convenience.

(2.27) **Can you** give *me* a sample of a recommendation letter? – beneficiary (speaker)
(2.28) **Can you** *please* take a look at the one linked below? – politeness

2.5 A Cognitive-Constructional Approach

Table 2.6 *Realisation procedures for the attributes of the ICM of requesting*

Beneficiary	Me/us, for me/for us E.g. *Can you give me a book? Can you find out the answer for me?*
Cost–benefit	If it is not too much trouble, if it doesn't bother you, if it's not too much to ask E.g. *If it's not too much to ask, can you find out the answer for me?*
Optionality	If possible, if you will, if you are able, maybe, perhaps E.g. *If possible, can you reach me the book?*
Mitigation	A bit, a little, a sec, for a second, just E.g. *Can you wait for a second?*
Politeness	Please, kindly, use of conditional modals (could), if you please E.g. *Could you please stay still for a sec?*

(2.29) **Can you** describe *a bit* more the problem with combat controls? – mitigation
(2.30) *If possible*, **can you** post the solution in the comments? – optionality
(2.31) Horace *if it's not too much trouble* **can you** post the locations of the events here? – cost–benefit

The words in italics activate additional specific attributes of the requesting ICM. In example (2.27), the personal pronoun *me* instantiates the speaker-as-beneficiary feature. In example (2.28), the adverb *please* instantiates the politeness attribute of requests. In example (2.29), *a bit* functions as a mitigator of the cost of the proposed action (i.e. mitigation attribute). In example (2.30), *if possible* presents the request as tentative thus increasing the freedom of the addressee to comply with it or to refuse to do it (i.e. optionality attribute). Finally, in example (2.31) the conditional phrase *if it is not too much trouble* directly alludes to the cost of the requested action, thus instantiating this specific attribute. It should be noted that the different attributes could be linguistically instantiated by other expressions with similar semantics. Although the inventory of realisation procedures for each attribute of the ICM of requesting will be dealt with in detail in Chapter 4, Table 2.6 includes some illustrative examples.

As shown in Section 2.5.5 in relation to examples (2.19)–(2.23), a single base construction can also be combined with a varying number of realisation procedures, thus metonymically activating a smaller or larger number of illocutionary attributes and yielding instances of requests that differ as to their degree of explicitness.

The different combinations of the base construction (CAN YOU DO X?) with specific realisation procedures for the attributes of the request

Table 2.7 *Number of occurrences in iWeb for the realisation procedures of the requests in examples (2.27)–(2.31)*

Base structure + realisation procedures for specific attributes	Number of occurrences (iWeb)
Can you do X? + beneficiary (me)	73,852
Can you do X? + politeness (please)	32,690
Can you do X? + mitigation (a bit)	4,577
Can you do X? + optionality (if possible)	197
Can you do X? + cost–benefit (if it's not too much trouble)	139

ICM conform to a family of constructions whose members display different degrees of conventionality. As shown in Table 2.7, different combinations have been found to have different degrees of productivity in the iWeb corpus, which suggests that some of them are more conventional than others.

The above data indicates that illocutionary constructions, just like constructions at other levels of linguistic description (Goldberg & Suttle, 2010), capture generalisations within a given language. The members of the CAN YOU DO X? family of request constructions are related via an inheritance hierarchy, with more abstract, productive constructions (i.e. base constructions) being directly related to their more conventional instantiations.

The description of the family of constructions for each speech act category should include its specific set of base constructions plus the inventory of realisation procedures that help instantiate further attributes of the corresponding illocutionary ICM. Table 2.6 captures an illustrative inventory of realisation procedures for the act of requesting. It is important to draw attention to the fact that the realisation procedures activate a very specific set of attributes (i.e. beneficiary, optionality, cost–benefit, mitigation, and politeness) among those that conform to the illocutionary ICM of requesting. Other attributes of the same requesting ICM, which do not function as realisation procedures, seem to have specialised as base constructions. These include the following: addressee-as-agent, addressee's capability, addressee's willingness, speaker's need, speaker's willingness, and possession of the requested object. An illustrative inventory of base constructions for requests is included in Table 2.8.

The attributes that activate base constructions correspond to essential aspects for the realisation of the requested action (i.e. capability, willingness,

2.5 A Cognitive-Constructional Approach

Table 2.8 *Base constructions for the act of requesting*

Attribute of the requesting ICM	Base constructions
Addressee-as-agent	IMPERATIVE CONSTRUCTION, YOU WILL DO X
Addressee's capability	CAN YOU DO X?, YOU CAN DO X
Addressee's willingness	WILL YOU DO X?, WOULD YOU BE WILLING TO DO X?, IF YOU WILL DO X
Speaker's willingness	I WANT X/I WANT YOU TO DO X, I'D LIKE X/I'D LIKE YOU TO DO X
Speaker's need	I NEED X/I NEED YOU TO DO X, I COULD DO WITH X
Possession of requested object	HAVE YOU GOT X?, YOU'VE GOT X

and possession). Thus, if the addressee cannot physically perform the requested action or is not in possession of the requested object, there is no point in addressing the request to him. Similarly, if the speaker has no desire or need for the requested object or action, there is no need for the performance of the request at all.

On the contrary, those attributes that correspond to additional realisation procedures that combine with base constructions are connected to dimensions of social behaviour and social expectations that could turn the request more or less successful (see Table 2.6). Thus, modulating the cost, optionality, mitigation, or politeness of the request may influence the addressee's decision as to whether or not to perform the request.

As was the case with the semantics of speech acts (see previous section), their constructional realisation should also be considered from a cross-linguistic perspective. Different languages offer diverse realisation procedures and favour different base constructions. Again, as with the attributes and variables that conform to the illocutionary ICMs, succeeding in teaching constructional families of speech acts in an L2 requires a previous comparison with those constructions available in L1, as well as explicit instruction aimed at making students aware of the similarities, differences, and mismatches between the constructions in each language.

Chapter 4 will offer detailed corpus-based inventories of the most prevalent base constructions and realisation procedures that English speakers use in their everyday life interactions for the expression of the directives under investigation. Illocutionary constructions will also be shown to be motivated by the semantics of speech acts as captured by the attributes conforming to their corresponding illocutionary ICMs. The constructional approach to

Table 2.9 *Summary of contemporary theoretical advancements on speech acts*

Functional paradigms	The notion of speech acts as social, as well as linguistic constructs
	The idea that the language system is capable of offering enough realisation procedures for the full codification of speech acts
Pragmatic-conversational paradigms	The realisation that speech acts show different degrees of conventionalisation and inference
	The focus on social/interactional aspects of illocution (i.e. pragmatic scales and variables)
	The relevance of conversational aspects of speech act performance (i.e. adjacency pairs, preference organisation)
	The relevance of the use of real data and sufficient contextual information
Cognitive-constructional paradigms	The realisation that speech act categories show prototype effects
	The realisation that codification, convention, and inferential processes are not discrete categories
	The realisation that the formalisation of the semantics of speech acts in terms of illocutionary ICMs makes it possible to capture their conceptual fabric and to distinguish prototypical cases of each illocutionary category
	The realisation that the formal side of illocutions is motivated by (multiple source)-in-target metonymical operations on illocutionary ICMs
	The description of the idiosyncratic nature of illocutionary constructions in terms of base constructions + linguistic realisation procedures, both motivated by the semantics of each illocutionary ICM
	Focus on the need of cross-cultural and cross-linguistic comparisons of the illocutionary ICMs and illocutionary constructional families in L1 and L2 for their successful teaching

speech acts that is advocated in this book accommodates the most relevant theoretical findings about the meaning and form of illocutionary acts that stem from the contemporary cognitive, pragmatic, and functional works revised in this chapter. By way of summary, Table 2.9 lists those theoretical advancements that shall guide our revision of the way in which speech acts are presently being represented in EFL textbooks (Chapter 3), as well as our pedagogical description of directive speech acts and the subsequent design of related teaching activities in Chapters 4 and 5, respectively.

3

Critical Assessment of the Representation of Speech Acts in Advanced EFL Textbooks

Chapter 2 offered a panorama of the main theoretical advancements on the study of speech acts stemming from a variety of linguistic traditions (i.e. functional, pragmatic, cognitive/constructional, and conversational paradigms). In the last sections of the previous chapter, those current theoretical findings were integrated into a new model of illocutionary description, in terms of illocutionary ICMs and illocutionary constructions, which has also been shown to be compatible with current experimental evidence about the performance of speech acts. The ultimate aim of this book is to translate this model of illocution, which captures current knowledge on illocutionary performance, into a cognitive pedagogical grammar of directive speech acts in English (Chapter 4) and a set of activities for its teaching to Spanish advanced EFL students (Chapter 5). It is mandatory, therefore, to justify the need for this endeavour. In this connection, one question needs to be answered: do current EFL textbooks offer a quantitatively faithful and qualitatively updated portrait of directive speech acts, one that is compatible with the theoretical and experimental findings reported in Chapter 2? Chapter 3 is devoted to providing an informed answer to this question.

Research on the adequacy of the representation of directive speech acts in EFL textbooks is not extensive, and it presents some significant weaknesses. To begin with, most studies on how directive speech acts are dealt with in EFL course books are based on the analysis of a few isolated speech act categories. Thus, as regards the general category of directives, which is the object of our analysis, EFL researchers have devoted considerable attention to analysing the portrayals of requests in EFL course books (Barron, 2007; Delen & Tevil, 2010; Koosha & Vahid Dastjerdi, 2012; Petraki & Bayes, 2013; Aksoyalp & Toprak, 2015; Ross, 2018) and, to a lesser extent, to studying the representation and instructional material of the act of suggesting (Jiang, 2006; Ekin, 2013). Data about how EFL textbooks approach other highly frequent directive categories, such as ordering, begging, advising, or warning, has received considerably less attention. As shall be shown in Section 3.2 this lack of research on how EFL textbooks deal with other speech act categories different from requests is likely to be a direct consequence of the fact that most course books do not actually include other directive speech act categories in their syllabus. In connection with this, the quantitative representation of speech acts in EFL textbooks (i.e. how many and which speech acts are actually being taught) has been poorly investigated to date. There are some notable exceptions such as the works by Soozandehfar and Sahragard (2011), Ulum (2015), Ren and Han (2016), and Pérez-Hernández (2019), whose findings will be compared with the data in Section 3.2 below.

Additionally, research on how EFL textbooks approach the teaching of speech acts is often limited to issues pertaining to a particular theoretical perspective. Thus, as pointed out in Pérez-Hernández (2019), most reviews of the treatment of speech acts in EFL textbooks take a conversational (Boxer & Pickering, 1995; Wong, 2002) or pragmatic stance (Vellenga, 2004; Soozandehfar & Sahragard, 2011; Diepenbroek & Derwing, 2013; Farashaiyan, Tan & Shahragard, 2018). Other relevant dimensions of the illocutionary phenomenon, such as its constructional nature, the cognitive operations that underlie its production and understanding, or the cross-cultural/linguistic aspects of its semantics and form, are not considered.

Finally, most previous studies on the treatment of illocution by EFL textbooks are based on exiguous amounts of data, usually comprising just one course book series (e.g. Soozandehfar & Sahragard, 2011; Akbari & Sharifzadeh, 2013; Ulum, 2015; Farashaiyan & Muthusamy, 2017; Farashaiyan, Tan & Shahragard, 2018).

This chapter reports the results of a qualitative and quantitative revision of directive speech acts in a richer collection of textbooks and through the application of a set of analytical categories with a broader theoretical scope (see Section 3.1), with a view to overcoming the aforementioned weaknesses. The conclusions drawn in Sections 3.2 and 3.3 offer a finer-grained portrayal of the present-day treatment of illocution in EFL textbooks for advanced students.

3.1 Analytical Categories and Corpus of Textbooks for Analysis

This chapter looks into a collection of textbooks for advanced EFL students and analyses their treatment of the set of directive speech acts chosen for this study. The chapter considers aspects related to (1) the quantitative

3.1 Analytical Categories and Corpus of Textbooks

representation of directive speech acts in the textbooks (i.e. determining if there is a balanced portrayal of the most frequent categories of directive speech acts) and (2) the qualitative treatment of directive speech acts. In relation to the latter, it has been argued in Chapters 1 and 2 that teaching how to perform directive speech acts correctly in a foreign language involves at least the following four main objectives.

1. Teaching the semantic and pragmatic attributes and variables that make up each directive illocutionary ICM.
2. Teaching the constructional nature of illocutionary acts.
3. Teaching the conversational structures in which illocutionary acts participate.
4. Teaching the areas of discrepancy between L1 and L2, which may result in difficulties to the EFL student.

These general theoretical hallmarks for the correct teaching of the illocutionary component of a language can be expanded into more specific teaching items that closely correspond to the latest theoretical advancements offered by the different linguistic traditions as revealed in our revision in Chapter 2.

1. Teaching the semantic and pragmatic attributes and variables that make up each directive illocutionary ICM:
   1.1. *transactional attributes*: agent, beneficiary, cost–benefit.
   1.2. *interactional attributes*: speaker/addressee's needs/willingness, optionality, mitigation, politeness.
   1.3. *social variables:* social power, social distance, formality.
2. Teaching the constructional nature of illocutionary acts:
   2.1. set of families of base constructions for each speech act category.
   2.2. inventory of realisation procedures that can be used to modulate the final illocutionary act as required by the interactional/contextual needs, as well as its degree of explicitness.
   2.3. cognitive operations that motivate illocutionary constructions, in general, and directive illocutionary constructions, in particular: (multiple source)-in-target metonymies and the specific force dynamics of each directive speech act.
3. Teaching the conversational structures in which illocutionary acts participate:
   3.1. use of real data and sufficient contextual information.
   3.2. adjacency pairs.
   3.3. preference organisation: preferred/dispreferred responses.

4. Teaching the areas of discrepancy between L1 and L2, which may result in difficulties to the EFL student:
   4.1. cross-cultural differences in the semantics/pragmatics of directive illocutionary ICMs, including culturally-based interactional/social mismatches (e.g. degree of politeness requirements typical of each culture).
   4.2. cross-linguistic differences in the collection of base constructions and in the inventory of realisation procedures for each directive speech act.

The theoretical points summarised above will be used as analytical categories in Sections 3.3.1–3.3.4 to qualitatively assess the EFL textbooks under scrutiny. The results of this analysis shall provide a comprehensive overview of the strengths and weaknesses of current treatments of illocution in contemporary teaching materials.

The ten EFL textbooks chosen for analysis are all currently being used in Spanish universities by undergraduate and graduate students of English studies, as well as in Spanish official language schools by advanced EFL Spanish students. The corpus of textbooks includes the following titles:[1]

Complete Advanced (Cambridge University Press)
English Unlimited Advanced (Cambridge University Press)
Face2face Advanced (Cambridge University Press)
Objective Advanced (Cambridge University Press)
Keynote Advanced (Cengage Learning. National Geographic Learning)
Outcomes Advanced (Cengage Learning. National Geographic Learning)
Navigate Advanced (Oxford University Press)
Solutions Advanced (Oxford University Press)
SpeakOut Advanced (Pearson)
Cutting Edge Advanced (Pearson)

All textbooks in the corpus correspond to the C1 level of proficiency as established by the Common European Framework of Reference for Languages (CEFR). As explained in Section 1.3, the type of explicit

---

[1] The aim of this revision is to offer a panorama of the treatment of directive speech acts in current EFL textbooks, not to single out any of the textbooks for their lack of quality regarding this issue. For this reason, the results reported in Sections 3.2 and 3.3 make use of anonymous acronyms (i.e. TB1, TB2, etc.), where TB stands for 'textbook', and the number is used simply to differentiate one from another. The numbers do not bear any relation to the order in which the textbooks have been listed above.

instruction advocated in this book is expected to be most useful for advanced EFL students, those who already have the necessary command of the English language to understand the explanations in the cognitive pedagogical description of directive speech acts offered in Chapter 4. For this reason and for the sake of exhaustiveness, the present review of EFL textbooks is restricted to this level of proficiency.

The collection of works chosen for analysis aims at being representative of present-day textbooks for the teaching of English to advanced students. Therefore, the pivotal criterion for corpus selection has been the variety of the textbooks in relation to their editorial houses, methodology, age-target, etc. There are course books from four mainstream publishing houses (i.e. Cambridge, Oxford, Pearson, and Cengage). Some of them are targeted to a specific age group, such as *Navigate Advanced, English Unlimited Advanced,* and *SpeakOut Advanced,* which are tailored for adult learners; while the rest target a broader audience. Some are exam-oriented (e.g. *Complete Advanced* and *Objective Advanced*), some give pride of place to communication skills and take on a top-bottom approach (e.g. *Outcomes Advanced*), and others approach language teaching with a bottom-up methodology (e.g. *Navigate Advanced*). Some highlight their use of real language (e.g. *Face2face Advanced*) and additionally promise a special focus on intercultural competence as a 'fifth skill' (*English Unlimited Advanced*). Finally, others place emphasis on their task-oriented methodology (e.g. *Solutions Advanced, Cutting Edge Advanced*). Altogether the collection of textbooks chosen for the study constitute a varied sample of the different methodologies, approaches, and trends in current instructional materials for the teaching of English as an L2 to advanced students.

3.2 Quantitative Assessment of the Treatment of Directive Speech Acts in Advanced EFL Textbooks

As Table 3.1 illustrates, the representation of directive categories in the textbooks under scrutiny is largely inconsistent. There is only one textbook that covers all six categories of directives (TB1). Most textbooks focus on the same three directives (i.e. requesting, suggesting, and advising) to the exclusion of others like begging, ordering, or warning, and some of them deal with only one or two directives (TB2, TB10). The number of activities devoted to teaching those speech acts is also scarce. In most cases, there is just one exercise aimed at practising the use of the directive, with only a few exceptions (e.g. TB4 and TB7) offering up to five exercises for the learning of advising and requesting acts, respectively. In these same textbooks, other

Table 3.1 *Range and distribution of exercises devoted to the teaching/practice of directive speech acts in advanced EFL textbooks*

	Ordering	Requesting	Begging	Suggesting	Advising	Warning
TB1	1	1	1	2	1	2
TB2					3	
TB3		1		2	3	
TB4	1	1		2	5	3
TB5	1	3		3	1	
TB6		2		1	1	
TB7	1	5		2	1	
TB8	1			2	1	1
TB9	1	1		1		
TB10		1		1		

directives receive considerably less amount of attention. Thus, the acts of ordering and suggesting, for instance, are approached in just one or two activities.

All in all, the data reveal that the representation of directive speech acts in the textbooks under analysis is fairly poor, at least from a quantitative point of view. In the majority of cases not all directive categories are included, and for those that are given consideration, the number of activities devoted to their learning varies considerably. In addition, it is observed that there is no overall logical or systematic planning for the teaching of directive speech acts at the C1 level of proficiency: which directives will be learned depends largely on the textbook chosen by each educational institution.

It could be argued that these data are limited to instructional material for advanced learning, and that the teaching of directives may have already been undertaken in previous academic stages. This hypothesis seems to be confirmed by Ulum's (2015) statistical analysis of the frequency of occurrence of each sub-category of Searle's (1976) speech act taxonomy in EFL textbooks at the starters level (A1 and A2). He concluded that the representation of illocutionary acts was unsystematic: only directive and commissive acts are present in the evaluated EFL textbooks, while assertives, expressives, and declarations are excluded. Thus, it could be concluded that if enough directives receive considerably attention at initial stages of the learning process (A1, A2), this makes it unnecessary to teach them again at more advanced levels, thus allowing space in the C1 and C2 levels of instruction for other illocutionary categories like assertives and expressives.

However, Ulum's (2015) analysis was restricted to just one course book series (i.e. *Yes You Can EFL*), and it did not specify which subtypes of directives were taught at the starters level. In fact, all the examples in his paper are instances of requests. No information is provided about whether other directive acts like begging, advising, ordering, or warning were included in the starters level textbooks. Contradictorily enough, requests are one of the directive subtypes that receives a higher amount of attention in our corpus of advanced level course books under analysis. This is not consistent, therefore, with the hypothesis that the underrepresentation of directives at the advanced level series is due to the fact that they had already been taught at earlier stages: requests are included both in the starters and again in the advanced level textbooks, while other directives are not.

Another piece of research carried out by Pérez-Hernández (2019) looked in detail into the types of directives taught at three different levels of proficiency (starters, intermediate, and advanced) in a larger collection of textbooks, including eight series of course books by mainstream editorial houses like Cambridge, Oxford, and Pearson. Her findings revealed that the representation of directives was poor at all three levels of instruction. Starters textbooks only dealt with requests and suggestions, leaving aside basic and highly frequent directives like ordering, warning, and advising. The intermediate level textbooks added some subtypes of orders (i.e. commands) and other directives like giving instructions, while still excluding some of the most common types of directive acts: advising, warning, and begging, among others. The advanced series were incapable of fully compensating for these gaps in previous levels. Most advanced textbooks included requests, suggestions, and advising, and only a few of them enlarged the inventory of directives to incorporate the acts of recommending or proposing future actions. Nguyen's (2011) and Ren and Han's (2016) papers provide similar data stemming from an analysis of lower-intermediate textbooks, which again focus on the acts of requesting, suggesting, and advising to the exclusion of other directives. These studies are largely compatible with this book's findings, which also shows that requesting, suggesting, and advising are the directive acts that receive the highest amount of attention in all advanced textbooks under scrutiny.

From the above considerations, it can be concluded that the limited representation of directive speech acts in advanced textbooks series is not because they have already been taught in previous academic stages. Acts like requests, suggestions, and, to a lesser extent, advising are taught at all levels of proficiency (i.e. starters, intermediate, and advanced), while others are simply and randomly left out in all three levels of instruction.

An extreme case is that of the act of begging, which has only been found in one advanced textbook (TB1). Warning and ordering are also largely underrepresented, with only half the textbooks in our corpus offering some kind of instructional material about them.

In addition, the amount of exercises made available for the learning of the six directive speech acts under enquiry was generally small with an average of just one or two exercises per speech act. In most cases, the space allowed for the teaching of a particular speech act within an exercise was shared with other linguistic issues. For example, those exercises that presented the use of modals like *must* and *have to* for the expression of the act of ordering, also included other uses of the modals, such as the deductive *must* (TB1). Some of the activities including directives did not even have the teaching of the speech act as their main focus. The few instances of warnings that have been found in the textbooks, for example, appear in exercises that are mainly concerned with reported speech: the student is given a direct form of warning (e.g. *Don't touch the stove, or you'll get burnt*) and is asked to use a performative verb (i.e. warn) to turn it into a reported speech expression (e.g. *He warned me not to touch the stove* …). Since the focus of the exercise is the teaching of reported speech, no information or instruction is provided about the directive speech act itself.

Turning to other quantitative dimensions of the data, it was observed that the amount of attention, understood in terms of the number of exercises/activities devoted to the teaching of a speech act, was randomly assigned and not justified from a theoretical or pedagogical point of view. One may wonder why some textbooks (TB4) offer up to five activities for the teaching of advising acts and only one for requests, while others (TB7) devote five exercises to latter and only one to the former. In any case, there is nothing intrinsically more complex in the conceptual nature of either of these speech acts that makes one of them more challenging than the other, or that makes one require deeper practice for its learning.

Although not the focus of this investigation, the planning of the teaching of directive speech acts throughout the different levels of proficiency also seems to be largely unsatisfactory. As already indicated in previous works (Moradi, Karbalaei & Afrad, 2013), a comparison of the request and advising formulae used in the starters, intermediate, and advanced instructional material for each of the course book series under enquiry reveals that the same linguistic expressions are being taught at all levels, following no specific pattern and with no significant increase in their difficulty or complexity. CAN / COULD YOU DO X? and I'D LIKE X requests are the linguistic formulae found in all textbooks. Whether both are used, or which one is used at either level of instruction varies greatly among editorial houses, which again suggests lack of planning based on pedagogical and/or theoretical criteria.

3.3 Qualitative Assessment of the Treatment of Directive Speech Acts in Advanced EFL Textbooks

The following subsections offer the results of a qualitative assessment of the EFL textbooks under scrutiny in relation to the analytical categories described in Section 3.1. They are summarised in Table 3.2 for convenience.

3.3.1 Inclusion of Semantic/Pragmatic Information about Speech Acts

In Chapter 2, the description of the semantic and pragmatic knowledge characterising each directive category in terms of illocutionary ICMs was proved to be one of the keystones of a sound theory of speech acts. In fact, the information comprised within each illocutionary ICM provides the grounding and motivation for the choice of speech act constructions and linguistic realisation procedures to be used in conversational interactions. Current functional and pragmatic research has evinced the roles and relevance of several types of attributes and variables in building the conceptual fabric of illocutionary ICMs (see Sections 2.2.2, 2.4.2, and 2.5.5 for detailed descriptions). By way of summary, *transactional attributes*

Table 3.2 *Analytical categories for the assessment of current EFL textbooks as regards their treatment of directive speech acts*

Semantic/pragmatic aspects	AC1. Transactional attributes (e.g. agent, beneficiary, cost)
	AC2. Interactional attributes (e.g. optionality, mitigation, politeness, etc.)
	AC3. Social variables (e.g. social power, social distance, formality)
Constructional aspects	AC4. Base constructions
	AC5. Realisation procedures
	AC6. Cognitive operations (metonymy, metaphor)
Conversational aspects	AC7. Adjacency pairs
	AC8. Preference organisation
	AC9. Use of real data and contextual information
Typological aspects	AC10. Cross-cultural mismatches in the semantics of illocutionary categories
	AC11. Cross-linguistic mismatches in the form of speech acts

inform about the agent, beneficiary, and cost–benefit of the transaction involved in the directive speech act; *interactional attributes* capture social and pragmatic conventions that regulate social exchanges and verbal interactions (e.g. politeness, optionality, mitigation); and *social variables*, like social power, social distance, and formality, have been shown to interact with the two previous sets of attributes and to be pivotal in determining their values (e.g. a large social distance increases the politeness, optionality, and mitigation requirements of the speech act). Altogether they conform to the ontology and structure of illocutionary ICMs (Section 2.5.5).

The extent to which these semantic and pragmatic items have been implemented in the textbooks under enquiry is disturbingly low, especially given the importance of mastering this type of information for the performance of socially and contextually felicitous speech acts, as has been extensively argued in the literature.

None of the textbooks under analysis offers information about the transactional attributes involved in the semantics of directive speech acts or their interconnections and synergies with interactional and social variables (e.g. the fact that as the cost of the requested action increases, the politeness of the act will need to be modulated accordingly). Interactional attributes and social variables are also largely overlooked. The only interactional attribute that is given any consideration is that of politeness. Only three of the textbooks in our corpus offer polite formulae for requests and suggestions, but they do not offer any instruction as to when such polite forms should be used (e.g. high cost of the requested action, large social distance, power asymmetries, etc.). It has also been observed that most of the illocutionary constructions included in the textbooks are highly polite (TB3, TB4, TB5, TB7, TB10). This is so especially in connection with the act of requesting (e.g. COULD / WOULD YOU DO X? forms). This type of polite requests, however, may not fit many of the everyday life interactional contexts in which a more relaxed register is expected and in which the use of such polite formulae may come through as odd, ironic, or straightforwardly clumsy. No information is offered about which contexts and which social variables license the use of those markedly polite illocutionary constructions. Other interactional attributes, such as those of mitigation and optionality, are not given any consideration.

Regarding social variables only two textbooks (TB3 and TB7) deal with the formality of the context, and just one of them introduces the variable of social distance in relation to requests (TB7). The variable of social power, an essential ingredient in the semantics of some directives (e.g. orders) does not receive any attention. Most textbooks teach linguistic formulae for the production of directive speech acts without instructing students about the fact that the power relations between the speakers, their social distance, or the formality of the context often have a bearing on their need for politeness, mitigation, and/or optionality.

The only exception to the lack of semantic/pragmatic information about the conceptual nature of directive illocutions is TB7, where a rich number of illocutionary constructions are offered with some explicit instruction about the contexts (formal/informal), social variables (distance), and some of the interactional attributes (politeness) that guide the speaker's choices in different situations. Unfortunately, this wealth of information is offered only in relation to the act of requesting. The rest of the directives included in this textbook do not display analogous explanations. There does not seem to be any sound reason why requests require explicit teaching about social and interactional aspects of their use, while other directives like advising, warning, begging, ordering, or suggesting do not. As pointed out at the beginning of this chapter, the act of requesting has received a significantly higher amount of attention in current theoretical and pedagogical research than other directives. The poor coverage of the semantic/pragmatic nature of directives different from requests in the textbooks under analysis may simply be a reflection of this situation. This brings to the front the need for detailed theoretical descriptions of speech acts like the one provided in Chapter 4 for their subsequent implementation in EFL textbooks and teaching materials.

Our findings on the lack of adequacy of the semantic/pragmatic descriptions of directive speech acts in the collection of textbooks under analysis are consistent with previous literature on this issue. Crandall and Basturkmen (2004), Vellenga (2004), Usó-Juan (2008), Nourdad and Roshani Khiabani (2015), Ren and Han (2016), and Pérez-Hernández (2019) apprise the lack of metapragmatic information in EFL textbooks. Diepenbroek and Derwing (2013: 1) point to the fact that 'the quality of the pragmatic information included in textbooks does not allow learners to develop their pragmatic competence in the target language'. More recently, Borer (2018) and Ton Nu (2018) not only confirm the paucity of explicit information on pragmatic aspects of illocutionary performance but also reveal that the few semantic/pragmatic aspects that are dealt with in the textbooks are inadequate according to current theories of L2 pragmatic teaching. Farashaiyan, Tan, and Shahragard (2018) also report a lack of cross-cultural perspective in the teaching of the pragmatic dimension of illocutionary acts.

All in all, the semantic and pragmatic knowledge of directive speech acts has been shown to be underrepresented in EFL textbooks: students are generally offered a limited number of linguistic forms for each directive, and related metapragmatic information is insufficient in terms of both quantity and quality. The amount of practice material is also scarce (Shimizu, Fukasawa & Yonekura, 2007).

3.3.2   Treatment of the Constructional Nature of Directive Speech Acts

Learning to form grammatically correct sentences is just the first step towards being able to communicate in a foreign language. As was made manifest in Chapter 2, however, learning to pair different linguistic formulae with specific communicative purposes, in particular contexts, and bearing in mind the interactional and social variables that are at work in each particular communicative exchange is what is actually needed in order to master the use of a second language. Examining how the formal, linguistic realisations of directive speech acts are presented in the textbooks, and whether they are taught in relation to their specific meanings, is essential in order to assess the adequacy and effectiveness of current teaching materials.

Previous research on this issue offers a bleak panorama that is confirmed by the data in our corpus. As already reported in the literature, the main focus is on the teaching of lists of expressions for the production of each directive speech act, which are randomly included in grammar sections or as part of dialogues and/or exercises (Farashaiyan & Muthusamy, 2017). The number and representativity of the linguistic expressions included in those lists does not follow any systematic pattern. There are textbooks (e.g. TB7) offering up to five different formulae for the expression of requests, three for the act of advising, and two for ordering. Alternatively, TB4 offers four expressions for the act of advising and only one for requests. Yet other textbooks (e.g. TB1) provide just one linguistic formula for each directive category. The theoretical description of directive speech acts that will be presented in Chapter 4 reveals that the English language does not discriminate among different directive acts as to the wealth of linguistic formulae that it offers for their realisations. The unbalanced portrayal found in the textbooks under scrutiny is likely to have a negative impact in the learning process of EFL students.

Aside from the above quantitative issues, Bouton (1996) points to another weakness of the treatment of formal and constructional aspects of speech acts in EFL textbooks: the lack of representativity of the formulae chosen as teaching targets. In his study on the act of inviting in EFL textbooks, the invitation formulae presented to the students were found to rarely occur in published native speakers' corpora. In this same vein, Nguyen (2011) reported that sometimes textbooks stress one formula over others which are equally or more frequent in real-life use, thus providing teachers and students with misleading information. This point has also been corroborated by the data in our corpus. By way of illustration, in relation to the act of ordering, all textbooks that include this directive in their syllabi offer the same two linguistic formulae for its expression, namely, the modal verbs *must* and *have to* (e.g. *You must study, You have to study*). A corpus search for the act of ordering (see Section 4.1.2 in the next chapter), however, reveals that these are neither the only, nor even the most frequent linguistic formulae for the communicative rendering of this directive. The IMPERATIVE construction and declarative-based constructions like YOU ARE TO DO X, for instance, which are also amply used by speakers, but are not considered in the textbooks.

In addition, none of the textbooks under scrutiny devotes specific sections to speech acts. The latter are introduced as part of the teaching of other grammatical issues. For instance, orders are dealt with when teaching modal verbs. Requests are introduced when teaching the uses of modal verbs in the past tense (e.g. could/would). Warnings have exclusively been found in connection with reported speech, when asking students to use the performative verb *warn* to report the corresponding indirect act. The fact that speech acts are always approached in relation to other linguistic issues, instead of being treated as independent teaching topics, may explain their shallow and partial representation in the textbooks under scrutiny.

The analysis of the textbooks chosen for this study also reveals that the linguistic formulae included in the teaching materials do not distinguish between illocutionary base constructions and realisation procedures. This distinction was shown to be relevant in Section 2.5.6, since realisation procedures act on base constructions to modulate their illocutionary force, so that they can fit different interactional/social contexts. Thus, the same base construction (e.g. CAN YOU DO X?) may be combined with different realisation procedures to modulate its levels of politeness (e.g. CAN YOU DO X, PLEASE?, COULD YOU DO X?) and even to change its illocutionary force from one of requesting to one of ordering or begging (e.g. CAN YOU DO X, PLEASE? versus CAN YOU DO X AT ONCE!! versus CAN YOU PLEASE, PLEASE, PLEASE DO X?).

Finally, the description of directive illocutionary constructions in the textbooks under scrutiny also fails to inform students about the cognitive operations that motivate them (see Sections 2.5.5 and 2.5.6). By way of illustration, students are unaware of the fact that questions about ability, willingness, or possession can metonymically activate a directive category simply because those are three basic components of the semantics of directive acts. Teaching the motivation of illocutionary expressions on the semantics of the corresponding illocutionary acts is likely to facilitate the memorisation of those formulae by L2 students, as has already been shown to be the case in other areas of L2 learning (e.g. prepositions, metaphors, idioms, etc.; Boers & Demecheleer, 1998; Shaffer, 2004; Boers & Lindstromberg, 2008; Tyler, 2012).

3.3.3 Treatment of Conversational Aspects of Directive Speech Acts

As explained in detail in Section 2.4.3, conversational approaches to illocution have highlighted the relevance of considering real language data in their analysis of speech acts. This theoretical postulate has also been assessed in relation to the portrayal of illocutionary acts in EFL textbooks, under the premise that the lack of real language examples can hinder the correct learning of a foreign language. As pointed out by Nguyen (2011), the literature provides ample evidence that EFL textbooks do not offer students adequate opportunities for learning authentic language (Bardovi-Harlig, 2001; Grant & Starks, 2001; Wong, 2002; Vellenga, 2004). In much the same vein, Jiang (2006: 36) points out that 'although the new generation textbooks introduce more linguistic structures … than the old generation textbooks, the discrepancies between real language use and EFL textbooks are still apparent'. This has also been made manifest in our assessment of the linguistic constructions and realisation procedures for directive speech acts included in our collection of textbooks (Section 3.3.2): the linguistic expressions that are currently being taught have been found to be highly formulaic and hardly representative of the wealth and variety of illocutionary constructions that the English language has to offer. In fact, out of the ten textbooks chosen for analysis, only five make it clear in their methodological descriptions that they make use of real language data in the texts and conversations included in the books. Authors like Bardovi-Harlig, Mossman, and Vellenga (2014a, 2014b) and Bardovi-Harlig and Mossman (2016), however, have provided ample evidence about the feasibility of using corpus-based authentic language for developing teaching materials. These authors have shown how to use language samples to help students identify pragmatic routines for speech acts and notice how they are used in context. The lack of a widespread corpus-based approach to the design of instructional material for the teaching of speech acts finds little justification in the time of digital humanities.

The use of real language examples as teaching material becomes pivotal when assessing the degree to which textbooks succeed in helping students

3.3 Qualitative Assessment

to master the conversational/discursive dimension of speech acts. In this connection, the use of naturally occurring conversations is essential for students to understand how interactions are locally managed by speakers by means of adjacency pairs, turn-taking strategies, pre-sequences, and preferred/dispreferred responses. Back in 2019, I reported on the assessment of eight EFL textbooks in relation to the attention devoted to three conversational aspects (i.e. adjacency pairs, pre-sequences, and preference organisation). My analysis revealed that coverage of these issues varied largely. In fact, the space devoted to them was found to be inversely proportional to the proficiency level of the textbooks under scrutiny, with advanced EFL textbooks paying the lowest degree of attention to these matters. As I concluded then (2019: 269), 'the focus of intermediate and advanced textbooks also shifts towards writing and reading comprehension tasks, thus focusing on assertive speech acts like those of describing, speculating, comparing, arguing, etc., which are less prone to a conversational handling'.

These findings are compatible with the results stemming from the analysis of the teaching material assessed in this book. As already pointed out in the two previous sections, the textbooks under scrutiny often introduce directive speech acts in connection with other linguistic aspects, such as modal verbs, hedging, or polite/tactful expressions. This approach generally limits the scope of the explanations to the phrase or sentence level. Suprasentential aspects of the performance of speech acts, such as adjacency pairs and preference organisation, are consequently left out.

In those few exceptions in which students are led to consider directive speech acts in conversations, the scarcity or lack of explicit instruction about their conversational and/or discursive functioning is recurrent. In TB2, students are asked to role play a conversation in which one of them is meant to advise the other. In order to do so, students are given just one example of a linguistic construction for the act of advising (i.e. I'D DO X, IF I WERE YOU). No information is added about the preceding or following conversational turns, and no explicit instruction is provided about the contexts in which offering a piece of advice is a preferred or dispreferred conversational move. In some extreme cases, students are asked to role play a particular directive in the absence of any information about its semantic, pragmatic, linguistic, or conversational workings. Thus, in one exercise in TB4, students are asked to formulate suggestions with no prior instruction about how to produce this speech act correctly and felicitously in the foreign language. Shockingly enough, this much-needed instruction is partially and implicitly offered in the following page of the textbook as part of an exercise about rephrasing and grammatical inversion (e.g. YOU SHOULD NOT DO X > UNDER NO CIRCUMSTANCES SHOULD YOU DO X).

As will be made apparent in Chapter 4, offering students corpus-based, real language examples of the conversational workings of directive speech acts is possible. More importantly, as regards some directives, looking beyond the sentence towards higher levels of language description is, in fact, necessary in order to achieve a realistic description of their formal layout. As reported in Chapter 4, the act of advising, for instance, is hardly ever performed within the scope of a single sentence in the data extracted from our corpus of real language examples. Pieces of advice are generally scattered in several subordinate and/or juxtaposed sentences and often realised through one or more conversational turns.

3.3.4 Treatment of Cross-Cultural and Cross-Linguistic Areas of Discrepancy between L1 and L2

Interest in cross-cultural and cross-linguistic aspects of the teaching of speech acts started as far back as the 1990s. In Bouton's (1996) classical volume on pragmatics and language learning, Cenoz and Valencia (1996) provide a case for taking into account cultural conventions on politeness and on the use of linguistic mitigation when teaching EFL students how to perform speech acts in a second language. According to their findings, Spanish students of English as a second language make use of less mitigating devices and more direct formulae for the expression of requests in their native language and in their conversations in English. The higher need for politeness and indirectness that characterises the use of requests in British English had not been properly acquired by the students taking part in this study, thus pointing to a failure in the teaching of pragmatic and cultural competence. As this type of socio-pragmatic, cultural competence is concerned, the comparison of native and non-native speakers of English and Spanish reveals that both groups are aware of the different situations and use different degrees of directness according to the context. These observations in the field of EFL teaching come to confirm the findings of an extensive body of theoretical research on cross-cultural variations in the performance of speech acts known as *interlanguage pragmatics* (Blum-Kulka, 1982, 1991; Blum-Kulka & House, 1989; Blum-Kulka, House & Kasper, 1989; Kasper, 1989; Rintell & Mitchell, 1989; among others).

Teachers and researchers of language learning and teaching often agree on the relevance of including intercultural dimensions of language in EFL instructional materials (Edelhoff, 1993; Byram & Risager, 1999; Sercu, 2002; Castro, Sercu & Garcia, 2004; Atay et al., 2009). With regard to this connection, Castro (1999: 92) points out that teachers are now expected not only to teach the foreign linguistic code but also to 'contextualise that code against the socio-cultural background associated with the foreign language and to promote the acquisition of intercultural communicative competence'. Nevertheless, as Neddar (2012) states, it is arguable to what extent the findings in interlanguage pragmatics have actually been given consideration in EFL textbooks, thus contributing to raising the learners' awareness of cross-cultural aspects of speech acts.

As early as the 1990s, authors like Kachru (1994) were pointing to the need to increase classroom practice on cross-cultural aspects of speech acts. The situation does not seem to have changed much since. More recently, in her masters' thesis on the pragmatics of EFL course books for Finnish students, Luomala (2010) points to the lack of explicit instructional and teaching materials devoted to making students aware of cross-cultural asymmetries in the conceptual and formal layout between speech acts in English and those in their native language. Loumala (2010: 7) remarks that 'although some of the necessary pragmatic knowledge can be transferred directly from the learner's first language (L1), more often than not the pragmatic rules and conventions in L1 and a foreign language differ significantly and, therefore, need to be consciously learned and practiced'. Neddar's (2010) study on cross-cultural pragmatic information in Algerian EFL course book series corroborates these findings. In much the same vein, our own assessment of advanced EFL textbooks shows that cross-cultural and cross-linguistic information is not included neither through explicit, nor through implicit instruction. Given the general consensus on the relevance of mastering this type of knowledge for the successful performance of speech acts in a foreign language, Neddar (2012: 5,691) rightly concludes that the exclusion of interlanguage pragmatics in current teaching materials has more to do with a lack of knowledge about its methodological implementation than with a denial of its effectiveness in inducing learning.

3.4 Conclusions and Way Forward: Explicit Instruction through a Corpus-Based Cognitive Pedagogical Grammar

This chapter has offered an assessment of current EFL advanced textbooks with a view to determining to what extent contemporary theoretical research advancements on speech acts have actually been implemented in the instructional material. As argued in Tomlinson, Dat, Masuhara, and Rubdy

(2001), textbook evaluation enables teachers, supervisors, administrators, and materials developers to make judgements about the effects of materials on the end-users (i.e. learners). The assessment of course books and teaching materials, as McGrath (2002) points out, is also an essential preliminary step in the development and administration of language learning programmes.

The findings reported in the previous sections reveal that the amount of instruction about the semantic, pragmatic, constructional, and cultural dimensions of directive speech acts in advanced EFL textbooks is unsystematic and scarce, ranging from limited to non-existent, and varying greatly depending on the textbook and the speech act under scrutiny. It is, therefore, necessary to take this attested weakness of present-day EFL instructional material into consideration in order to make a conscious move towards the teaching and dissemination of explicit information about the many sides involved in the performance of directive speech acts in the language classroom. In this connection, Tan and Farashaiyan (2016) draw additional attention to the fact that instructors should also be given sufficient input in guides and relevant materials to facilitate the teaching of this significant constructs, so that learners can acquire intercultural communicative competence, and due emphasis can be given to illocutionary acts performance in teacher training courses.

Section 1.3 has already highlighted the advantages of an explicit approach to the teaching of pragmatics (i.e. speech acts) in a foreign language. In general, there is agreement in the literature that pragmatic aspects of language, like speech acts, are teachable across culturally diverse students (Grossi, 2009), and that instruction and, more particularly, explicit metapragmatic instruction, is more effective than other approaches, such as implicit teaching (Rose & Ng, 2001; Tateyama, 2001; Alcón, 2005; Rose, 2005; Takahashi, 2005). Reza and Zohreh (2016) offer an exhaustive bibliographical revision on this matter. As Tello Rueda (2016: 170) summarises in his review on this issue:

> recommendations have been made since the late 1980s, for the inclusion of explicit pragmatic instruction as part of foreign and second language (L2) curricula (e.g. Blum-Kulka, House & Kasper, 1989). … Empirical studies on this direction have analysed the effect of instruction in the development of pragmatic knowledge dealing with a multiplicity of features. The results from most of these studies are promising with regard to the positive effect of pedagogical intervention.

Bringing explicit instruction into the EFL classroom has two main goals, which closely correspond to Wildner-Bassett's (1994) distinction between the development of metapragmatic declarative knowledge, on the one

3.4 Conclusions and Way Forward

hand, and metapragmatic procedural knowledge, on the other. The first goal involves the development of the students' awareness about all factors involved in the successful performance of speech acts in the target foreign language (i.e. semantic, pragmatic, formal, and cross-linguistic knowledge). This goal will be addressed in Chapter 4 of this book, which offers a cognitive pedagogical grammar of directive speech acts that attempts to capture their multi-sided, kaleidoscopic nature and, thus, to pave the way to a more faithful representation of this linguistic phenomenon in future EFL instructional materials. The second goal deals with practising the knowledge acquired through the instruction. To this aim, Chapter 5 suggests samples of activities and exercises that exploit on the conceptual information included in the directive illocutionary ICMs and on the formal aspects of the production of directive speech acts (i.e. base constructions and realisation procedures) provided in Chapter 4.

4

A Cognitive Pedagogical Grammar of Directive Speech Acts I: Know-What and Know-How of Directives

Chapter 4 provides a cognitive pedagogical grammar of six frequently used directive speech acts: ordering, requesting, suggesting, begging, advising, and warning. Following the pragmatic and cognitive theoretical postulates laid out in Chapter 2, both the conceptual layout and the formal/constructional nature of these acts will be included in the explanation. The description of the semantics/pragmatics of the directive illocutionary acts under scrutiny makes use of the information included in their corresponding *illocutionary ICMs*. As explained in detail in Section 2.5.5, illocutionary ICMs are exhaustive collections of semantic and pragmatic attributes (i.e. agent, beneficiary, capability, willingness, possession, need, cost–benefit, optionality, mitigation, politeness) and variables (i.e. power, social distance, formality) that capture the knowledge that native speakers have about each speech act category. The formal/constructional side of each directive will be dealt with in terms of *base constructions* and *realisation procedures*, as shown in Section 2.5.6.

All the information reported in this chapter stems from a corpus-based study on the meaning and form of each directive speech act (see Section 1.3 for a description of the corpora used in the analysis, and Sections 2.5.5 and 2.5.6 for the theoretical basis of the analysis). The present account of directive speech acts is intended for advanced Spanish students of EFL. It is also directed at teachers and publishers who intend to include speech acts in their teaching practice and materials. For this reason, the information is provided in the form of a pedagogical grammar (see Section 1.3), which attempts to avoid technical jargon as much as possible. Thus, terms like illocutionary ICM, illocutionary construction, or realisation procedure have been substituted for more transparent, lay expressions. Illocutionary ICMs, for instance, are nothing but collections of semantic/pragmatic bits of knowledge that speakers need to acquire in order to be capable of understanding and performing directive acts successfully in a particular language. Thus, in the ensuing sections we refer to them as the *know-what* of directive speech acts (e.g. knowing what an act of order is and what social, interactional, and transactional attributes and variables define it in English). The linguistic jargon that characterises the description of the illocutionary ICMs has also been avoided as much as possible. Specific terms such as the variables and attributes involved in the description (e.g. mitigation, optionality, etc.) have been introduced in the form of questions that clarify their meaning for non-expert readers (e.g. mitigation = does the speaker attempt to minimise the cost of the requested action?). Likewise, illocutionary constructions and realisation procedures are just the linguistic forms that the English language offers for the realisation of each of the variables/attributes of the illocutionary ICMs. For this reason, they are labelled as the *know-how* of directives (i.e. the linguistic kits that English offers speakers for the expression of those acts). Students, teachers, and publishers need not know the technical, expert terms, but they do need the knowledge that lies behind them.

4.1 Orders

Cognitive linguists use a metaphor to describe speech acts. Johnson (1987: ch. 3) argued that our understanding of speech acts, like that of other linguistic phenomena (i.e. modality), is metaphorically grounded on the notion of force:

> It should not be surprising, then, to find similar force structures operating in the structure of speech acts themselves. After all, speech acts are actions; and since our 'physical' and 'social' actions are subject to forces, we should expect that our 'linguistic' actions are also subject to forces, metaphorically understood.
>
> (Johnson, 1987: 57)

Pérez-Hernández and Ruiz de Mendoza (2002) expanded on this idea and showed how different directive speech acts seem to be grounded on specific types of forces. Thus, an order is presented as a type of unstoppable force that pushes a speaker to do something.[1] Figure 4.1 visually represents the underlying force metaphor based on the compulsion force schema (Johnson, 1987: 45).

H represents the hearer, and the vector F_1 represents the order uttered by the speaker (S). As a result of the force of the order, the hearer is pushed into

---

[1] See Johnson (1987: 57), Talmy (1988), and Pérez-Hernández and Ruiz de Mendoza (2002) for in-depth accounts of the force dynamics underlying speech acts.

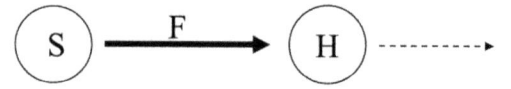

Figure 4.1 Force schema underlying the conceptualisation of orders

action. The fact that orders are conceptualised as unstoppable, compulsive forces is neither arbitrary nor inconsequential: this metaphor derives from some of the attributes conforming to the semantics of orders, and it is manifested in their linguistic forms, prototypical orders displaying specific characteristics of their own. For their orders to be successful and to move the hearer into action, students need to master the *know-what* (i.e. what an order is and which pieces of transactional, interactional, and social knowledge are involved in its conceptualisation by English speakers) and the *know-how* (i.e. the linguistic expressions that the English language offers for its performance) of this directive speech act category. These are spelled out in the next two sections.

4.1.1 *The Know-What of Orders*

What is an order? The speech act of ordering is semantically complex. It is like a kaleidoscope made up of many little bits and pieces: some of them are brighter or bigger, some almost go unnoticed. When the viewer turns the kaleidoscope, the little crystals move around and create new patterns. In much the same way, not all attributes and variables involved in the conceptualisation of an order are equally important. Some are shared with other directives, while others are central to their characterisation as orders. In addition, as the context changes, those attributes and variables also move around and produce new patterns, which will require different linguistic expressions for their correct realisation depending on the power/social relations between speakers, the formality of the context, or the cost of the action, among other situational and transactional factors.

Let us then see which pieces of knowledge conform to the meaning of an order in English, and how their value may vary in different contexts.

Who is to do the action expressed in the order?
The person who is to carry out the action expressed by a speech act is called the agent, and orders present the hearer(s) as the expected agent:

(4.1) 'Act like a grown-up,' Judge Ward **ordered** Aguilera at one point (iWeb)

4.1 Orders

In this respect orders are similar to other directive speech acts under scrutiny such as those of requesting and begging, which also have the hearer as their agent. Advising, warning, and suggesting, however, may differ in some cases in which the proposed action is to be jointly carried out by the speaker and the hearer (e.g. *Let's get our feet back under us on some solid ground, he suggested*; iWeb).

Who will benefit from the action expressed in the order?
Traditional accounts have argued that prototypical orders represent a benefit for the speaker and a cost for the hearer (Leech, 1983; Pérez-Hernández, 2001; Del Campo, 2013). However, the data in our corpus shows that this is not always the case. In most orders in our corpus, the benefit is, in fact, for the speaker, as in example (4.2):

(4.2) 'Stay away from my personal effects!' the pirate **ordered**, not liking the idea of having her clothing searched through or touched by anyone but herself … (iWeb)

However, it can also be the case that the benefit is not just for the speaker but for other people under his protection as well:

(4.3) 'The more prosperous the powerful become, the more distressed the poor turn. We beg things to be replaced.' The Emperor **ordered**. 'It is against the public benefit that the powerful intimidate the poor. It must be stopped and never be allowed to happen.' (iWeb)

Additionally, in a small number of examples, the beneficiary of the action is a third person, as in example (4.4), and even the hearers themselves, as in example (4.5):

(4.4) 'Give the boy a pair of shoes with good thick soles and big enough so he can grow into the them,' my father **ordered** (iWeb)
(4.5) 'Well wait till the sun comes up. Oh geez, get back to the truck guys! Don't catch a cold in this fucking rain!' the captain **ordered** (iWeb)

Can the hearer do the action expressed in the order?
According to our corpus data, the capability of the hearer to carry out the ordered action is taken for granted. The speaker either knows for certain or assumes that the hearer can do the action and does not entertain any other scenario. In this, orders differ from requests, for instance, which

often ask about the hearer's ability to perform the action as a means of increasing their politeness (e.g. *So as Nguyen requested: can you please set us up wp-admin and ftp access to your site?*; iWeb).

Do speaker and hearer want the action to be carried out?
Whether the speaker and the hearer want the ordered action to take place or not correlates with whom benefits from the action. As shown above, in most cases the speaker is the beneficiary, either on her own or in conjunction with others. On these occasions, the speaker clearly wants the action to be carried out, as it is sometimes even made manifest in the expression of the order itself:

(4.6) 'Your father has finally found a bride for your brother, Itachi is going to be married soon and when his betrothed comes **I want** you to be on your best behaviour, you're going to have to share your brother and I don't want you clinging to him when his bride arrives,' the matriarch **ordered** (iWeb)

When the beneficiary of the order is the hearer or a third party, the speaker's wanting the action to take place becomes less relevant. Still, when ordering someone to do something, the speaker expects the hearer to comply, even if the proposed action is not in her own benefit.

As regards the hearer, his wanting to carry out the ordered action is prototypically low, since it generally involves a cost to him. Only in those situations in which the order is in his benefit (see example (4.5) above), will his desire to perform the action increase. What is important to highlight, however, is that whether or not the hearer wants to do the action is irrelevant for the speaker. When ordering, the latter does not take into consideration the hearer's disposition and only expects compliance. This explains that there is not one single instance of order construction in our corpus based on the hearer's willingness to perform the action. Expressions like WILL YOU DO X? (e.g. *Will you vacuum the house for me?*) have not been found in the corpus in relation to the act of ordering. It could be argued that, when used by a powerful speaker, these expressions could be understood as orders. Our corpus study shows that, even if the notion of order is a prototypical category and WILL YOU DO X? instances of orders could be accommodated as peripheral (polite) instances of the category, the fact is that native speakers do not prototypically use these expressions when they want to order someone to do something. The attested lack of occurrences of order constructions exploiting the hearer's willingness or lack of it to carry out the action correlates with the results

4.1 Orders

of the analysis of the conceptual layout of orders, according to which the hearer's willingness to perform the action is irrelevant to the speaker, who just expects compliance with her order.

Is the action expressed in the order necessary?
In most instances of orders, the speaker needs the action to be carried out because he is to benefit from it:

(4.7) 'Shut up. **We need to** keep going!', Hou Qing **ordered** as he took the lead once more (iWeb)

Still, even in those cases in which he does not have a strict necessity that the action is carried out, he still expects compliance with the order.

How much freedom does an order allow the hearer?
Whether or not the hearer follows an order is beyond the speaker's control, but when a speaker gives an order, he presents it as non-negotiable. Orders communicate the idea that the hearer has no freedom to choose a path of action different from the one expressed in the utterance:

(4.8) '… I want you to be on your best behaviour, you're going to have to share your brother and I don't want you clinging to him when his bride arrives.' The matriarch **ordered**. She was sweet and caring like every other mother, but she was also an Uchiha and she didn't ask for things, she's demanded for them. **Sasuke wasn't being given an option; his mother's words were law** (iWeb)

As shall be made apparent in Section 4.1.2, this attribute of the meaning of orders largely influences the formal traits of order constructions.

Does the speaker attempt to minimise the cost of the action?
When giving an order, the speaker does not make any explicit attempt to bring down the cost of the proposed action. In fact, it is usually the case that such cost is increased by adding a requirement of immediateness:

(4.9) 'Get your hands up and against that wall,' the woman **ordered**, stepping away from her slightly. '**Now**!' (iWeb)

Does the speaker attempt to be polite?
Politeness can be found in any type of speech act. Even threats can be polite (i.e. *Honey, please, if you don't finish up your soup, I will have to punish you without playtime*). However, as the data in our corpus shows,

orders are not prototypically polite. Over 99 per cent of the orders in our data show no overt attempt at being polite. The opposite is usually the case. Most order constructions include strategies that highlight their impositive nature and, therefore, render them fairly impolite (e.g. expressions of immediateness, forceful intonation, vocatives stressing the hearer's inferiority, etc.):

(4.10) 'Girls, into your room, **now**.' Her father **ordered sternly** as he rose to the door (iWeb)
(4.11) 'Finish it, **NOW!!!**', Alice **ordered grimly** (iWeb)
(4.12) 'Sit down, **you moron!**' Herrera **ordered** (iWeb)

In fact, in connection with orders the use of politeness strategies is anecdotal and, when they are used, they often yield peripheral examples of ironic, sarcastic, or even humiliating orders, such as the following example in which politeness is used in an order addressed to a hearer who is clearly being denigrated by the speaker:

(4.13) 'Shelby walked over to Sara with a dog leash in her hand. She clipped the leash to Sara's collar […] she went to her knees and crawled behind Shelby. The house was so big that her knees were very sore by the time they got to the main dining room […] Under the table please,' Shelby **ordered**. (iWeb)

Is social power relevant to the act of ordering?
The power relationship that holds between the speakers is central to the act of ordering. Orders are about power. An unstoppable force can move an object if it is strong enough to counteract the weight of the object. Likewise, a directive speech act is an order if the speaker has enough power over the addressee to impose her willingness on him. Other directive acts also exercise power onto the addressee. Threats, for instance, are also impositives. In this case the power of the speaker comes from the fact that she can somehow harm or wrong the hearer if he does not comply with her wishes. The power involved in the act of ordering does not imply this type of retaliation.

All instances of orders in our corpus are uttered by speakers who either are socially more powerful than the hearers or who adopt a position of superiority in relation to the latter. The notion of social power has been found to be quite heterogeneous. The power of the speaker may be physical, granted by social institutions (a company, the military, the family hierarchical structure), or linked to social conventions (age, social class,

4.1 Orders

knowledge). Examples (4.14)–(4.17) illustrate different sources of the power exhibited by speakers uttering orders:

(4.14) 'Itee! Make some tea for your grandfather. Its five o'clock', **ordered** her *father* (iWeb)
(4.15) 'Go, find out where he is,' the *king* **ordered** (iWeb)
(4.16) 'Sign to them to keep off,' *Colonel* Forsyth **ordered** (iWeb)
(4.17) 'So, now tell me in full detail everything you thought and felt while you sat within the chamber,' the *Doctor* **ordered** (iWeb)

The power of the speaker may even arise from the moral superiority stemming from the knowledge that the action expressed in the order is in the benefit of the hearer or a third party. Example (4.18) illustrates this: a brother orders his sibling (an equal) to stop seeing her girlfriend under the premise that it is not good for him to do so. What seems essential is that the speaker makes use of a real or perceived superiority to present the action as an imposition that leaves the hearer little freedom to refuse to comply:

(4.18) 'You must stop seeing that Russian girl,' I **ordered my brother** [...] Echoing the prejudiced, ignorant sentiment that I had grown up with, I believed it was wrong to become seriously involved with a person who does not follow the Hindu religion and is not a member of the Indian race (iWeb)

Is the social distance between the speakers relevant to the act of ordering?
Our data shows that orders can be performed regardless of the social distance that exists between the speakers: as long as the speaker has the necessary power, she can direct her order to people who are socially close to her (relatives, friends, colleagues) or far away in the social scale (strangers). EFL learners need to be aware, however, that the closer the speakers are socially, the higher the need to soften its force and the less impositive the order tends to be perceived. As example (4.19) shows it is not socially acceptable to impose on people who are socially close to us, even if we have the power to do so. The use of the vocative signalling social closeness (i.e. *sweetie*) helps to soften the impositive force of the order by acknowledging the closeness between the speakers:

(4.19) 'Ok **sweetie** let me go to sleep on this cloud you've given me ...' she *softly* **ordered**. Turning her head to the side she continued, '... but first give me a kiss Goodnight.' (iWeb)

Table 4.1 *The know-what of orders*

Orders are strong directive speech acts in which a speaker tries to impose a course of action on the hearer(s). When someone orders someone else to do something, they communicate the following:

'I have the necessary power/authority to impose on you a particular course of action. I want you to do it because it is beneficial to me or to someone that I want to benefit from the action. I know it is costly to you, but I still expect you to comply with my order.'

What you need to bear in mind to perform a successful order:
- The proposed action may benefit the speaker, the hearer, a third party, or a combination of the former.
- Orders stem from a need or a desire on the part of the speaker, who takes for granted that the hearer is capable of performing the action.
- Whether or not the hearer wants to do as told is irrelevant for the speaker, who assumes that she has the power (either real or perceived) to impose her wishes on the former.
- Prototypical orders are not polite, they do not attempt to minimise the cost of the proposed action, and they offer little or no freedom to the hearer to refuse to do as told.
- Orders can be performed in all contexts regardless of their formality, and they can be directed to hearers regardless of the social distance that separates them from the speaker.

BE AWARE!!!
- Orders are prototypically not polite and unmitigated. The overt use of politeness or mitigation gives way to peripheral instances of orders that may be felt as ironical or may be mistaken for requests.
- You can perform an order regardless of the social distance that separates you from the hearer, but you should bear in mind that the smaller the social distance between the participants, the less impositive and forceful your order will be perceived. It is not socially acceptable to impose on people to which we feel emotionally attached.

Is the formality of the context relevant to the act of ordering?
Orders are not tied to a specific type of context. Around 50 per cent of the orders in our corpus take place in formal contexts and the other half in informal situations (see Table 4.1).

4.1.2 The Know-How of Orders

How are orders expressed in English? The analysis of the first 500 instances of orders returned by the iWeb corpus offers the following portrait of how English speakers realise this speech act linguistically (see Table 4.2).

Looking at the data, it comes as no surprise that the imperative sentence type has traditionally been associated with the speech act of ordering. Over

Table 4.2 *Base constructions for the act of ordering in English*

Base constructions	Occurrences	Percentage
IMPERATIVE	436	87.2
YOU DO X	6	1.2
X SHALL BE/DO	6	1.2
YOU ARE (NOT) TO DO X	5	1
YOU MUST DO X	4	0.8
YOU HAVE TO DO X	4	0.8
X MUST DO Y	4	0.8
LET X DO Y	4	0.8
GO DO X	4	0.8
I WANT YOU TO DO X	4	0.8
I WANT YOU + PREPOSITION	3	0.6
SEE THAT X IS DONE	2	0.4
I'D LIKE X	2	0.4
X MUST BE DONE	2	0.4
X WILL BE DONE	2	0.4
YOU HAD BETTER DO X	2	0.4
I ORDER YOU TO DO X	2	0.4
X IS PROHIBITED TO DO X	2	0.4
X IS DIRECTED TO DO Y	2	0.4
X WILL (NOT) BE REQUIRED TO DO Y	2	0.4
THERE BETTER BE X	2	0.4
Total	**500**	**100**

87 per cent of the instances of orders in our corpus make use of imperative sentences as their base constructions:

(4.20) (BARE IMPERATIVE) '*Release* the lady,' the soldier **ordered** (iWeb)

(4.21) (SEE THAT X IS DONE): 'These men will not be required to work for two weeks,' he **ordered** sternly. 'And *see that good provisions are handed out to them*,' he added (iWeb)

(4.22) (GO DO X): 'Right. *Go lock* the door then so mother won't be disturbing us,' he **ordered** (iWeb)

The rest of the orders in our corpus make use of a varied array of base constructions that activate different elements of the meaning of orders, therefore metonymically activating their interpretation as such. Thus, there are some constructions that focus on the speaker's desire that the action is carried out by the hearer:

(4.23) (I WANT YOU TO DO X) When she **ordered**: '*I want you* out of here now ...' (iWeb)

(4.24) (I'D LIKE X / I'D LIKE YOU TO DO X) '*I'd like* a rowboat ready to cast off, mister Quidd,' the Admiral **ordered** (iWeb)

There are also some base constructions focusing on the lack of freedom of the hearer to refuse to comply with the order:

(4.25) (YOU DO X) '*You stay* here and find one,' he **ordered** (iWeb)

(4.26) (YOU HAVE TO DO X) '*You have to* taste it before complaining,' she **ordered** him (iWeb)

(4.27) (YOU ARE ORDERED TO DO X) '*You are ordered to* co-operate ...' (iWeb)

Others exploit the impositive flavour of orders and present the realisation of the action as unavoidable:

(4.28) (X SHALL DO Y) '*Defendant School District shall pay a fine* per infraction to the Plaintiff ...' the judge **ordered** (iWeb)

(4.29) (X WILL BE DONE) '... whatever we find in the shape of an upper class in Poland *will be liquidated*,' Hitler had **ordered** (iWeb)

With the exception of those constructions which have a marked impositive flavour (e.g. YOU ARE TO DO X, YOU HAVE TO DO X, YOU DO X, X SHALL DO Y, X WILL BE DONE, etc.), the rest of the base constructions for ordering found in our corpus are also used in the expression of other speech acts (see sections in relation to requests, beggings, suggestions, advice acts, and warnings). Imperatives simply present the content of a proposition for realisation, and this is a goal that is shared by all directive speech acts. However, as shown in Section 2.5.6, base constructions rarely appear on their own. They combine with other linguistic strategies that further activate other aspects of the meaning of illocutions, thus clarifying the nature of the intended speech act. How is the imperative used when the aim of the speaker is to perform an order? Table 4.3 summarises the linguistic strategies that accompany the IMPERATIVE base construction in the expression of orders.

A central characteristic of the linguistic strategies that combine with the base constructions used in the expression of orders is that they generally aim at increasing the imposition and the force of the act. Thus, the three

Table 4.3 *Imperative base construction + realisation procedures for orders*

Imperative constructions	Occurrences	Percentage
BARE IMPERATIVE	254	58.2
IMPERATIVE + IMPOSITIVE INTONATION	116	26.7
IMPERATIVE + EXPRESSION OF IMMEDIATENESS	29	6.7
IMPERATIVE + EXPRESSION DOWNGRADING THE HEARER	17	3.9
IMPERATIVE + EXPRESSION OF SOCIAL CLOSENESS	17	3.9
IMPERATIVE + EXPRESSION OF POLITENESS	3	0.6
Total	**436**	**100**

main realisation procedures that combine with IMPERATIVE base constructions in the production of orders are (1) a forceful/impositive intonation, (2) expressions of immediateness, and (3) vocatives downgrading the hearer and, hence, pointing to the superiority of the speaker, as illustrated by examples (4.30)–(4.32), respectively.

(4.30) 'Come on!' he **ordered** *roughly* (iWeb)
(4.31) 'Get your hands up and against that wall,' the woman **ordered**, stepping away from her slightly. '*Now!*' (iWeb)
(4.32) 'Open your mouth *whore!*' he **ordered** (iWeb)

Still, around half of the IMPERATIVE base constructions used in the expression of orders in our corpus are bare imperatives. The use of bare imperatives, deprived of any other lexico-grammatical forms that help to specify the type of directive involved, can be an economic strategy for performing directives, as long as the semantic attributes of the speech act that is to be communicated are contextually activated. As regards orders, EFL students should be aware of the fact that the use of a bare imperative will be successfully interpreted as an order in contexts in which the power of the speaker is known to all participants. In relation to the act of ordering, the superiority of the speaker leads him to not even entertain the possibility of a refusal to comply by the hearer. Hence, when this is clear from the context, he does not feel the need to make use of any of the strategies included in Table 4.3 to force the hearer to obey his order. If speakers are socially equal, however, the interpretation of the IMPERATIVE base construction as an order will be ruled out in favour of alternative directive readings like requests, beggings, suggestions, etc. The examples in which politeness strategies (i.e. use of the adverb *please*) are used in connection with the imperative for the expression of an order are either sarcastic polite orders (see example (4.13) above), camouflaged orders, or cases in which the social distance between the speakers is small (i.e. they are friends, relatives, long-time colleagues). With respect to the latter, students need to be aware of the fact that the impositive force of an order is sensitive to the social distance that exists between speakers. As explained in Section 4.1.1, when the speakers are socially close (friends, relatives), the imperative is perceived as less forceful because it is taken for granted that it is not socially acceptable to impose on people who are close to us. In these cases, if the speaker wants to maintain the impositive flavour of an order, she should make use of one of the strengthening strategies described above (i.e. forceful intonation, expression of immediateness, downgrading vocative). If, on the contrary, she wishes to soften the strength of the order to adapt it to the requirements of a short social distance, he can either make use of politeness strategies (example (4.33)) or simply use expressions that signal the social closeness with the hearer (example (4.19), reproduced below as example (4.34) for convenience):

(4.33) 'I wrote it up myself,' Harper's secretary replied. [...] 'Dig it out for me and bring it in here, *please*,' Harper **ordered** (iWeb)

(4.34) 'Ok *sweetie* let me go to sleep on this cloud you've giving me ...' she *softly* **ordered**. Turning her head to the side she continued, '... but first give me a kiss Goodnight.' (iWeb)

The data reported in this section suggests that teaching Spanish EFL students to perform orders in English should necessarily include the most frequent constructions in Table 4.2. In addition, it would be useful to explain in detail the use of the IMPERATIVE base construction in the production of orders, since this has turned out to be the most frequent linguistic strategy for their expression in English. In this respect, two issues should be highlighted: (1) if the features included in the know-what of an order are evident from the context, a bare imperative is one of the preferred, most prototypical linguistic strategies for ordering someone to do something in English; and (2) in a less informative context, the order interpretation of an IMPERATIVE construction can be secured by making use of additional strategies aimed at increasing its impositive character (i.e. expressions of immediateness, forceful intonation, downgraders, etc.) or by avoiding those that soften its force (i.e. politeness strategies, expressions of social closeness).

The strategies offered by the English language for the expression of orders have been compared with those that are most frequent in Spanish. Such comparison allows us to alert EFL learners to possible mismatches between both languages.

Table 4.4 shows the number of occurrences and percentages of the different order constructions in our English and Spanish corpora. The data

Table 4.4 Comparison of base constructions for the act of ordering in English and Spanish

Orders base constructions (English)	Number	Percentage	Number	Percentage	Orders base constructions (Spanish)
IMPERATIVE	436	87.2	380	76	IMPERATIVE
YOU ARE TO DO X	5	1	13	2.6	VAS A HACER X
YOU MUST DO X	4	0.8	4	0.8	DEBES HACER X
YOU HAVE TO DO X	4	0.8	5	1	TIENES QUE HACER X
YOU (WILL) DO X	6	1.2	29	5.8	(TÚ/VOSOTROS/USTEDES) HARÁS/HARÉIS X
X WILL/SHALL BE/DO X	6	1.2	3	0.6	(ÉL/ELLA/ELLOS/AS) HARÁ(N) X
X MUST DO Y	4	0.8	2	0.4	DEBE HACER X
GO DO X	4	0.8	1	0.2	VE Y HAZ X
I WANT YOU TO DO X	4	0.8	1	0.2	QUIERO QUE HAGAS X
I WANT YOU + PREPOSITION	3	0.6	1	0.2	TE QUIERO + PREPOSITION
X MUST BE DONE	2	0.4	9	1.8	(SE) DEBE HACER(SE) X
I ORDER YOU TO DO X	2	0.4	13	2.6	TE ORDENO QUE…
LET X DO Y	4	0.8	0	0	Possible but not productive
SEE THAT X IS DONE	2	0.4	0	0	Possible but not productive
I'D LIKE X	2	0.4	0	0	Possible, but not productive
X WILL BE DONE	2	0.4	0	0	Possible but not productive
YOU HAD BETTER DO X	2	0.4	0	0	Possible but not productive
X IS PROHIBITED TO DO X	2	0.4	0	0	Possible but not productive
X IS DIRECTED TO DO Y	2	0.4	0	0	Possible but not productive
X WILL BE REQUIRED TO DO Y	2	0.4	0	0	Possible but not productive
THERE BETTER BE X	2	0.4	0	0	Possible but not productive
Not possible	0	0	30	6	QUE HAGA(N) X
Not possible	0	0	9	1.8	A + HACER X
TOTAL	500	100	500	100	

reveals that there are some parallel constructions for the expression of orders that have a similar frequency of occurrence in both languages. Among them, the most frequent are the IMPERATIVE, YOU MUST DO X, YOU HAVE TO DO X, and YOU ARE TO DO X constructions (white rows in Table 4.4).

Many others are found in both languages, but they are more frequently used in one of them (light grey rows in Table 4.4). Thus, order constructions that refer to the speaker's wanting the action to take place (e.g. I WANT YOU TO DO X, I WANT + PREP) are found in both languages, but are slightly more frequent in English. Spanish, on the contrary, displays a preference towards the use of direct performatives (e.g. TE ORDENO QUE (I ORDER YOU TO DO X)).

Finally, there are constructions that only arise in the corpus for one of the languages (dark grey rows in Table 4.4). In some cases, this is so because there exists no direct counterpart in the other language. Spanish, for example, makes use of empathic order constructions like QUE HAGA(N) X (THAT THEY DO X) and A HACER X (TO DO X) that have no parallel linguistic expression in English. The English corpus also contains some specific constructions (e.g. THERE BETTER BE X, I'D LIKE X, and several passive constructions Y IS DIRECTED TO DO X, Y WILL BE REQUIRED TO DO X) that, although possible, yield no occurrences in the Spanish corpus, thus indicating that Spanish speakers do not favour the use of those particular constructions.

The above information about the preferences displayed by each language in the expression of orders is key to their efficient teaching. Depending on the target level of proficiency of their students, teachers and textbook designers can adapt the scope of their teaching content on the basis of the information included in Table 4.4. Order constructions that are more frequent and which are similar in both languages can be introduced at the starter and intermediate levels, while those constructions that display mismatches between the two languages in terms of frequency of use, and those that do not exist in the students' native language, can be dealt with at latter stages of instruction.

4.2 Requests

The force metaphor is also pervasive in our understanding of requests. Everyday life expressions like *His request moved me to … / pushed me to …* are grounded on the idea that requests metaphorically function as (linguistic) forces that cause the hearer to carry out the specified action. If orders were conceptualised in terms of a compulsion force (i.e. a powerful,

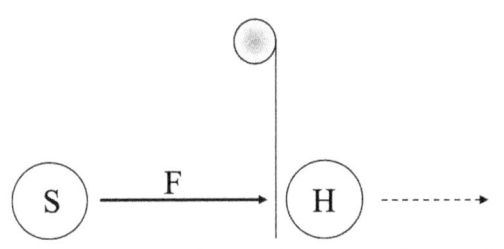

Figure 4.2 Force schema underlying the conceptualisation of requests

unstoppable force as shown in Section 4.1.1), the force schema on which requests are grounded is characterised by the potential existence of a blockage or restraint that needs to be removed. Figure 4.2 illustrates the removal of restraint image schema (Johnson, 1987: 45) that underlies the conceptualisation of requests according to Pérez-Hernández and Ruiz de Mendoza (2002: 275).

The restraint needs to be removed so that the force (i.e. linguistic request uttered by the speaker) can have an effect on the hearer and move him into action. This restraint metaphorically stands for some of the potential obstacles that may prevent a request from being successful. Among others, these may be the lack of capability or willingness of the hearer to comply with the action, his lack of possession of the object being requested, the cost of the requested action, etc.

As far as orders are concerned, the higher social power of the speaker leads him to disregard those potential obstacles. As a consequence, a speaker issuing an order expects no other move but compliance on the part of the hearer. The freedom of the latter to decide whether or not to obey the order is either very low or inexistent. The speaker uttering a request, however, does not have enough power to issue a compulsive unstoppable force like that of orders. He is well aware of the fact that he does not have the necessary power to disregard potential obstacles that may affect the success of the requestive force of his utterance. Therefore, he needs to acknowledge them and to try to remove them in order for his request to be effective. This metaphorical conceptualisation of requests, grounded on the removal of restraint force schema, helps to understand their semantic make-up (i.e. their know-what), and it is also manifested in their linguistic forms (i.e. their know-how), as will be explained in the following two sections.

4.2.1 The Know-What of Requests

Among directive speech acts, requests have attracted a large amount of research interest both in English and Spanish by most relevant pragmatists

(Searle, 1969; Brown & Levinson, 1987; Leech, 1983, 2014), cognitivists (Pérez-Hernández, 1996, 2001, 2012, 2013, 2019; Stefanowitsch, 2003; Ruiz de Mendoza & Baicchi, 2007; Pérez-Hernández & Ruiz de Mendoza, 2011; Del Campo, 2013; Vassilaki, 2017), and intercultural linguists (Blum-Kulka, 1987, 1991; Blum-Kulka & House, 1989; Blum-Kulka, House & Kasper, 1989; Fukushima, 2000; Schauer, 2009), among others.

As opposed to the initial Searleian definition of requests as a classical all-or-nothing category (1969: 66), nowadays, there is large consensus that speech acts constitute prototypical categories, which include both central and peripheral members (Leech, 2014: 137) forming a continuum between different illocutionary acts. In this section, we present the know-what of the act of requesting, which spells out the main semantic attributes that conform to prototypical members of the category and motivate their linguistic realisations (i.e. their know-how), which shall be described in Section 4.2.2.

Who is to do the action expressed in the request?
The data in our corpus confirms findings by previous authors (e.g. Pérez-Hernández, 2001; Del Campo, 2013; Leech, 2014) that all requests are hearer-focused (i.e. they intent the hearer to be the agent of the requested action). Even requests for permission, whose linguistic forms present the speaker as the agent (e.g. *Can I use your phone to call him?)* or those request constructions that have an impersonal *it* as subject (e.g. *Is it possible to get a copy of that?*) are ultimately meant for the hearer to perform an action. As Leech (2014: 141–142) notes, this is made manifest by their compatibility with the politeness marker *please* (e.g. *Can I use your phone to call him, please?, Is it possible to get a copy of that, please?*).

Who will benefit from the action expressed in the request?
Previous studies argue that prototypical requests imply a benefit to the speaker and a cost to the hearer (Leech, 2014: 137), the size of the cost and the size of the benefit being scalar and varying from minimal to very large. According to the data in our corpus, most requests do involve a benefit to the speaker, as in example (4.35), but they may simultaneously benefit others as well, as in examples (4.36) and (4.37), both the speaker and the hearer (e.g. example (4.38)), or the hearer exclusively (as in example (4.39)):

(4.35) 'Feed *me*,' Sadiq Ali **requested** playfully, when Kamala allowed the two hours to stretch into lunch (iWeb)
(4.36) 'So, Bella, tell *us* a little bit about yourself.' He **requested** politely (iWeb)

(4.37) 'Let *us* go,' she **requested** (iWeb)
(4.38) 'Gentlemen, *we need* to start getting ready so if you will all follow me please?' he **requested** (iWeb)
(4.39) 'Please, Mr Darcy. Your head is bleeding. It is not safe for you to sit up at this time.' She put her soaked handkerchief down on the ground. 'I am afraid my handkerchief was not sufficient, do you have your own?' **she requested**, trying to see if he could comprehend her. # Mr Darcy hesitated for a moment, then produced one from his coat pocket (iWeb)

As was the case with orders, all instances of requests share the fact that the hearer is presented as the agent of an action that has a beneficiary, which is prototypically the speaker, but could be other people as well.

Whether requests imply a cost to the hearer or not is a more complex issue. At first sight, since they always require an action by the hearer, they could be thought to be costly to her at least in the minimal sense of having to carry out the requested action. However, on some occasions, such action may result in a benefit for the agent (i.e. hearer herself), as in example (4.39) above. In these cases, requests could not be properly said to be costly to the hearer. In example (4.39), the speaker benefits minimally (i.e. by obtaining compliance with her request), and the hearer is the one that fully benefits from the action she has been asked to perform. These cases of requests, which involve a minimal benefit for the speaker and a maximal benefit for the hearer, together with those which involve a similar benefit for both speaker and hearer, are peripheral exemplars of the category, which approximate other directive categories like those of advising and suggesting, respectively.

Can the hearer do the action expressed in the request?
When a speaker asks someone to do something, he is usually previously informed about the hearer's ability to do the action. Otherwise, it would make no sense to ask him. Thus, in all instances in our corpus, the hearer is capable of performing the requested action. However, while the speaker issuing an order takes for granted the capability of the hearer to perform the proposed action (e.g. *Feed me!*), requests often question it (e.g. *Can / Could you feed me?*). This is done as a means to increase the hearer's freedom to opt out from doing the action without infringing social norms of politeness. Acknowledging the freedom of the hearer to do the requested action is a direct consequence of the lack of power of the speaker uttering a request, as opposed to the superiority of that issuing an order.

Do speaker and hearer want the action to be carried out?
Prototypical requests are uttered by speakers who have a strong desire that the proposed action is carried out. This is sometimes used as the conceptual motivation underlying some request constructions:

(4.40)   '*I wish* they'd stop, really,' he **requested** (iWeb)
(4.41)   '*I would like* chocolate mint ice-cream!' The boy **requested** to the clerk (iWeb)

In both examples (4.40) and (4.41) the mere expression of the speaker's desire counts as a request for action on the part of the hearer.

    Whether the hearer is equally willing to do as requested depends greatly on who is to benefit from the action and varies largely. If the hearer herself is among the beneficiaries of the action, then her willingness to act as requested may increase, as in example (4.42) in which the benefit of looking for a quality beer benefits both the speaker and the hearer:

(4.42)   'Could *we*,' he **requested** in a typically dismissive way, 'meet at a place that serves imported beer as opposed to the s--t that Americans drink?' (iWeb)

Otherwise, the hearer's willingness to do as requested is expected to be low. Interestingly enough, as opposed to orders, where the fact that the hearer might not be willing to perform the action was irrelevant to the speaker, requests are characterised by displaying concern about this potential lack of willingness to comply. In fact, the hearer not wanting to perform the requested action is one of the potential obstacles that may block the success of the request. Impediments like this can be disregarded when the speaker has enough social or knowledge power to impose on the hearer a certain course of action (i.e. orders, pieces of advice). However, as regards requests, since the speaker does not have such power, the willingness of the hearer or the lack of it become relevant and, as shall be illustrated in Section 4.2.2, this serves as conceptual motivation for several request constructions (e.g. WILL YOU DO X?, WOULD YOU MIND DOING X?).

Is the action expressed in the request necessary?
Prototypically, requests stem from the need of the speaker for an object or from his need that a particular action is carried out in his benefit. This semantic attribute motivates some linguistic constructions associated with requests (e.g. I / WE NEED YOU TO DO X):

(4.43)   'And we did this all by ourselves. But now *we need you to* edit this and maybe help us with words that just don't sound right before the class sees it on Thursday,' Cole **requested** (iWeb)

4.2 Requests

How much freedom does a request allow the hearer?
The lack of power of the speaker to impose her will on the hearer leads to a prototypically high freedom of the latter to comply with the request or not. Unlike orders, which have been shown to be non-negotiable, requests are typically characterised by allowing ample freedom of action to the hearer. This high optionality is one of the central semantic features of requests and motivates many linguistic constructions of the declarative and interrogative sentence types that serve as vehicles for the expression of this speech act. Declarative sentences simply present a proposition for consideration, and interrogative sentences characteristically present a proposition as (partially) open (Risselada, 1993: 71), thus offering the optionality needed in the expression of requests:

(4.44) 'Could you teach me how to dance, Misty?' He **requested** (iWeb)
(4.45) 'Would you pass the grated cheese?' I **requested** (iWeb)
(4.46) 'Yeah, good idea. But before you do, I want you to just stand up and turn around, Stacy.' He **requested** (iWeb)

As opposed to the imperative sentence type, both declaratives and interrogatives highlight the freedom granted to the hearer to comply with the request or to opt out and are, therefore, better suited as vehicles for the expression of this directive speech act. The impositive nature of imperatives needs to be soften in order to be able to function well as requests, as shown in examples (4.47)–(4.49). This is done by means of increasing the politeness or tentativeness of the act (i.e. *please, if you can*), or by decreasing the cost of the action (i.e. *a little bit*).

(4.47) The man **requested**, 'Sir, *please* have my dowry returned to me.' (iWeb)
(4.48) 'While you're out, *if you can*, take some pictures of the birds and send them to me.' She **requested** and watched him nod (iWeb)
(4.49) 'So, Bella, tell us *a little bit* about yourself.' He **requested** politely (iWeb)

The optionality of the hearer only decreases in specific situations. For instance, when the request is invited by the hearer (as in example (4.50)), where the hearer would lose face if he refused to grant the speaker's wish after offering to give her anything she needs, or in highly structured settings where the hearer is expected to comply with the speaker wishes by virtue of social conventions (as in the commercial setting depicted in (4.51)):

(4.50) *'Anything you need Lute.'* # Luticia's eyes began to close as her head turned to the side, a bit of blood started to slip out of her mouth. 'One story, please one more story,' she **requested** of me (iWeb)

(4.51) We smiled eagerly at the young cashier as he rung up our purchase. # 'Eighty-seven cents, please,' he **requested** (iWeb)

Optionality also decreases in fake requests, those uttered in a polite fashion by a powerful speaker. As remarked by Leech (2014: 138), a boss addressing her employee may say something along the line of *You might want to collect those documents before the bank close*. In spite of the freedom conveyed by the tentativeness of the linguistic form, the hearer is well aware of the superiority of the speaker and of his obligation to comply. These are, in fact, orders camouflaged as requests or polite orders. Students should be aware of interactions of this type between the semantic attribute of optionality and the semantic variable of social power, to the effect that asymmetrical power relationships may override the effect of the optionality conveyed by the linguistic form.

Does the speaker attempt to minimise the cost of the action?
Among the obstacles that may lead to an unsuccessful request there is also the cost of the action. Since the speaker is not powerful enough to impose her will on the hearer, she needs to carefully consider the cost of the requested action and attempt to minimise it as much as possible to secure the hearer's compliance. The minimisation of cost serves as the grounding for some request constructions (i.e. IF ONLY YOU COULD DO X, IF ONLY YOU DID X). It can also be achieved by the use of a particular set of realisation procedures, mainly adverbs like *a little, a bit, just, simply, a minute, only*, etc. By means of illustration, see examples (4.52) and (4.53).

(4.52) 'When they see a plow truck, *just* give us the opportunity to do what we need to do to help them get where they're going,' **requested** Maroon (iWeb)

(4.53) Simba **requested**: 'Taraja, could you stay here *a bit* while Akili and I climb out.' (iWeb)

Does the speaker attempt to be polite?
Politeness has traditionally been considered a defining trait of requests. However, as was the case with optionality, politeness *per se* may not lead to a request interpretation, especially in those cases in which the speaker is

clearly more powerful than the hearer, and it is obvious from the context that she has reasons to use such power to coerce the hearer's course of action. In asymmetrical relationships, politeness, without optionality, leads to fake requests or polite orders such as the one in example (4.54):

(4.54) (Team captain to players) 'Would players three and eleven please step forward?' Caius **requested** (iWeb)

Being aware of this overriding effect of the social power variable, students will be able to understand that the use of politeness is only a straightforward signal of requests when the speaker is either socially equal to or inferior than the hearer. When this situation holds, politeness is an effective way of overcoming some of the obstacles that may prevent the request from succeeding (e.g. the hearer's unwillingness to do the action or the high cost of the action). This is the reason for the pervasiveness of politeness in the realisation of requests. However, as shown by the data in our corpus, the politeness of requests may decrease in several circumstances, such as when the speaker is more powerful than the hearer (example (4.55)), and when the beneficiary of the requested action is the hearer himself (example (4.56)), or both speaker and hearer (example (4.57)). Politeness is also taken for granted when the speaker and the hearer are socially close (example (4.58)).

(4.55) 'STEWARDESS SNIPPEE!' Captain boomed. 'YOU ARE REQUESTED ON FLIGHT DECK!' (iWeb)
(4.56) Then Jill took off her pants and handed them to Jack, as she said, 'Here, you try on mine!' As she **requested**, he tried them (iWeb)
(4.57) 'Keep our studio clean,' another sign **requested** (iWeb)
(4.58) 'Go down to Thomas and get me some more,' his father **requested** (iWeb)

Is social power relevant to the act of requesting?
Requests can be uttered regardless of the power relationship that holds between the speakers. Nevertheless, as explained above, students should be aware of the fact that as the power of the speaker increases, (1) the need for politeness to secure compliance from the hearer decreases, and requests gradually fade into more impositive speech acts like orders or commands, and (2) the optionality of the hearer to decide whether to act as requested decreases in spite of the politeness used in the expression of the request. Mutual knowledge of the speaker's superiority overrules the effects of politeness and limits the freedom of the hearer to decide on his course of action, thus turning those instances of requests into more peripheral members of the category.

Is the social distance between the speakers relevant to the act of requesting?
Requests can be addressed to people who are both close and distant to the speaker on the axis of social relationships. Still, students should be aware of the interaction of this social variable with the semantic attribute of politeness. As shown above, the closer the speakers are, the lower the need for overt politeness in the expression of requests will be. In conversations among socially close people, politeness is taken for granted, since the unwritten rules of social interaction already apply, and people are not expected to impose on others who are socially or emotionally close to them (see example 4.58).

Is the formality of the context relevant to the act of requesting?
Requests are performed in all contexts regardless of their degree of formality. The use of politeness tends to increase with the formality of the context. Formal contexts often also imply a larger social distance between speakers, which also favours the aforementioned increase in the use of politeness (see Table 4.5).

4.2.2   The Know-How of Requests

Studies on the linguistic formulae used by speakers of different languages to request someone to do something have flourished since the beginning of speech act theory. It is possible to distinguish four main lines of research on this matter, including pragmatic, interlinguistic, cognitive, and conversational approaches. Within the pragmatic strand, Leech (2014) has provided one of the most comprehensive works to date, devoting a full chapter of his book to a qualitative, corpus-based taxonomy of the different linguistic realisation procedures for requests or, in his own words, the pragmalinguistic strategies and lexico-grammatical forms available for the expression of requests in English. His main classification criterion is based on the degree of directness/conventionalisation of the different formulae. It does consider some motivating factors, such as cost–benefit, social distance, and power but ignores others like the capability and willingness/need of the participants, the formality of the context, and the potential interactions between semantic variables and attributes, thus falling short of offering a comprehensive picture of the semantic motivation that underlies the diverse range of linguistic constructions at hand for the realisation of requests.

   Blum-Kulka, House, and Kasper (1989) have delved into the interlinguistic issues affecting the production of requests, with a view to identifying

Table 4.5 *The know-what of requests*

Requests are directive speech acts in which a speaker asks the hearer(s) to carry out an action. When someone requests someone else to do something, they communicate the following:

'I want you to do something because it is beneficial to me or to someone whom I also want to benefit from the action. I know it is costly to you, and I do not have the necessary power to impose the action on you. I acknowledge your freedom to comply or to opt out.'

What you need to bear in mind in order to perform a successful request:

- Prototypically, the requested action benefits the speaker, but more peripheral instances of requests may be intended to benefit the hearer, a third party, or a combination of the former.
- Requests stem from a need or a desire on the part of the speaker, who does not have the necessary social power to impose his will on the hearer and who is, therefore, aware of the fact that he may need to overcome some obstacles in order to get the hearer to comply with his wish.
- Among the obstacles to overcome, there is the willingness and ability of the hearer to carry out the proposed action and the cost of the action itself.
- To overcome the aforementioned obstacles, prototypical requests are polite, they attempt to minimise the cost of the proposed action, and they offer freedom to the hearer to refuse to do as told.

BE AWARE!!!

- Prototypical requests are uttered by speakers who do not have the necessary power to impose their will on the hearers. If you are a socially powerful speaker, be aware that your social power may overrule the effect of politeness and of the prototypical optionality of a requestive act, thus giving way to cases of fake requests or camouflaged orders.
- You can perform requests in all contexts regardless of their formality, and they can be directed to hearers regardless of the social distance that separates them from the speaker. Nevertheless, you should be aware that the higher the formality of the context or the larger the social distance between the participants, the politer the request will need to be to secure compliance. Remember that politeness can also be achieved indirectly by means of minimising the cost of the action and/or increasing the optionality of the hearer to do as told.
- You should be aware of the fact that the higher the cost of the action, the higher the need to be polite, to acknowledge the freedom of the hearer to refuse, and/or to minimise the cost of the action.

---

cultural idiosyncrasies that need to be taken into account when attempting to perform a request in a second language.

Cognitive approaches offer a more detailed account of the experiential grounding (i.e. removal of restraint force schema), cognitive operations (i.e. illocutionary metonymy), and cultural conventions (ICMs) that motivate the strategies for requesting (Pérez-Hernández, 2001, 2013, 2019; Ruiz de Mendoza & Baicchi, 2007; Del Campo, 2013; Vassilaki, 2017).

Finally, conversational approaches have shown that the expression of requests often exceeds the limits of a single utterance and have also looked into the supportive moves and preferred-dispreferred conversational turns in which requests are involved (Blum-Kulka, House & Kasper, 1989; Faerch & Kasper, 1989).

In the framework adopted for this book (see Chapter 2), the portrayal of request constructions brings together these four essential aspects of the expression of requests. There are not many studies on frequency data for different request constructions. Not even Leech's (2014) comprehensive taxonomy of requesting strategies provides information about their frequency of use. This type of information, however, is essential for teaching purposes. Owing to space limitations, EFL course books cannot possibly cover every single request strategy, which makes it important to know which are the most frequently used by native speakers in order to include them in the teaching materials. This information is also useful when planning the teaching of speech acts throughout the different levels of instruction. Frequency data can help teachers and editors to choose the most common constructions for the starters' level and gradually increase the difficulty with less frequently used constructions at the intermediate and advanced levels. Based on the London-Lund corpus of spoken English, Aijmer (1996: 157) reports two constructions (i.e. YOU COULD DO X and COULD YOU DO X?) as those showing a higher frequency of occurrence among educated British speakers from the 1950s–1970s generation which populated the data of that particular corpus. Along this line, as shown in Chapter 3, textbooks of English as a second language offer a very limited number of canonical formulae for requesting such as CAN / COULD YOU DO X?, IMPERATIVE + PLEASE, OR WOULD YOU MIND DOING X? The iWeb corpus, containing fourteen billion words, offers a slightly different picture and paves the way for a richer approach to the programming of the teaching of requests in EFL textbooks.

As can be seen in Table 4.6, the data in this corpus yields a large number of linguistic constructions with varied rates of occurrence in the expression of requests in English.

The request strategies taught in EFL textbooks are often restricted to CAN / COULD YOU DO X?, WILL / WOULD YOU DO X?, WOULD YOU MIND DOING X? constructions. The use of the IMPERATIVE construction in association with the politeness adverb *please* is also a typical request construction taught to EFL students. The data in our corpus, however, should lead to reconsider present-day approaches to the teaching of request strategies.

4.2 Requests

Table 4.6 *Base constructions for the act of requesting in English*

Base constructions	Occurrences	Percentage
IMPERATIVE	280	56
CAN YOU DO X?	45	9
COULD YOU DO X?	25	5
I WOULD LIKE X		
I WOULD LIKE YOU TO DO X	20	4
I WISH X		
I WISH YOU TO DO X	15	3
IF YOU WILL DO X	15	3
WILL YOU DO X?	10	2
WOULD YOU DO X?	10	2
DO YOU HAVE X?		
HAVE YOU GOT X?	10	2
CAN WE NOT DO X?	5	1
COULD WE NOT DO X?	5	1
MAY YOU DO X?	5	1
I WANT YOU TO DO X	5	1
I NEED YOU TO DO X	5	1
IT'S TIME FOR YOU TO DO X	5	1
IT WOULD BE GOOD IF YOU COULD DO X	5	1
YOU THINK YOU COULD DO X	5	1
WOULD YOU MIND DOING X?	5	1
ANY CHANCE YOU COULD DO X?	5	1
I DIRECT THAT YOU SHALL DO X	5	1
I ASK YOU TO DO X	10	2
I ASK THAT YOU DO X		
YOU ARE REQUESTED TO DO X	5	1
Total	**500**	**100**

As illustrated in Table 4.6, the IMPERATIVE construction is by far the most common linguistic formula for the expression of requests in English with over 50 per cent of the total number of occurrences. The canonical CAN / COULD YOU DO X?, I WOULD LIKE X, or I WOULD LIKE YOU TO DO X constructions, among others, occupy secondary distant positions.

The high frequency of use of the IMPERATIVE construction, however, calls for a closer examination of its particular use in the realisation of requests. As can be observed in Table 4.7, bare imperatives constitute over 40 per cent of the total number of the occurrences of imperative-based request constructions in English.

Using a bare imperative for requesting is an effective strategy but also a complex and risky one, since imperatives can realise any type of

Table 4.7 *Imperative base construction + realisation procedures for requests*

Imperative constructions for requests	Occurrences	Percentage
BARE IMPERATIVE	115	41
IMPERATIVE + EXPRESSION OF POLITENESS (PLEASE)	65	23
IMPERATIVE + EXPRESSION OF OPTIONALITY	30	11
IMPERATIVE + EXPRESSION OF SOCIAL CLOSENESS	30	11
IMPERATIVE + EXPRESSION OF MINIMISATION OF COST	20	7
IMPERATIVE + EXPRESSION OF SUPERIORITY OF HEARER	10	3.6
IMPERATIVE + REASON CLAUSE	5	1.7
IMPERATIVE + EXPRESSION PRAISING THE HEARER	5	1.7
Total	**280**	**100**

directive (see the know-how sections for other directives in this chapter). A successful use of bare imperatives as requests will depend on whether the semantic attributes of the ICM of requesting (see Section 4.2.1) are activated contextually. If it is clear that the action is in the speaker's benefit, that participants are equals, and that the speaker does not have enough power to impose his will on the hearer, the bare imperative will be effective as a request. This is illustrated by example (4.59), in which a lover asks her partner to tell her that he loves her:

(4.59) 'Sirius', meekly she **requested**, 'Tell me you love me.' (iWeb)

Otherwise, alternative directive interpretations may be activated. The student should also be made aware of the fact that in some contexts, especially those that are highly formal (e.g. legal documents), the use of a bare imperative may be a dispreferred construction for requesting even if all semantic attributes of requests are clearly activated by the context. Compare the formal request in example (4.60) with a fabricated alternative that makes use of a bare imperative in example (4.61).

(4.60) 'I direct that my executors shall arrange for my remains to be taken to the country of Bali and to be cremated there in accordance with the Buddhist rituals of Bali', Bowie allegedly **requested** in his last will testament (iWeb)

(4.61) 'Take my remains to the country of Bali and cremate them there in accordance with the Buddhist rituals of Bali', Bowie **requested** in his last will testament

4.2 Requests

Mastering the use of bare imperatives for the performance of the different types of directives is a highly complex task. Fortunately, the language system offers a myriad of lexico-grammatical realisation procedures that can be used to secure a requestive use of the imperative. These are different from the lexico-grammatical realisation procedures that lead to an order interpretation of the IMPERATIVE construction (see Section 4.1.2), and they are semantically grounded in the semantics of requesting (see the know-what of requesting in Section 4.2.1). Thus, the lack of social power of a speaker issuing a request prevents her from being able to impose her will on the hearer as is the case with other directives like orders and threats. For this reason, when requesting something, speakers attempt to achieve the hearer's compliance through other means. The most frequent lexico-grammatical realisation procedures used in connection with an IMPERATIVE construction to secure a request interpretation are those that express (1) politeness, (2) mitigation of cost, (3) optionality, and (4) social closeness. As captured in Table 4.7, the most widespread one among them is the use of politeness through the use of the adverb *please* or alternative expressions (e.g. *if you please*).

(4.62) '*Please*, make way,' I **requested** (iWeb)

Also highly frequent is the use of the IMPERATIVE construction together with expressions of optionality (e.g. *if you can / will, if you don't mind*, question tags like *can / could / will / would you?*), aimed at enhancing the freedom of the hearer to refuse to carry out the requested action, and thus, indirectly, at increasing the tact and politeness of the act:

(4.63) 'While you're out, *if you can*, take some pictures of the birds and send them to me.' She **requested** (iWeb)

IMPERATIVE constructions with vocatives signalling social closeness and affection also point towards a request interpretation, since imposing on people who are close to us is generally not socially acceptable:

(4.64) '*July*, wait,' he **requested** politely (iWeb)

Likewise, lexico-grammatical forms that mitigate the cost of the proposed action help to guarantee a request interpretation of IMPERATIVE constructions. If the speaker had the power to impose his will (as happens with orders), he would not need to consider the cost of what he asks for or attempt to mitigate it. In fact, as shown in Section 4.1.2, IMPERATIVE constructions for orders were not mitigated in the data from our corpus. Requests realised through IMPERATIVE constructions, on the contrary, often show mitigation of the cost of the required action through the use of adverbs like *just* and *only*, diminutives, expressions of diminishing like *a little*, *a bit*, *a little bit*, etc., or a combination of one or more of these linguistic resources:

(4.65) 'So, Bella, tell us *a little bit* about yourself.' He **requested** politely (iWeb)
(4.66) '*Just a little* off the bottom please,' **requested** the unsuspecting lady (iWeb)

Signalling the superiority of the hearer by means of vocatives expressing the asymmetric power relationship between participants is also an indirect way of acknowledging that the hearer is free to comply (i.e. optionality), thus tilting the interpretation towards that of a request:

(4.67) '*Sir*, come over to our vigil,' she **requested** in vain (iWeb)

Another less frequent means of acknowledging lack of power to impose an action is by alluding to rational arguments in order to persuade the hearer to comply. Thus, some request IMPERATIVE constructions are either preceded or followed by reason clauses stating the motives that lead the speaker to ask the hearer to do something:

(4.68) 'Ok, look, *I'm not good with words* so bear with me here,' I **requested** (iWeb)

Finally, IMPERATIVE constructions with vocatives praising the hearers are also prototypically interpreted as requests because they come through as polite:

(4.69) 'Tell me more, *you big handsome sailor*,' she **requested** (iWeb)

All in all, if compared to the IMPERATIVE constructions for orders (Section 4.1.2) and other directive types (see following sections), the realisation procedures accompanying IMPERATIVE constructions for requests are specific enough for hearers to identify them as such and for speakers to grant the intended interpretation.

While over 80 per cent of order constructions in our corpus are based on the use of the imperative, the act of requesting offers a more varied range of construction types for its expression. Nearly 50 per cent of requests in our corpus are realised by means of declarative or interrogative-based constructions. The most frequent of them are those that question the ability of the hearer to perform the requested action (i.e. CAN / COULD YOU DO X?)

4.2 Requests

(4.70) 'Can you tell me where the bathroom is on this ship?' She nervously **requested** (iWeb)
(4.71) 'Could you teach me how to dance, Misty?' He **requested** (iWeb)

This type of interrogative-based constructions, grounded on an essential semantic attribute for directives (i.e. the fact that the hearer has to be able to perform the requested action), gives the latter freedom to refuse compliance without losing face. In this way, one of the key semantic attributes of requests (i.e. the fact that they allow optionality to the hearer) is activated. If the past modal is used, the politeness of the act increases, thus further activating another essential feature of requesting (i.e. its polite nature).[2] Through the metonymic activation of three nuclear semantic variables of requesting (i.e. ability of the hearer to perform the action, optionality, and politeness) CAN / COULD YOU DO X? constructions constitute a very effective means of conveying a request, which explains their productivity in actual use as shown by the data (see Table 4.6).

In his taxonomy of request strategies, Leech (2014: 148–149) includes declarative-based ability constructions (i.e. YOU CAN / COULD DO X) as strategies for requesting. These could, in fact, be used as requests in a proper context, however, our corpus yields no occurrences for constructions of this type, except for two variants in which the politeness and optionality of the act is highlighted through other means. Thus, the constructions IT WOULD BE GOOD IF YOU COULD DO X and I THINK YOU COULD DO X activate the politeness and optionality variables by means of past modals (i.e. it *would* be good if …) and expressions of tentativeness (i.e. I think …), respectively. Affirmative ability-based constructions with no overt politeness or optionality markers are hardly used as requests, probably because they feel too impositive. Other ability-based interrogative constructions, like CAN / COULD WE / YOU NOT DO X? (as in *Can we not use that phrase, please?*) are far from polite and, as explained in detail in Leech (2014: 156), are accompanied by a tone of annoyance.

Another group of fairly productive constructions for requesting is formed by declarative constructions expressing the willingness of the speaker that the action is carried out (i.e. I WOULD LIKE YOU TO DO X, I WISH YOU TO DO X):

(4.72) 'And now, if you will examine the floor,' the magician **requested**. 'All of it. I *wish you to assure* the audience that there are no hidden trapdoors.' (iWeb)

---

[2] For explanations on the politeness of past modals, see Pérez-Hernández (1996) and Leech (2014: 153–155).

This type of construction also activates the politeness and optionality variables through the use of past modals or lexical means (i.e. *wish* is more tentative than *want*). The present tense variant (i.e. I WANT YOU TO DO X), which does not activate the key request attributes of optionality or politeness, is much less productive in the corpus.

Interrogative constructions that activate the attribute concerning the willingness of the hearer to perform the requested action are also fairly frequent (i.e. IF YOU WILL DO X, WILL YOU DO X?, WOULD YOU DO X?):

(4.73) '*Would* you pass the grated cheese?' I **requested** (iWeb)
(4.74) '*If you will* examine the floor,' the magician **requested** (iWeb)

Both the interrogative sentence type and the conditional phrase activate the optionality of the speaker to comply and, in turn, the politeness of the request. In example (4.73) politeness is also overtly expressed by means of the use of a past modal.

Finally, requests for objects often make use of interrogative-based constructions that question the hearer's possession of the requested object:

(4.75) She put her soaked handkerchief down on the ground. 'I am afraid my handkerchief was not sufficient; *do you have your own?*' she **requested** (iWeb)

The rest of the constructions found in our corpus are much less productive. This may be due to the fact that some of them are restricted to formal use (i.e. constructions with performative verbs such as I ASK YOU TO DO X, YOU ARE REQUESTED TO DO X) or to contexts that require higher amounts of politeness (i.e. a large social distance between speakers, for instance, requires the use of formulaic constructions like WOULD YOU MIND DOING X?; requests involving a very high cost for the hearer also ask for an increase in the tentativeness, optionality, and politeness of the construction, e.g. ANY CHANCE YOU COULD DO X?).

All in all, while orders showed a clear preference for imperative base constructions (around 87 per cent of the total), requests make use of imperative base formulae (56 per cent) but also of interrogative and declarative base constructions (44 per cent). The less impositive nature of declarative and interrogative sentences suits well the necessary optionality and politeness of requests. As shown above, IMPERATIVE constructions are generally accompanied by optionality, politeness, and mitigation realisation procedures which activate the request interpretation and rule out impositive readings (orders, threats). These same realisation procedures can be used in combination with declarative and interrogative-based constructions to modulate the politeness, optionality, and cost conveyed by a request, as well as to increase its degree of explicitness.

A comparison of the request constructions in our English and Spanish corpora yields some asymmetries between the two languages that are also of interest for EFL teachers and students.

As reported in Chapter 3, the most common request constructions found in EFL textbooks are the ability-based interrogative formulae CAN / COULD YOU DO X? and the volitional construction I'D LIKE X / I'D LIKE YOU TO DO X. Nevertheless, our data from the English corpus shows that IMPERATIVE constructions clearly outnumber the latter in actual use. This comes to confirm Bouton's (1996) and Nguyen's (2011) observation that there is a lack of representativity of the formulae chosen as teaching targets. The request constructions used in EFL textbooks do not match the actual preferences of real native speakers. In this respect, it would be more realistic to teach students how to use IMPERATIVE constructions together with the proper realisation procedures (see Table 4.7) that help speakers secure a request interpretation.

In addition, it can also be observed that Spanish shows a marked preference for IMPERATIVE constructions (71 per cent) and direct questions about the hearer's course of action (around 11 per cent; E.g. ¿ME HACES X? = *DO YOU DO X FOR ME?) over other formulae for the expression of requests. This can be expected from a language that has already been shown to make a less use of indirectness and politeness than English (Blum-Kulka & House, 1989; Blum-Kulka, House & Kasper, 1989; Márquez-Reiter, 2002; Bataller, 2013). Choosing CAN / COULD YOU DO X? or I'D LIKE YOU TO DO X constructions as teaching targets for Spanish students of English, when their native language favours other construction types, does not seem a very effective way of approaching the teaching of English requests to Spanish speakers. On the contrary, teaching them the realisation procedures that guarantee a request interpretation of IMPERATIVE constructions appears as a more natural approach for students of a language that already displays a preference for this base construction.

Spanish students would also have to be made aware of the fact that although the COULD YOU DO X? construction has a similar frequency of occurrence to that of its Spanish counterpart (¿PODRÍAS HACER X?), the same construction with a present modal (CAN YOU DO X?) is also widely used in English. In fact, more widely used than its Spanish counterpart (¿PUEDES HACER X?).

There are some English constructions that are easy to teach to Spanish students, since there exist parallel Spanish forms with a similar rate of occurrence (white rows in Table 4.8). However, Spanish students of English should be taught that other constructions show different rates of preference in each language (light grey rows in Table 4.8). Thus, some are more widely used in English (e.g. I'D LIKE X / YOU TO DO X; I WISH X / YOU TO DO X), and others are favoured in Spanish (e.g. IMPERATIVE, QUIERO QUE HAGAS X (I WANT YOU TO DO X)).

Finally, there are constructions that only arise in the corpus for one of the languages under scrutiny (dark grey rows in Table 4.8). The English corpus displays some specific constructions (e.g. IF YOU WILL DO X, ANY CHANCE YOU WOULD DO X, YOU THINK YOU COULD DO X, etc.) that, although possible, yield no occurrences in the Spanish corpus, thus indicating that Spanish speakers do not favour the use of those particular constructions. More relevant for teaching purposes are those cases in which there exists no direct counterpart in the other language. Spanish, for example, makes use of request constructions like ¿ME HACES X? and ¿ME HARÍAS X? (as in *¿Me abres la puerta?* = *Do you open the door for me?) that have no parallel linguistic expression in English. Students should be made aware of these mismatches in order to prevent mistakes based on interlanguage interferences.

4.3 Beggings

In comparison to the extensive existing bibliography on requests, the act of begging has attracted virtually no attention in the literature. A simple search in Google Scholar retrieves no specific research articles on begs, other than some scattered mentions of this illocutionary act as an example of directive speech act. This lack of research interest in the act of begging parallels its poor treatment in EFL textbooks. As shown in Chapter 3, only one out of the ten textbooks under scrutiny offered specific teaching on this illocutionary act with just one passing reference to it. Begging, however, is not uncommon in everyday life interactions, and reaching proficiency in a second language should involve the knowledge of how to properly and effectively produce this speech act.

Like other directives, begs are grounded on force dynamics and metaphorically conceptualised as a specific type of weak force that needs to be repeated several times to achieve its aim. This iterative force acts on the rationality and/or social conscience of the hearer (i.e. $H_{R/S}$) and, if successful, turns him into an agent (i.e. H_A) and moves him

Table 4.8 Comparison of base constructions for the act of requesting in English and Spanish

Requests base constructions (English)	Number	Percentage	Number	Percentage	Requests base constructions (Spanish)
COULD YOU DO X?	25	5	25	5	¿(ME) PODRÍAS HACER X?
DO YOU HAVE X?					
HAVE YOU GOT X?	10	2	9	1.8	¿TIENES X?
I ASK YOU TO DO X					
I ASK THAT YOU DO X	10	2	9	1.8	(YO) TE PIDO QUE HAGAS X
I NEED YOU TO DO X	5	1	6	1.2	(LO QUE) YO NECESITO ES QUE HAGAS X
COULD YOU/WE NOT DO X?	5	1	7	1.4	¿NO PODRÍAS/PODRÍAMOS HACER X?
IMPERATIVE	280	56	355	71	IMPERATIVE
CAN YOU DO X?	45	9	10	2	¿(ME) PUEDES HACER X?
I WOULD LIKE X			5	1	ME GUSTARÍA X
I'D LIKE YOU TO DO X	20	4			ME GUSTARÍA QUE TÚ HAGAS X
I WISH X					ESPERO X
I WISH YOU TO DO X	15	3	5	1	ESPERO QUE HAGAS X
I WANT YOU TO DO X	5	1	8	1.6	QUIERO QUE HAGAS X

Table 4.8 (cont.)

Requests base constructions (English)	Number	Percentage	Number	Percentage	Requests base constructions (Spanish)
CAN YOU/WE NOT DO X?	5	1	0	0	Possible but not productive
MAY YOU DO X?	5	1	0	0	Possible but not productive
IF YOU WILL DO X	15	3	0	0	Possible but not productive
WILL YOU DO X?	10	2	0	0	Possible but not productive
WOULD YOU DO X?	10	2	0	0	Possible but not productive
IT'S TIME FOR YOU TO DO X	5	1	0	0	Possible but not productive
IT WOULD BE GOOD IF YOU COULD DO X	5	1	0	0	Possible but not productive
YOU THINK YOU COULD DO X	5	1	0	0	Possible but not productive
WOULD YOU MIND DOING X?	5	1	0	0	Possible but not productive
ANY CHANCE YOU COULD DO X?	5	1	0	0	Possible but not productive
I DIRECT THAT YOU SHALL DO X	5	1	0	0	Possible but not productive
YOU ARE REQUESTED TO DO X	5	1	0	0	Possible but not productive
Not possible	0	0	57	11.4	¿ME HACES X?
Not possible	0	0	4	0.8	¿ME HARÍAS X?
Total	500	100	500	100	

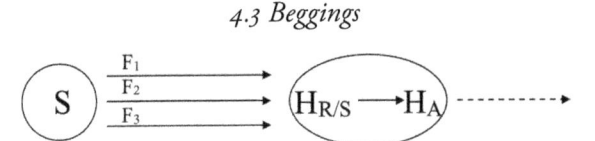

Figure 4.3 Force schema underlying the conceptualisation of beggings

into action. Figure 4.3 illustrates the iteration image schema underlying beggings, as proposed by Pérez-Hernández and Ruiz de Mendoza (2002: 278–279).

In the world of physics, the repeated exertion of a force generally leads to a larger effect. Likewise, the repetition of the linguistic act in the case of beggings is expected to result in a higher likelihood of success. In Pérez and Ruiz de Mendoza's (2002: 278) words, 'linguistic insistence increases the chances of a speech act being successful'. The reasons why beggings require this type of insistence will be explained in the know-what of the act of begging.

4.3.1 The Know-What of Beggings

The act of begging has been defined as 'an insistent, continual harrying of someone who is in a position to grant a favour' (Hayakawa, 1969: 449). To this, Leech (1983: 219) adds that beggings are also characterised by a marked use of linguistic courtesy, the lack of power of the speaker to impose her will seemingly being the reason behind this increase in politeness. Wierzbicka (1987: 53) also states that, when begging, the speaker assumes that the hearer is not willing to do as required, which motivates the implementation of two further tactics on the part of the speaker: (1) letting the hearer know that she is not going to give up easily and (2) adopting a humble, abject attitude. The inferiority of the speaker to impose her will and the assumption that the hearer is not willing to comply, however, cannot justify by themselves the prototypical insistence and higher politeness of this illocutionary act. Other directives, like requests or suggestions, also share these attributes, but they do not exhibit the insistence and extreme use of politeness that characterises beggings. As shall be argued below, the data in our corpus comes to confirm Pérez-Hernández's (2001: 209–233) proposal on the centrality of yet another semantic attribute for the correct conceptualisation of beggings: the fact that the speaker has a strong desire that the proposed action is carried out. Additionally, the know-what of beggings also comprises the following knowledge.

Who is to do the action expressed in the act of begging?
Like most directives beggings present the hearer as the agent of the action:

(4.76) 'Daddy, please stay,' she **begged**, 'Please stay like mommy used to.' (iWeb)

Who will benefit from the action expressed in the begging?
Beggings prototypically have the speaker as the beneficiary of the action:

(4.77) 'Girls, can you bring me something to drink … pretty pleaseeeee?' she **begged**. (iWeb)

There are, however, some peripheral cases in which both the speaker and the hearer benefit from the action, as illustrated by example (4.78), in which the speaker begs the hearer to not commit suicide.

(4.78) In the wake of Sam's suicide, Brittany couldn't seem to stop crying […] 'Promise me you won't take your life,' her father **begged**. 'Promise you'll come to me before anything.' (iWeb)

The speaker (i.e. father) benefits because he does not want to lose her daughter, and the hearer (i.e. Brittany) benefits because she remains alive. The fact that both speaker and hearer benefit from the action has some bearings on the form of the act, which though insistent, does not make use of the politeness mechanisms that characterise those prototypical instances in which the speaker is the only beneficiary. The fact that the hearer also benefits from the action makes politeness less necessary and brings insistence to the front.

Can the hearer do the action expressed in the act of begging?
According to the data in our corpus, speakers uttering beggings prototypically work under the assumption that the hearer is perfectly capable of doing the required action, hence the extensive use of imperative-based instances of begging that simply point the hearer to the desired action. However, as was the case with requests, when the context requires higher doses of tentativeness, it is also possible to question the hearer's ability to perform the action as a means to increasing the latter's freedom to comply (see example (4.77) above).

Do speaker and hearer want the action to be carried out?
Our data confirms previous studies to the effect that the act of begging displays the highest degree of speaker's will among directives (Verschueren,

1985: 153–154). Speakers uttering a beg have a strong desire that a particular action is carried out:

(4.79) 'No, please, *I would really like* to be left out!' the man **begged**. (iWeb)

In this, as remarked by Pérez-Hernández (2001: 209), beggings equal threats, though each of these speech acts makes use of different strategies in order to materialise the speakers' desire that the action is performed. Thus, while beggings make use of strategies based on insistence, negotiation, and politeness, among others (see Section 4.3.2 for a detailed inventory), threats are more prone to resort to blackmailing and coercive means (see Pérez-Hernández, 2001: ch. 10). Speakers uttering beggings also work under the assumption that the hearer's willingness to comply with their proposal is low (Pérez-Hernández, 2001: 211).

The speaker's strong desire that the action is carried out, his lack of power to impose his will on the hearer, and his assumption that the hearer is probably not willing to comply explain the insistence and higher use of politeness that characterises the act of begging. Example (4.80) clearly illustrates these semantic traits:

(4.80) Given Jacob's history with hobbies, it was no surprise that *Jacob's father was reluctant* to buy him a magician's kit for his birthday. 'Geez, Jacob ... You sure you wouldn't rather I got you more guitar lessons?' He suggested. *Jacob was insistent*. 'Dad, you've got to get me the magician's kit. This time I'll stick with it for real. I promise! Come on, Dad.' Jacob **begged** (iWeb)

In fact, in those cases in which the hearer makes his willingness and/or disposition to comply explicit in advance, politeness and insistence are not deem so necessary, and the act of begging tends to resemble an average request for action. This is the case with example (4.81), which is much less insistent (i.e. there are no repetitions) and less polite (i.e. no overt use of politeness markers like *please*) than prototypical pleas like in example (4.76).

(4.81) A cyclist lying on his deathbed asked his best friend to do him a favour when he'd gone. '*Anything*,' replied his friend. 'Just don't let my wife sell my bikes for what I told her I paid for them,' he **begged** (iWeb)

Is the action expressed in the act of begging necessary?
Like orders and requests, begs may also stem from the speaker's needing an object or from his needing an action to be carried out. This semantic

attribute motivates some begging constructions based on the expression of necessity:

(4.82) 'Please sir, I *need* medical help,' I **begged**, barely able to speak (iWeb)

How much freedom does an act of begging allow the hearer?
The speaker uttering a begging does not have the necessary power to impose his will on the hearer. The freedom of the latter to do as asked is therefore high by default. This was also the case with requests, which respected that optionality and even attempted to increase it as an indirect means of enhancing the politeness of the act (see Section 4.2.1). Beggings work differently. Motivated by her strong desire that the proposed action is carried out, the speaker attempts to somehow limit the chances of the hearer refusing to comply. Limiting the optionality of the hearer cannot be done through imposition (as in the case of orders) or through coercion (as in threats) because of the lack of power that characterises speakers uttering beggings. Consequently, the powerless but eager speaker favours other strategies to secure the hearer's compliance. Among them, she will make extensive use of a combination of insistence (to make her degree of desire clear to the hearer) and politeness (to gain the hearer's compliance while avoiding imposition). Increasing the expressiveness of the act (by means of interjections, forceful intonation, lengthening of sounds, etc.) may also help to increase the hearer's compliance. These realisation procedures allow the speaker to convey her strong desire that the action is carried out. The overt expression of the speaker's wishes puts the hearer in the position of having to comply if she does not want to contravene the social expectations included in the Politeness Principle (Leech, 1983). To a lesser extent, other strategies, like negotiating, minimising the cost of the action, pampering, or appealing to justifying reasons, have also been found to be effective in restricting the hearer's optionality and moving her to comply with the speaker's begging. Example (4.83) illustrates several of them (i.e. politeness, insistence, negotiation, mitigation, expressiveness):

(4.83) 'Oh, please don't Aunt Lucy! I promise I won't do it again. I'll give you everything I have. Just please don't tell Mum,' he **begged** (iWeb)

Does the speaker attempt to minimise the cost of the action?
Previous studies based on more limited data have suggested that beggings, like requests, minimise the cost of the requested action as a way of persuading the hearer to comply (Pérez-Hernández, 2001: 214–215). The results of this corpus analysis, based on 500 instances of beggings, contradict previous

findings. Minimisation of cost, although a possible strategy compatible with the aim of beggings (example (4.81): *Just don't let my wife sell my bikes for what I told her I paid for them*), is not extensively used by English speakers. When begging, they do not rely on this strategy to achieve their goal, favouring others such us the use of politeness, negotiation, or the offering of justifications. It is only natural that minimisation of cost should not be central to the conceptualisation of beggings. Minimising the cost involves asking for less, and this contradicts one of the essential semantic attributes of begging: the fact that the speaker has a strong desire to achieve his goal. It makes no sense, therefore, to ask for less than what is actually wanted in order to minimise the cost of the action. The hearer's compliance is therefore searched through other means (e.g. politeness, negotiation, etc.).

Does the speaker attempt to be polite?
Politeness, in combination with directness and insistence, has been found to be a characterising semantic feature of the act of begging. The lack of social power of the speaker, his high desire to get the hearer to carry out the proposed action, and his assumption that the hearer may not be willing to comply motivate the use of politeness as a means to persuade him into action. Politeness is also a way of humbly acknowledging the inherent freedom of the hearer to decide for or against carrying out the required action. Example (4.84) illustrates the extensive use of politeness found in prototypical beggings:

(4.84) '*Please, please*' she **begged**, 'Rape me, take my money but *please* don't kill me *please*.' (iWeb)

The need for politeness decreases when the beneficiary of the action includes the hearer as well as the speaker (see example (4.78) above), as well as when the power of the speaker increases or the social distance between speakers is smaller, as in examples (4.85) and (4.86), respectively:

(4.85) 'Tell me who you are,' the King **begged**, for he was amazed by her beauty and magic (iWeb)
(4.86) 'Mama, get me out of here,' the girl **begged** (iWeb)

Is social power relevant to the act of begging?
As illustrated by examples (4.76)–(4.86), beggings can be performed regardless of the power relationship between speakers. Even kings, who represent a clear-cut instance of social power, may find themselves in the need of begging in certain contexts (see example (4.85)). Nevertheless, we have argued that speakers uttering beggings typically lack the power to

impose their will. As explained in Pérez-Hernández (2001: 216), the hearer's power need not arise from an institution. In the case of beggings, the hearer is the person who has the ability to grant the speaker's wishes, and this endows her with an ad hoc superiority over the latter. Thus, in example (4.85), in spite of his institutional power, the king, who is in love with the hearer, finds himself in a position of inferiority because of this, being aware of the fact that his power as king does not grant him control over the woman's emotions).

This inferiority of the speaker, whose wishes depend on the hearer's disposition, is one of the motivating factors that explains the insistence and higher levels of politeness that characterise beggings, two strategies used to overcome this inferiority and to persuade the hearer into compliance.

Is the social distance between the speakers relevant to the act of begging?
Beggings can be performed regardless of the social distance that exits between speakers. One can beg to a stranger and to an intimate alike. EFL students, however, should be aware of the interactions of the variable of social distance with other semantic attributes of the act of begging. Thus, the data in our corpus suggests that, when begging, the larger the social distance between the speakers, the higher the need to increase the politeness of the act will be:

(4.87) The old beggar woman saw Calista and began speaking. 'Oh m'lady, *would you be so kind as to …*'. 'Get out,' Calista demanded. '*Please*, I am not asking for much, just food scraps, maybe an old blanket …' the old woman **begged** (iWeb)

On the contrary, example (4.86) above showed how short social distances are linked to smaller needs of politeness. Pérez-Hernández (2001: 217) has explained that small social distances correlate with a higher predisposition of the hearer to grant the speaker's wishes. In these contexts, the familiarity between the participants gives the speaker reasons to expect collaboration on the part of the hearer. This makes politeness and insistence less necessary, unless the speaker asks for something too costly or too important for the hearer.

Is the formality of the context relevant to the act of begging?
The corpus under scrutiny yields instances of begging in all types of contexts, regardless of their formality, though this directive tends to be more common in informal contexts.

4.3 Beggings

Formal contexts are generally more structured and less prone to expressions of subjectivity or emotions. In our corpus, those beggings found in formal contexts tend to be less insistent and to rely on negotiation strategies to secure the hearer's compliance. Example (4.88), set in the formal context of a royal audience, illustrates this use of negotiation, in which the speaker promises something back in return for the king's compliance. In addition, this instance of begging does not display the insistence (i.e. repetitions, intensifiers) or expressiveness (i.e. exclamations, interjections) that characterise its informal counterparts.

(4.88) Shaqiq went to the Prince. 'Give me three days, and I will bring your dog back to you. Set my friends free,' he **begged** (iWeb)

Table 4.9 summarises the conceptual layout of the act of begging.

Table 4.9 *The know-what of beggings*

Beggings are directive speech acts by means of which a speaker insistently asks the hearer(s) to carry out an action. When someone begs someone else to do something, they communicate the following:

'I really want you to do this. I know you have the power to decide for or against doing it. I acknowledge your power, but I have to keep trying hard to persuade you to do it because I really want to achieve my goal.'

What you need to bear in mind in order to perform a successful act of begging:

- The speaker, who is the prototypical beneficiary of the action, has a strong desire to achieve his goal (i.e. to get the hearer to do as told), which leads him to be direct, unambiguous, and insistent in the expression of his begging.
- The hearer is perceived as being more powerful than the speaker. This power need not be institutional. Simply the fact that he is the one who can make the speaker's wishes come true endows him with an ad hoc superiority.
- The speaker feels that he lacks the necessary power to impose his will on the hearer.
- The hearer is largely free to decide for or against doing what the speaker says.
- The speaker acknowledges and respects the hearer's optionality by being overtly polite, but he also keeps trying to achieve his goal by insisting, negotiating with him, pampering him, and to a lesser extent, minimising the cost of the required action.

BE AWARE!!!

- Politeness is not so necessary when the benefit is for both the speaker and the hearer, and/or the action is not very costly.
- You can beg someone to do something regardless of how powerful you may be, but the less (social, institutional) power you have, the more polite you need to be.
- You can beg someone to do something regardless of the social distance that separates you from the hearer, but the larger the social distance, the more polite you need to be.
- You can beg someone to do something in all contexts regardless of their formality, but the more formal the context, the less insistent you have to be, and the more extensive your use of negotiation strategies should be.

4.3.2 The Know-How of Beggings

The lack of research on linguistic constructions and realisation procedures for the expression of beggings parallels the virtually inexistent attention devoted to the teaching of this directive speech act in the ten textbooks analysed for this study.[3] As reported in Chapter 3, only one of them takes into consideration this speech act. This is done in passing, as part of a reported speech activity in which students are asked to rephrase a direct act of begging (i.e. *Please, please, don't wear those old jeans*) using the speech verb *to beg*. There is no explicit explanation about the semantics of this directive act, much less about the characteristics of the linguistic construction that is used as illustration. As shall be made apparent in this section, the English language offers a rich array of base constructions and realisation procedures to allow the expression of the act of begging, all of which find a motivation in the semantic description of the act provided in Section 4.3.1. EFL students at the advanced level of instruction would surely benefit from the teaching of at least the most frequent among these constructions. Table 4.10 summarises

Table 4.10 *Base constructions for the act of begging in English*

Base constructions	Occurrences	Percentage
IMPERATIVE	374	74.8
I BEG YOU TO DO X	46	9.2
CAN I/YOU/WE DO X?	28	5.6
CAN'T I/WE/YOU DO X?	16	3.2
I WANT/NEED X		
I WANT/NEED YOU TO DO X	10	2
YOU HAVE/MUST DO X	8	1.6
COULD YOU DO X?	4	0.8
WON'T YOU DO X?	4	0.8
WILL YOU DO X?	2	0.4
WOULD YOU DO X ?	2	0.4
DO YOU THINK YOU COULD DO X?	2	0.4
YOU'LL DO X (WON'T YOU?)	2	0.4
YOU CAN DO X	2	0.4
Total	**500**	**100**

---

[3] The only previous in-depth study of beggings dates from the beginning of the century (Pérez-Hernández, 2001: ch. 8), and it is based on a smaller collection of examples. The present study comes to confirm Pérez-Hernández's (2001) initial conclusions regarding the realisation procedures that activate each attribute of the begging ICM (i.e. each piece of knowledge included in the know-what of beggings). In addition, it offers a collection of base constructions for the expression of beggings in English and a comparison with those of the Spanish language.

4.3 Beggings

the quantitative data on begging constructions resulting from the analysis of the first 500 random occurrences of beggings in the iWeb corpus.

With nearly 75 per cent of the total number of occurrences, IMPERATIVE base constructions clearly outnumber other linguistic constructions in the expression of beggings. This is only to be expected since the speaker uttering a begging has a strong desire to achieve her goal. In turn, this motivates the use of the imperative as a direct, unambiguous way for the speaker to communicate the hearer the action that she expects him to carry out.

As has previously been shown to be the case with orders and requests, IMPERATIVE constructions for the expression of beggings display some specific characteristics of their own, which constitute an essential teaching target for EFL students. The realisation procedures that combine with IMPERATIVE base constructions in the expression of beggings (see Table 4.11) can be divided into two main groups: (1) those that, assuming the lack of power of the speaker to impose his will, attempt to persuade the hearer to do as asked, and (2) those that communicate the speaker's strong desire that the action is carried out. Let us see each of them in turn.

How can a powerless, but eager to achieve his will, speaker attempt to persuade the hearer to do as told? The data in our corpus shows that in many cases this is done by making use of politeness. The use of the IMPERATIVE base construction in combination with the adverb *please* amounts to over 15 per cent of the total number of beggings in our corpus:

(4.89) The brother then **begged** him: '*Please*, father, intercede for me to God that I may be allowed *a little more* time in which to amend my life'

Table 4.11 *Imperative base construction + realisation procedures for beggings*

Imperative construction for begging	Occurrences	Percentage
BARE IMPERATIVE	13	3.4
IMPERATIVE + EXCLAMATIONS/INTONATION	70	19
IMPERATIVE + EXPRESSION OF POLITENESS (PLEASE)	60	16
IMPERATIVE + REPETITION	36	9.6
IMPERATIVE + NEGOTIATION (PROMISES)	17	4.5
IMPERATIVE + REASON CLAUSE	7	1.9
IMPERATIVE + EXPRESSION OF MINIMISATION OF COST	5	1.3
IMPERATIVE + A COMBINATION OF 2 OR MORE OF THE REALISATION PROCEDURES ABOVE	166	44.3
Total	374	100

The speaker in example (4.89) also attempts to minimise the cost of the required action (i.e. *a little more time*). Mitigation of cost was shown to be a pervasive strategy in relation to requests. This realisation procedure is also used in some instances of beggings in our corpus but to a lesser extent (around 2 per cent). As explained in the know-what of beggings, since the speaker has a strong desire that the action is carried out, it does not make much sense to ask for less than what is actually wanted. The higher degree of speaker's will that characterises beggings, as compared to that of requests, provides an explanation for the more limited use of this realisation procedure. In begging, speakers seem to prefer other persuasive strategies that do not imply minimising the desired objective. Thus, around 7 per cent of the IMPERATIVE constructions in our data make use of negotiation or reasoning strategies as a way to get the hearer to comply. Consider examples (4.90) and (4.91), respectively:

(4.90) 'Turn yourself in,' Phil Vetrano **begged** his daughter's killer two weeks after her death. 'I will make sure the reward money goes to the person of your choice. Your sister, your brother, your mother. It's a life changer.'
(4.91) 'Simon, put him down. You'll hurt him!' Sean **begged**

In example (4.90) the speaker attempts to persuade the hearer to comply with his wish by promising to reward one of his relatives. The use of the IMPERATIVE base construction followed or preceded by a promise that benefits the hearer is a fairly frequent realisation procedure for begging. In example (4.91), the speaker's strategy of persuasion is based on the provision of rational arguments for him to do as asked. Thus, the speaker points out that someone is to be hurt if the hearer does not carry out the required action. Appealing to the hearer's rationality by means of a reason clause, either before or after the IMPERATIVE base construction, is another common mechanism for begging.

A second group of realisation procedures that combine with imperatives to render a begging interpretation is grounded on the strong desire of the speaker to achieve his goal, which is a central aspect of the meaning of beggings. Examples (4.92)–(4.95) illustrate those realisation procedures that enable its linguistic instantiation:

(4.92) 'Oh God,' the grave keeper **begged**, praying. 'Save me.'
(4.93) 'Don't do that! Don't do that! I'll die.' He **begged** *hard*, but no use
...

4.3 Beggings

(4.94) 'NOOOOOOO!!!! PLEASE, Aaron, STO-HAHAHAHA-P!!! Stop tickling me, please!' Mike **begged** with tears starting to come out of his eyes

(4.95) 'Please, don't murder me? Pretty-pretty-please?' he **begged**

The above examples illustrate some recurrent linguistic resources that accompany IMPERATIVE base constructions when used as beggings. There are exclamations and interjections (e.g. *Oh God, NOOOOO!!!*), the use of a particular type of intonation that may range from persuasive to insistent (see example (4.95)), and above all the use of repetitions (examples (4.93)–(4.95)). These realisation procedures allow the speaker to convey his strong desire that the required action is carried out. In addition, as explained in detail in Pérez-Hernández (2001: 224–226), linguistic strategies of this kind exploit the *Tact Maxim* of the general Politeness Principle (Leech, 1983), according to which participants are expected to maximise benefit to others. By stating his wishes clearly through an imperative sentence and by communicating how strong those wishes are by means of exclamations, interjections, repetitions, etc., the speaker is pragmatically constraining the hearer's freedom to opt out. In fact, a refusal to comply on the part of the hearer would involve a breach of the *Tact Maxim* and would make her lose face.

Some of the realisation procedures described above have already been shown to co-occur with the IMPERATIVE base construction in the expression of other directives. For example, making use of politeness (e.g. *please*) or minimising the cost involved in the action (e.g. *just, only*) are strategies that have previously been shown to direct hearers to a request interpretation of the imperative (see Section 4.2.2). How can we help EFL students to produce clear-cut instances of beggings that differ from those of requests that use similar realisation procedures? As shown in Table 4.11, over 44 per cent of the instances of begging in our sample make use of a combination of an IMPERATIVE base construction and two or more realisation procedures among those of the two main groups of resources describe above. Native speakers favour this mechanism, which is only natural given that the use of a combination of two or more realisation procedures together with the IMPERATIVE base construction manages to activate all the essential key attributes of the act of begging: the speaker's strong desire to achieve her goal and the acknowledgement of her inferiority and lack of ability to impose her will on the hearer. Example (4.96) illustrates a clear-cut instance of begging that makes use of a combination of several linguistic resources to activate the meaning essentials of the directive under consideration:

(4.96) 'Oh, please don't Aunt Lucy! I promise I won't do it again. I'll give you everything I have on you. Just please don't tell Mum', he **begged**

Thus, in example (4.96) the speaker's high desire that the hearer complies with his wishes is conveyed by means of interjections (i.e. *Oh*), exclamations, and repetitions (i.e. *please ... please*). In addition, example (4.96) also exhibits attempts at persuading the hearer to do as told by means of negotiation strategies (i.e. promises in return of his compliance) and of the minimisation of the cost of the required action (i.e. *just*).

All in all, this combination of an IMPERATIVE base construction plus several realisation procedures manages to activate a clear begging interpretation and represents a good teaching target for EFL advanced students.

The rest of the base constructions for begging that have been found in the data under study display a lower frequency of occurrence. Advanced students could also be taught that it is possible to beg by means of base constructions that make use of explicit performatives (i.e. I BEG YOU TO DO X) or that activate the ability variable (i.e. CAN / CAN'T / COULD YOU DO X?), the speaker's willingness (i.e. I / WE WANT YOU TO DO X), the need for the action to be carried out (i.e. I / WE NEED YOU TO DO X), or the hearer's volition (i.e. YOU'LL DO X and WILL / WON'T / WOULD YOU DO X?). As can be observed in examples (4.97)–(4.99), these base constructions also combine with the realisation procedures described in relation to IMPERATIVE base constructions to secure a clearer begging interpretation:

(4.97) CAN YOU DO X? base construction + expressions of politeness (*please*), exclamations/intonation, negotiation (promise):'Mom, can you *please* stop buying store brand sausage? *I will pay* for Jimmy Dean!' she **begged**

(4.98) I/WE NEED X base construction + repetition, expression of politeness (*please*):'We need to go to the club now. Please. Please. Right now,' she **begged** and pleaded

(4.99) YOU'LL DO X base construction + repetition (tag question):'You'll come out after supper, won't you?' he **begged**

Comparison with the constructions for beggings in the Spanish corpus yields relevant information for EFL professionals. The first four base constructions in Table 4.12 are used in both languages. The first two

Table 4.12 Comparison of base constructions for the act of begging in English and Spanish

Beggings base constructions (English)	Number	Percentage	Number	Percentage	Beggings base constructions (Spanish)
YOU HAVE/MUST DO X	8	1.6	15	3	TIENES QUE HACER X
I WANT/NEED X	10	2	10	2	QUIERO QUE HAGAS X
I WANT/NEED YOU TO DO X					
IMPERATIVE	374	74.8	275	55	IMPERATIVE
I BEG YOU TO DO X	46	9.2	135	27	TE/LE RUEGO QUE HAGAS X
CAN I/YOU/WE DO X?	28	5.6	0		Possible but not productive
CAN'T I/WE/YOU DO X?	16	3.2	0		Possible but not productive
COULD YOU DO X?	4	0.8	0		Possible but not productive
WON'T YOU DO X?	4	0.8	0		Possible but not productive
WILL YOU DO X?	2	0.4	0		Possible but not productive
WOULD YOU DO X ?	2	0.4	0		Possible but not productive
DO YOU THINK YOU COULD DO X?	2	0.4	0		Possible but not productive
YOU'LL DO X (WON'T YOU?)	2	0.4	0		Possible but not productive
YOU CAN DO X	2	0.4	0		Possible but not productive
Not possible	0		30	6	¡QUÉ + PRESENT SUBJUNCTIVE (2ND PERSON)!
Possible but not productive	0		20	4	SE RUEGA X/HACER X
Possible but not productive	0		9	1.8	TE/LE ROGARÍA QUE HICIERA(S) X
Not possible	0		5	1	OJALÁ + SUBJUCTIVE (2ND PERSON)
Possible but not productive	0		1	0.2	SI USTED PUDIERA HACER X
Total	500	100	500	100	

(white rows) have a similarly low frequency of occurrence in English and Spanish. The constructions in the light grey rows (i.e. the imperative and the explicit performative verb *beg*) show different rates of occurrence in the two languages, but they are the most productive base constructions for EFL teaching purposes. Both languages display a more extensive use of the imperative than of the performative, although in Spanish the use of the performative almost triples that in English. The explicit performative is a very direct, unambiguous way of performing a begging, and the Spanish language has often been characterised as having a higher tendency to directness than English.

The dark grey rows in Table 4.12 show those constructions for which our corpora only yield occurrences for either English or Spanish. All the base constructions in English are possible in Spanish although, under the light of the data, they are not particularly productive in the latter language. In addition, some of the Spanish base constructions not only do not yield any occurrences in the English corpus, but they do not even have a direct counterpart in English. This is the case with the ¡QUÉ + PRESENT SUBJUNCTIVE (2ND PERSON)! base construction:

(4.100)   '¡Qué no hable, por favor, qué no hable!' **rogué**
          'That he PRESENT SUBJECTIVE NEGATIVE-speak, please, that he PRESENT SUBJECTIVE NEGATIVE-speak!' I begged

Constructions of this type should be red flagged in EFL textbooks to avoid potential interferences with the students' L1.

4.4   Suggestions

Searle (1979: 356) defined suggestions as 'a weak attempt to get the hearer to do something' and included them in the category of directive speech acts. Other authors have questioned the directive status of suggestions, arguing that they simply intend to get the hearer to consider the potential benefits of a particular course of action, rather than attempting to get her to do the action (Fraser, 1974; Verschueren, 1985; Wierzbicka, 1987). Yet others have regarded suggestions as components of a broader speech act that involves the act of advising, using the terms suggesting and advising almost interchangeably (Hinkel, 1997; Matsumura, 2001, 2003). In fact, suggestions are often so similar to other directives that some authors have posed the question of whether suggesting is a speech act category or simply a mode of illocutionary performance (Pérez-Hernández, 2001: 236–237). The data in our corpus reveals that the act of suggesting has enough unique semantic characteristics to be considered a directive category of its own that differs from those of ordering, requesting, begging, etc. (see Section 4.4.1). These meaning traits also provide the motivation for the specific formal features of the base constructions and linguistic realisation procedures that the English language offers for the expression of suggestions (Section 4.4.2).

4.4.1 The Know-What of Suggestions

The experiential grounding of the act of suggesting could be represented by a force vector that works in two times. Initially, the force pushes the rational hearer (i.e. H_R) to consider the suggested action (see Figure 4.4). This initial force (F), which needs to go through the filter of the hearer's rationality and consideration, is thus weakened, and it could even be blocked by the hearer's decision. If successful, however, it could turn the hearer into an agent (i.e. H_A) and move her into action.

The fact that the initial force is mediated by the hearer's consideration explains some of the semantic characteristics of suggestions as will be explained below.

Who is to do the action expressed in the suggestion?
The agent of the suggested action can be either the hearer, or both the speaker and the hearer, as illustrated by examples (4.101) and (4.102), respectively:

(4.101) 'If you want, you can skip school today and rest or maybe even go somewhere fun,' she **suggested** (iWeb)
(4.102) 'Suppose we call the field mice,' she **suggested**. 'They could probably tell us the way to the Emerald City.' (iWeb)

As will be made apparent in Section 4.4.2, the identity of the agent has direct consequences on the type of linguistic formulae used by native speakers in the expression of this act, with a marked tendency towards the use of comparatively more tentative constructions when the hearer is the only agent of the suggested action.

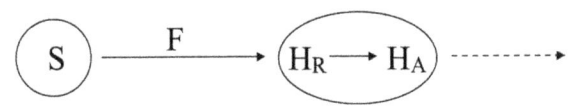

Figure 4.4 Force schema underlying the conceptualisation of suggestions

Who will benefit from the action expressed in the suggestion?
Previous accounts (Haverkate, 1984; Martínez-Flor, 2005) describe suggestions as non-impositive directive speech acts that are aimed at benefitting the hearer. The data in our corpus, however, shows that suggestions are very little constrained as regards the identity of the beneficiary of the action. While it is true that a vast majority of the suggestions in our data involve a benefit for the hearer or for both the hearer and the speaker (see examples (4.101) and (4.102)), there are also instances in which the speaker is the only beneficiary (example (4.103)) and others in which the beneficiary is a third person (example (4.104)).

(4.103) 'Pretend I am a visiting ambassador from Akram,' Leo **suggested**. 'Why do you get to be the visiting ambassador?' (iWeb)

(4.104) 'So, get him another,' Niklas **suggested**. 'He could make a few credits up there.' (iWeb)

As pointed out by Pérez-Hernández (2001: 242), this variability in the identity of the beneficiary makes suggestions 'a highly heterogenous group, different instances of which may closely resemble other illocutionary types'. Examples (4.103) and (4.104), by way of illustration, could be interpreted as instances of requests. As shall be shown below, however, there are certain semantic traits that set suggestions apart from other directives.

Can the hearer do the action expressed in the suggestion?
The speaker who suggests a future action works under the assumption that the chosen agent(s) are capable of carrying it out. In this respect, suggestions do not differ from other members of the category of directive illocutions. The ability of the agents to carry out the action motivates some of the base constructions for suggesting (e.g. YOU CAN DO X, as in 'You can do something as simple as lighting a candle in their honour,' Kessler **suggested**; see Section 4.4.2).

Do speaker and hearer want the action to be carried out?
Whether the speaker and the hearer want the suggested action to be carried out could be expected to depend mostly on whether the action results in a benefit to them or not. In this regard, suggestions have been shown to be a rather heterogeneous group that sometimes resembles requests (i.e. in those cases in which the speaker benefits from the action) and sometimes advising or offering (i.e. if the hearer is the main beneficiary).

4.4 Suggestions

However, the *modus operandi* of this semantic variable displays some interesting traits. The data in our corpus reveals that, regardless of who is to be the beneficiary of the action, the hearer's willingness is generally unknown and irrelevant to the speaker. In fact, there are no instances in our corpus in which this meaning attribute is explicitly activated. Constructions based on the hearer's wanting to do the action, which are common in the expression of requests and beggings (i.e. WILL YOU DO X?, IF YOU WILL DO X, WOULD YOU MIND DOING X?) are not used in suggesting.

The fact that the speaker uttering a suggestion is not concerned with the hearer's disposition to carrying out the action parallels his own indifference regarding the realisation of the action. When the intended beneficiary is the hearer or a third person, this could only be expected. However, the ratings of the speaker's willingness are kept low even in those situations in which he is the only beneficiary or the joint beneficiary of the action. This particularity, which has already been described in previous works (Fraser, 1974; Verschueren, 1985; Pérez-Hernández, 2001), stands out as one of the main distinguishing characteristics of the act of suggesting. Holmes (1983) and Richards (1985) stated that the speaker's low degree of wanting/interest that the suggested action is performed explains the weaker force of suggestions as compared to that of other directives (e.g. requests, orders, threats, and beggings, among others). It also explains Wierzbicka's (1987) observation that suggestions do not require a reply, as opposed to similar speech acts, like proposals, which do ask for a response in the form of compliance or refusal.

As will be shown below, the low degree of speaker's willingness also explains the workings of other semantic attributes of suggestions, such as their low minimisation of cost and their scarce use of politeness (see Section 4.4.2). The latter are defining features of requests and beggings, in relation to which they act as persuasive strategies that aid the speaker to move the hearer into compliance. When suggesting, the speaker's interest in achieving compliance is lower, and hence his use of persuasive strategies is also more limited.

Is the action expressed in the suggestion necessary?
In the context of suggestions, the speaker does not have an acute necessity that the proposed action is carried out. As was the case with the speaker's low interest in the performance of the action, this variable triggers low degrees of minimisation of cost and politeness.

How much freedom does a suggestion allow the hearer?
Suggestions are non-impositive speech acts. According to some authors, such as Haverkate (1984), this is due to the fact that they generally involve a benefit for the agent (i.e. hearer). However, as shown above, suggestions can also have the speaker and a third person as beneficiaries. Regardless of who is to obtain the benefits of the action, suggestions still fall within the group of face-threatening speech acts (Brown & Levinson, 1987) since, by asking the hearer to consider a future action for realisation, the speaker is somehow intruding into the hearer's world and trying to direct his future course of action. This leads the speaker to attempt to soften his speech act through enhancing the hearer's optionality. Since his interest in the action being carried out is also low, he does not feel the need to force the hearer into compliance. Thus, the optionality of the hearer is not constrained neither through persuasion (as in requests or beggings), nor through imposition (as in orders). On the contrary, his freedom is enhanced through tentativeness and indirection. Among directive speech acts, suggestions offer the highest amount of optionality to the hearer. As shall be shown in more detail in Section 4.4.2, this motivates an extensive use of modal verbs in the past tense and/or interrogative formulae like the following:

(4.105) 'Perhaps you *could* discuss the problem with your wife,' Blalock **suggested** (iWeb)
(4.106) 'Well now, sweetie, how about this?' Niecy **suggested**, 'how about we sell or give away all the stuff that Xander and the rest don't need, and we use the money to get them new stuff?' (iWeb)

Even in those cases in which imperatives are used, the optionality of the hearer is maximised through the limitation or altogether avoidance of the use of persuasive or impositive realisation procedures. Thus, examples (4.107) and (4.108) illustrate the lack of overt politeness (e.g. adverb *please*), minimisation of cost (e.g. *just, a little*), and minimisation of optionality (i.e. expressions of immediateness, forceful intonation) markers. In fact, the lack of imposition of the imperative in example (4.108) is signalled by the use of an interrogation mark.

(4.107) 'Let's head for the beach,' Kukui **suggested** (iWeb)
(4.108) 'Well, get up and go finish in the toilet?' I **suggested** as I once again closed my eyes (iWeb)

As shown in previous sections, this was not the case with orders, requests, and beggings. The imperatives used for the expression of these directives were characteristically accompanied by different types of realisation procedures intended to coerce the hearer's optionality through imposition, persuasion, or insistence.

Does the speaker attempt to minimise the cost of the action?
The high degree of freedom and low degree of imposition that characterise suggestions make the minimisation of cost largely unnecessary. In addition, most instances of suggestions involve a benefit for the agent (i.e. hearer), which makes it even less necessary to reduce the cost of the proposed action. As will be shown in Section 4.2.2, suggestions display virtually no overt minimisation of cost. There are, however, some factors that may prompt the speaker to attempt to cut down the cost of his suggestion. Among these, there are those cases in which the suggestion involves a clear cost for the hearer, as in example (4.109) where the speaker attempts to minimise it through the use of the expression *a bit*. Minimisation is also activated when the social distance between the speakers is large (i.e. when suggesting something to a stranger as in example (4.110)), when there is a power asymmetry between the participants, or when the formality of the situation increases.

(4.109) 'We can go down that little draw and sift *a bit*,' Ernie **suggested**. 'If that quartz vein ever had anything in it, that's where it'll be.' (iWeb)
(4.110) I turned and faced him [a stranger]. 'Why don't we talk *a little*, then?' I **suggested**. 'You can tell me *a bit* about yourself and how you manage to defeat formidable foes in gym battles.' (iWeb)

Does the speaker attempt to be polite?
Suggestions are characterised by their lack of overt politeness. None of the suggestions in our corpus displays the use of the adverb *please* or is realised by means of formulaic expressions of politeness (e.g. WOULD YOU MIND DOING X?). If at all, politeness is conveyed through indirection (i.e. interrogative sentence types, use of modals in the past tense). These resources are primarily aimed at increasing the optionality of the agent. Only secondarily, by decreasing the imposition of the act, they increase its politeness. The lack of deference is a feature of suggestions that has been identified in different languages as noted in cross-cultural studies like those of Rintell (1979), who observed that suggestions were less polite than requests in both English and Spanish. Politeness is a persuasive strategy aimed at gaining the hearer's compliance. Since the speaker uttering a

suggestion is not as concerned or interested in obtaining such compliance as is the case with requests or beggings, politeness is not felt as necessary.

Is social power relevant to the act of suggesting?
Suggestions can be performed regardless of the power relation that holds between participants. Students should be aware, however, that if there is an asymmetrical power relationship, the speaker may want to attempt to minimise the cost and/or increase the tentativeness of the act. If the speaker is more powerful than the hearer, this will help to avoid imposition and to keep the optionality of the hearer within the limits expected in the act of suggesting.

(4.111) '*Why don't you* go ahead and take *a little bit of* a swim anyway?' He **suggested**. 'Maybe it'll cool you off.' (iWeb)

In example (4.111) a father avoids the imposition that may characterise a paternal command by increasing the tentativeness (i.e. *Why don't you …?*) and by minimising the cost of the action he suggests to his son (i.e. *a little bit*).

If the speaker is less powerful, the minimisation of cost and/or an increase in tentativeness will help keep the imposition of the act low and avoid the negative consequences of a face-threatening act (see House & Kasper (1981: 143) for similar conclusions). This is the case with example (4.112) in which the hearer has a higher social status than the speaker. The latter's suggestion relies on tentativeness (i.e. *Why don't you …?*) and minimisation of cost (i.e. *a bit*) to avoid imposition.

(4.112) Somehow Amanda had a hard time thinking of this poor unhappy girl as a recording star, even though she was clutching a guitar case to her chest. 'Why don't you sit down and rest a bit,' **suggested** Amanda, adopting a solicitous attitude (iWeb)

Is the social distance between the speakers relevant to the act of suggesting?
Most suggestions in our corpus display participants who are socially close. It is also possible to perform the act of suggesting when the social distance between participants is large. Students should be reminded that these situations require higher dose of tentativeness and of minimisation of cost to avoid imposing on the hearer. See examples (4.110) and (4.112) above.

Is the formality of the context relevant to the act of suggesting?
Most suggestions in our corpus take place in informal contexts. Those uttered in more formal settings have been found to display higher levels of minimisation of cost and tentativeness; or alternatively to make use of

4.4 Suggestions

Table 4.13 *The know-what of suggestions*

Suggestions are weak directive speech acts by means of which a speaker asks the hearer(s) to consider the merits or benefits of a potential course of action. When someone suggests someone else to do something, he communicates the following:

'I believe that a particular course of action may be positive for you, for both of us, or for someone else. You could consider doing it. I have no particular interest in you carrying out that action, neither do I have the social, institutional, or experiential power to impose the action on you, but I share it with you for your consideration.'

What you need to bear in mind in order to perform a successful suggestion:

- The beneficiary of the action may be the speaker, the hearer, both of them, or a third person.
- Regardless of who is to benefit from the action, the speaker shows no special desire or interest in its materialisation. He merely presents it for the hearer's consideration.
- Whether or not the hearer wants to do as told is unknown or irrelevant for the speaker, who respects the hearer's freedom to comply or refuse to do as suggested.
- In order to respect the optionality of the hearer, the speaker makes no overt attempt to minimise the cost of the action or to persuade the hearer to comply through insistence, imposition, or the use of politeness.

BE AWARE!!!

- You can make suggestions in all contexts, regardless of their formality and of the power relationship or social distance that separates you from the hearer(s). However, if there are power asymmetries between the speakers, if the social distance between them is large, or if the context is formal, your suggestions will need to include attempts to minimise their cost and/or exhibit a higher use of tentativeness.

---

unambiguous performative verbs that have lexicalised the non-impositive nature of suggestions (i.e. I SUGGEST THAT YOU DO X). Formal contexts, by default, tend to be politer. In this regard, suggestions do not differ from other directives (see Table 4.13).

4.4.2 The Know-How of Suggestions

Research on the linguistic constructions available for the expression of suggestions is scarce. One of the few existing taxonomies in English is based exclusively on a compilation of those formulae found in theoretical works (Martínez-Flor, 2005) and offers no information as to which constructions are preferred by native speakers. Jiang's (2006) more extensive corpus-based classification of suggestions provides quantitative data about the frequency of occurrence of each construction, as well as a comparison between those found in real language and those that appear in EFL textbooks. He concludes that there is a relevant gap between the way native speakers perform this speech act, and the linguistic strategies included in EFL teaching materials. Jiang's (2006) taxonomy, however, is restricted to suggestions produced in a very specific setting (i.e. student study groups and student–teacher office hour interactions), in which speakers have a fixed social and power status. In this particular setting, the LET'S DO X construction and performative structures like I SUGGEST YOU DO X, which do not appear in the textbooks under his analysis, are found to be some of the most frequently used structures for suggestions. Jiang (2006) also notices that all textbooks emphasise the use of the modal *should* (YOU / WE SHOULD DO X), while his corpus shows that constructions with *have to* and *need to* are used much more often in the registers under examination. Finally, Jiang (2006) points out that the formulaic expressions HOW ABOUT DOING X?, WHY DON'T YOU DO X?, etc., which are ubiquitous in EFL textbooks, are not common at all as expressions for suggestions in the academic settings under analysis. As Table 4.14 illustrates, the analysis of a larger and more varied corpus, which is not limited to a single situational setting, yields somehow different results.

Table 4.14 *Base constructions for the act of suggesting in English*

Base constructions	Occurrences	Percentage
IMPERATIVE	88	17.6
LET'S DO X	78	15.6
WHY DON'T YOU/WE DO X?	70	14
YOU/WE SHOULD DO X	52	10.4
YOU/WE OUGHT TO DO X	10	2
YOU/WE CAN DO X	46	9.2
HOW ABOUT DOING X?	45	9
YOU/WE COULD DO X	34	6.8
WHY NOT JUST DO X?	15	3
YOU/WE NEED TO DO X	12	2.4
YOU MIGHT DO X YOU MIGHT WANT TO DO X YOU MIGHT WANT TO TRY TO DO X	10	2
I SUGGEST YOU/WE DO X	9	1.8
YOU/WE CAN/COULD ALWAYS DO X	7	1.4
YOU/WE'D BETTER DO X	7	1.4
WHAT IF YOU/WE DO X?	7	1.4
WHAT ABOUT DOING X?	5	1
BETTER DO X	4	0.8
WHAT DO YOU SAY TO DOING X?	1	0.2
Total	500	100

4.4 Suggestions

The IMPERATIVE and the LET'S DO X base constructions stand out from the rest as regards their frequency of occurrence in our corpus. This could be shocking under the traditional speech act theory view of imperatives as impositive strategies. Following this line of reasoning, Koike (1994), Hinkel (1997), and Martínez-Flor (2005), among others, state that imperatives are regarded as the most direct and impolite forms of making a suggestion. If IMPERATIVE base constructions were actually as impolite as traditional pragmatists deem them to be, we may wonder why so many native speakers chose this linguistic strategy for the performance of an intrinsically non-impositive speech act like suggesting. As was explained in detail in Chapter 2, however, it is possible to adopt a weaker version of the literal force hypothesis, according to which imperative sentences are defined simply as those which present the content of a proposition for realisation (Risselada, 1993: 71). Under the light of a weaker literal force hypothesis, imperatives are not impositive *per se*. In previous sections, it has also been shown how the combined use of the IMPERATIVE base construction with specific realisation procedures for the semantic variables of different directive categories leads to a metonymic activation of specific speech acts. IMPERATIVE base constructions are combined with impositive linguistic strategies (e.g. expressions of immediateness, forceful intonation, etc.) to activate orders; with strategies of mitigation and politeness (e.g. adverb *please*, expressions of optionality, mitigation, and social closeness) to yield requests; and with a combination of strategies of persuasion and insistence (e.g. repetitions, adverb *please*, negotiation, and reasoning) to prompt a begging interpretation. The use of the imperative for the expression of suggestions also displays some peculiarities of its own as captured in Table 4.15.

As the data in our corpus reveal, what characterises IMPERATIVE base constructions in relation to the act of suggesting is their use in isolation. As defined by Risselada (1993: 71) the imperative simply presents the content of

Table 4.15 *Imperative base constructions + realisation procedures for suggestions*

Imperative constructions for suggestions	Occurrences	Percentage
BARE IMPERATIVE	78	88.6
IMPERATIVE + REASON CLAUSE	6	6.8
IMPERATIVE + INTERROGATIVE INTONATION	2	2.3
IMPERATIVE + EXPRESSION OF PROBABILITY	2	2.3
Total	88	100

a proposition for realisation, and that is precisely the aim of a suggestion: to present an action for the consideration of the hearer. Bare imperatives used with a neutral, non-impositive intonation suit well the nature of suggestions, and this is, in fact, the way in which native speakers use them. In those rare occasions in which the IMPERATIVE base construction is found in combination with other linguistic strategies, these are aimed at increasing the tentativeness of the act (e.g. use of interrogative intonation or adverbs of probability like *maybe, perhaps*, etc.). The six occurrences in which the speaker provides the reasons that motivate him to ask the hearer to perform the proposed action imply benefits either to a third person (as in example (4.113)) or both to speaker and hearer (as in example (4.114)), and they constitute peripheral instances of suggestions which could be also interpreted as weak requests or pieces of advice, respectively:

(4.113) 'So, get him another,' Niklas **suggested**. '*He could make a few credits up there.*' (iWeb)

(4.114) 'Then don't bother,' Ginger **suggested**. 'Use the museum as an excuse to raise the front gate price, to maybe five-fifty, or even six bucks. *A buck isn't going to cut the traffic down much, especially since you can advertise the museum as part of the gate price. That would also help cover the cost of the back-pit improvements.*' (iWeb)

Declarative sentences with modal verbs of ability, necessity, probability, and obligation are also extensively used as strategies for the expression of suggestions. Altogether they amount to 32 per cent of the suggestions in our corpus. Native speakers show a preference for constructions including the modal verbs *should* (i.e. YOU / WE SHOULD DO X) and *can* (i.e. YOU / WE CAN DO X), which amount to roughly 10 per cent each of the total number of suggestions:

(4.115) 'Perhaps you should go to the military museum and see it,' I **suggested** (iWeb)

(4.116) 'You can tell us about the time you fell into Clearedge Lake,' Pip **suggested** (iWeb)

This contrasts with Jiang's (2006) findings. According to this author, declarative base constructions with the modals *have to* and *need to* outnumber those with *should*. However, it should be taken into account that his corpus included a limited set of situations (i.e. study groups and student–teacher interactions). In addition, student–teacher interactions involve an asymmetrical relationship in which the teacher has a higher institutional and knowledge power. This could explain the higher frequency

4.4 Suggestions

of occurrence of more impositive modals, like *have to*, in this particular setting. In our corpus, however, there are no instances of suggestions with the modal verb *have to*, and those with *need to* are just a little over 2 per cent of the total number of examples. These results, which are in line with those of Edmondson & House (1981), Banerjee and Carrell (1988), Koike (1994), Bardovi-Harlig and Hartford (1996), and Alcón and Safont (2001), seem more compatible with the non-impositive nature of suggestions. Ability modals and the tentative modal *should* respect the freedom of the hearer to choose whether to do the action or not, which is a central characteristic of suggestions. In this connection, it has been attested that constructions for suggestions based on modal verbs tend to combine with an additional linguistic strategy: the use of expressions of tentativeness and probability. Thus, 62 out of the 171 constructions based on the use of modal verbs include adverbs of probability like *maybe* or *perhaps*, expressions of tentativeness (e.g. YOU MIGHT *TRY AND* DO X), or an interrogative intonation. These linguistic strategies are used to further increase the optionality granted to the hearer.

The third group of constructions for the expression of suggestions that stands out in our data comprises a rich collection of interrogative-based formulae like WHY DON'T YOU / WE DO X?, WHY NOT (JUST) DO X?, HOW ABOUT DOING X?, WHAT ABOUT DOING X?, WHAT IF YOU / WE DO X?, etc. Altogether they represent nearly one-third of the examples in the corpus. Most authors agree that the interrogative forms employed by using these formulae are typical of suggestions (Wardhaugh, 1985; Wierzbicka, 1987; Koike, 1994). The vast majority of them are highly tentative since they do not even make explicit the identity of the agent of the suggested action (e.g. HOW ABOUT DOING X?, WHAT ABOUT DOING X?, WHY NOT JUST DO X?), which again suits well the fact that suggestions are characterised by allowing high doses of optionality to the hearer. These constructions were not common in Jiang's (2006) corpus of teacher–student interactions. The asymmetrical power relationship between the participants in Jiang's corpus, where teachers have knowledge authority over their students, explains that their suggestions were on average less tentative and made a lesser use of interrogative formulae like the ones under consideration. In situations in which the speaker has a higher status than the hearer, the dividing line between a suggestion and a piece of advice or an order becomes blurry.

The last set of strategies found in our corpus represents a heterogeneous group that includes constructions based on the use of performative verbs (e.g. I SUGGEST YOU DO X) and declarative sentences expressing the benefits of a certain action (e.g. IT MIGHT BE WORTHWHILE TO DO X, YOU'D BETTER DO X, BETTER DO X, etc.). None of these constructions is very productive. Koike (1996) and Koester (2002) have already argued that performatives are not widely used as suggestions, since they are felt as too direct and impositive. Martínez-Flor (2005: 175) found these formulae mainly in formal contexts.

Table 4.16 compares the constructions used in Spanish and English for the expression of suggestions. The constructions in the white rows have a similar number of occurrences in the corpora for both languages. As can be observed, IMPERATIVE base constructions, including LET'S DO X performatives, which in Spanish correspond to both the first-person plural of the present subjunctive and the VAMOS A HACER X formula, take pride of place in both languages with a similar number of tokens. The conventional formulae for suggestions (i.e. WHY DON'T YOU / WE DO X?, WHAT ABOUT DOING X?) also have counterparts in Spanish (i.e. ¿POR QUÉ NO HACES / HACEMOS X?, ¿QUÉ TE PARECE HACER X?). These constructions show a similar number of occurrences in both languages, the first one being much more productive in both of them. Likewise, the use of performative verbs for the expression of suggestions is possible in both languages, displaying a similarly low degree of occurrence. Given their existence and their similar degree of occurrence in both languages, these constructions are expected to be easy for Spanish speakers to learn. This should be taken into account by EFL teachers and professionals in order to schedule the teaching of suggestion constructions throughout the different levels of instruction. The easiest constructions could be programmed for the initial levels. Those constructions that show differences between the two languages (light grey and dark grey rows in Table 4.16; see explanation below) should be dealt with in subsequent years and would most likely require a larger amount of teaching time and resources.

Suggestion constructions based on the use of modal verbs (i.e. YOU SHOULD DO X, YOU CAN / COULD DO X, YOU NEED TO DO) are found in both languages. The English language shows a preference for the use of modal verbs within declarative sentences, while Spanish displays a more varied range of formulae based on the use of modal verbs, including declarative, but also impersonal forms (i.e. LO QUE DEBERÍA HACERSE ES X (WHAT SHOULD BE DONE IS X), LO QUE SE DEBE HACER ES X (WHAT HAS TO BE DONE IS X), SE PUEDE / PODRÍA HACER X (X CAN / COUND BE DONE), and interrogative-based constructions (i.e. ¿NO PODEMOS HACER X?, ¿NO TENDRÍAS QUE HACER X?)). The last two do not yield any occurrences in the English

Table 4.16 Comparison of base constructions for the act of suggesting in English and Spanish

Suggestions base constructions (English)	Number	Percentage	Number	Percentage	Suggestions base constructions (Spanish)
IMPERATIVE	88	17.6	136	27.2	IMPERATIVE (2nd person)
LET'S DO X	78	15.6	41	8.2	VAMOS A HACER X
			28	5.6	HAGAMOS X (1st person plural Present Subjunctive)
WHY DON'T YOU/WE DO X?	70	14	50	10	¿POR QUÉ NO HACES/HACEMOS X?
WHAT ABOUT DOING X?	5	1	4	0.8	¿QUÉ TAL SI HACES/HACEMOS X?
I SUGGEST YOU/WE DO X	9	1.8	6	1.2	SUGIERO QUE HAGAS/HAGAMOS X
YOU/WE SHOULD DO X	52	10.4	34	6.8	(LO QUE) DEBERÍAS/DEBERÍAMOS HACER ES X
YOU/WE OUGHT TO DO X	10	2			
YOU/WE CAN DO X	46	9.2	26	5.2	PUEDES/PODEMOS HACER X
YOU/WE COULD DO X	34	6.8	20	4	PODRÍAS/PODRÍAMOS HACER X
WHY NOT JUST DO X?	15	3	8	1.6	¿POR QUÉ NO HACER X?
YOU/WE NEED TO DO X	12	2.4	2	0.4	NECESITAS/NECESITAMOS HACER X
WHAT IF YOU/WE DO X?	7	1.4	20	4	¿Y SI HACEMOS/HICIÉSEMOS X? Verb in 1st person pl. Present Simple Indicative or Past Simple Subjunctive
YOU/WE'D BETTER DO X	7	1.4	16	3.2	MEJOR HAZ/HAGAMOS X LO MEJOR ES QUE HAGAS/HAGAMOS X
BETTER DO X	4	0.8	10	2	LO MEJOR ES HACER X ES MEJOR HACER X QUIZÁS SEA MEJOR HACER X

Table 4.16 (*Cont.*)

Suggestions base constructions (English)	Number	Percentage	Number	Percentage	Suggestions base constructions (Spanish)
WHAT DO YOU SAY TO DOING X?	1	0.2	0		Possible but not productive
HOW ABOUT DOING X?	45	9	0		Not possible
YOU/WE CAN/COULD ALWAYS DO X	7	1.4	0		Not possible
YOU MIGHT DO X					
YOU MIGHT WANT TO DO X	10	2	0		Possible but not productive
YOU MIGHT WANT TO TRY TO DO X					
Not possible	0		29	5.8	HAY QUE HACER X
Possible but not productive	0		17	3.4	TIENES/TENEMOS QUE HACER X
Possible but not productive	0		12	2.4	(LO QUE) DEBES/DEBEMOS HACER ES X
Possible but not productive	0		10	2	(LO QUE) DEBERÍA HACERSE ES X
Possible but not productive	0		10	2	(LO QUE) SE DEBE HACER ES X
Not possible	0		10	2	¿HACEMOS X? ¿ [Present Indicative 1st person pl.] X?
Not possible	0		8	1.6	SE PUEDE/PODRÍA HACER X
Possible but not productive	0		2	0.4	¿NO PODEMOS HACER X?
Possible but not productive	0		1	0.2	¿NO TENDRÍAS QUE HACER X?
Total	500	100	500	100	

corpus, thus suggesting a low productivity in this language. Spanish also makes quite a significant use of the modal verb TENER QUE (HAVE TO) in constructions like TIENES / TENEMOS QUE HACER X (YOU / WE HAVE TO DO X). At first sight, it may strike as odd that this impositive modal is used for suggesting. However, a closer look at the examples shows that their impositive force is generally softened by means of a reason clause justifying the command and/or pointing out the benefits that the hearer may obtain if he decides to comply (e.g. *¡Está casi lloviendo! Tenemos que llegar cuanto antes a un lugar habitable* (It's almost raining! We have to get to a shelter as soon as possible!)).

Interrogative-based constructions that are possible in both languages include WHY NOT DO X? and WHAT IF YOU / WE DO X? formulae, both displaying slightly different amounts of productivity in each language. Likewise, some declarative constructions based on the statement of what is considered to be the best course of action according to the speaker (i.e. YOU'D BETTER DO X, BETTER DO X) are found in both languages with a slightly higher number of occurrences in the Spanish corpus.

Finally, there is a number of constructions that either are not possible in one of the languages or are not productive in the corpora (dark grey rows in Table 4.16). Among these, the HOW ABOUT DOING X? construction stands out from the rest. This formula has a significant presence in English (9 per cent of the suggestions in the corpus) but shows no counterpart in Spanish. This is an English construction to which EFL materials should, therefore, devote special consideration. EFL textbooks should also make Spanish EFL students aware of the fact that some constructions for suggesting that are common in their language (i.e. HAY QUE HACER X, ¿HACEMOS X?) do not have a direct counterpart in English. Thus, the impersonal HAY QUE HACER X construction corresponds to personal constructions like YOU HAVE TO / MUST DO X in English. The latter do not show productivity in the English corpus, which is only to be expected since this type of personal constructions are highly impositive. The impersonal formula in Spanish, on the contrary, suits well the non-impositive nature of suggestions. Not making explicit the identity of the agent increases the freedom of the hearer to choose whether to comply with the suggestion or not. Posing a simple question in the present indicative tense (i.e. ¿HACEMOS X?) also respects the hearer's optionality and, therefore, is useful in the expression of suggestions. These constructions, however, are not possible in English (**Do we play cards after dinner?*). Spanish EFL students should be made aware of this to avoid faulty realisations.

4.5 Advice Acts

Searle (1969) defined the speech act of advice as 'a weak directive whose illocutionary force is to suggest a future action to the hearer that the adviser believes will benefit the former'. Searle used the speech act verb *suggest* in the definition of advice acts. In fact, the defining line between these two illocutionary acts is very thin, and some authors include both within the group of advice acts (Wierzbicka, 1987: 181–190). Suggesting and advising also share similar force dynamics. In both cases the speaker directs a force towards the hearer with the aim of getting her to consider a beneficial future course of action. If this force succeeds in persuading the hearer that the action is in her benefit, then it can eventually move her into action. The initial force (F), which needs to go through the filter of the hearer's consideration and rationality (i.e. H_R), could be blocked by the latter if deemed unnecessary or not beneficial (see Figure 4.5). In Section 4.4.1, it was argued that the speaker uttering a suggestion does not make any overt attempt to persuade the hearer about the benefits of the suggested action. As will be shown below, this is the main difference with advice acts. When advising, the speaker does attempt to persuade the hearer about the benefits of the action, and he does so by appealing to his rationality (i.e. by presenting the reasons, advantages, and benefits of the proposed action).[4] As a result, the initial force of an advice act is stronger than that of suggestions and more likely to achieve its goal of turning the hearer into an agent that moves into action (i.e. H_A). Since the force still needs to go through the filter of the hearer's consideration, however, it is not felt as impositive as that of orders or threats.

4.5.1 The Know-What of Advice Acts

Advising is a complex illocutionary category which includes both those pieces of advice which have been asked for (i.e. solicited advice) and those which have been uttered spontaneously by the speaker (i.e. unsolicited

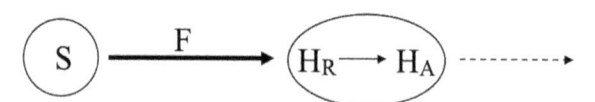

Figure 4.5 Force schema underlying the conceptualisation of advice acts

[4] In this respect, advice acts differ from requests, which are aimed at the social dimension of the hearer rather than to his rationality, thus exploiting well-established conventions of politeness and correct social behaviour, as shown in Section 4.2.1.

advice). As shall be explained below, it is important to bear this distinction in mind, since it triggers some special functioning of several semantic attributes of the act of advising.

Who is to do the action expressed in the advice act?
In accordance with previous accounts, the advice acts in our corpus prototypically present the hearer as the agent of the proposed action:

(4.117) 'Move fast and break things,' as Mark Zuckerberg **advised** (iWeb)

However, there are also some instances of advice which put forward a joint action by the speaker and the hearer (example (4.118)), or even an action that should be carried out by a whole group of people different from them (example (4.119)):

(4.118) 'We must be model Christian leaders,' he **advised** (iWeb)
(4.119) 'Businesses have got to start planning for this,' Kimball **advised** (iWeb)

Reformulating Searle's definition of advice acts under the light of the corpus data, it can be concluded that advising involves an attempt to get someone to consider the realisation of a future beneficial action, regardless of whether the prospective agent of the advice act is exclusively the hearer, both the speaker and the hearer, or a third person or group of people.

Who will benefit from the action expressed in the advice act?
According to most accounts of advising (Searle, 1969; Tsui, 1994; Trosborg, 1995; Mandala, 1999), this directive act implies a future course of action that is in the sole interest of the hearer. As can be observed in examples (4.117)–(4.119) the beneficiary of the action can be either the hearer, both the hearer and the speaker, or a third party. What seems to define an advice act is that agent and beneficiary are the same entity. Thus, in example (4.117), if the beneficiary of the action were the speaker (or someone different from the agent-hearer), then the speech act would lose its advising force and turn into an order or request.

Can the chosen agent do the action expressed in the advice act?
According to the corpus data, speakers uttering a piece of advice work under the assumption that the chosen agent is capable of carrying out the proposed action. Advising someone to perform an action that he does not have the ability to carry out would be nonsensical or even ironic in certain contexts. Thus, the assumption that the agent is capable of carrying out the

action is sometimes found to be the underlying motivation of some advice constructions (e.g. YOU CAN DO X, as in *'You can offer free shipping or discounts on their first order,'* Smale **advised**).

Do speaker and hearer want the action to be carried out?
The distinction between solicited and unsolicited advice acts becomes relevant in relation to whether the speaker and/or hearer are willing to see the advised action take place.

In the case of solicited advice acts, since it is the prospective agent himself who asks for advice, her wanting to follow the proposed course of action is expected to be high. The speaker is also expected to want the action to be performed. If someone asks for advice and then does not follow it, the advice giver is entitled to get offended. Compliance is the preferred turn for solicited advice acts, as illustrated in example (4.120):

(4.120) *'Do I have to go with them?'* she asked. 'Yes, you must go,' they **advised**. 'But Sulaiman will go with you.' She stepped *obediently* into the other boat (iWeb)

Unsolicited advice acts, on the contrary, have traditionally been considered as non-wilful acts (Merin, 1991), that is to say, as directive acts concerned not with the wishes of the speaker but with those of the hearer (or prospective agent). In these cases, the speaker assumes that the hearer will be willing to follow his advice, since it is in his benefit, but the actual degree of willingness of the hearer is unknown. Additionally, since the advice has not been asked for, non-compliance is not felt as impolite as was the case with solicited advice acts.

(4.121) *'You want* to choose a standard size, such as 24 by 36, or 18 by 24,' he **advised**. 'That way your customers can purchase ready-made frames for less money.' (iWeb)

All other things being equal, our data also shows that the speaker's wanting the action to be carried out increases as social distance shortens. This is probably due to the fact that the smaller the social distance between the speakers, the greater their emotional attachment is. In turn, this explains that the speaker has a higher desire for the hearer to comply with his piece of advice. The speaker's involvement motivates a higher use of politeness as a means to get the hearer to obey. Example (4.122) illustrates an interaction between two close friends, where one of them politely advises the other to lie down after the latter had fainted. Since the speaker is emotionally

4.5 Advice Acts

involved with the hearer and wants him to be ok, he also indirectly benefits from the hearer's compliance.

(4.122) 'Bloom, please you'd better lie down.' Flora **advised**. 'No, I'm fine.' (iWeb)

Is the action expressed in the advice act necessary?
The speaker uttering a piece of advice does so under the assumption that the proposed action is somehow necessary for the hearer (or designated agent). This assumption serves as metonymical motivation for some advice constructions (see Section 4.5.2):

(4.123) 'You *need* to test and learn and start small,' **advised** Martin (iWeb)

How much freedom does an advice act allow the hearer?
Like suggestions, advice acts are regarded as non-impositive acts by Haverkate (1984), because the speaker does not aim at imposing her will on the hearer. Nevertheless, despite the fact that the speaker does not attempt to constrain the hearer's freedom of action, advice acts are still traditionally regarded as face-threatening acts (Brown & Levinson, 1987). This is so because they do intend to at least influence the hearer's future behaviour and, therefore, they can be perceived on occasions as somehow impositive. According to our data, advice-givers attempt to guide the hearer's future course of action by appealing to his rationality and presenting her with arguments that support the need/benefits of the proposed action. As will be argued in Section 4.5.2, those linguistic constructions (e.g. IMPERATIVE construction, constructions based on modal verbs like YOU MUST / SHOULD DO X) used in advice acts are seldom found in isolation. They are systematically accompanied, in the same or different conversational turns, by clauses stating the purpose of the advice act (example (4.124)), the reasons why it is beneficial (example (4.125)), and sometimes even by promises about the positive outcome that will derive from following the piece of advice (example (4.126)):

(4.124) 'Make sure you add the .au,' Joyce **advised**, '*in order to* avoid a similarly addressed US website for a Missouri B'n'B offering romantic …' (iWeb)

(4.125) 'My advice would be to really consider it before you friend anyone,' she **advised**. '*Because* once you have, it's a tough spot to get out of. isn't the best thing to do.'

(4.126) 'Be professional, yet impersonal,' he **advised** me, 'and you'll get solid results.' (iWeb)

This suprasentential characteristic of advice strategies sets them apart from other impositive uses of the same constructions for the expression of orders and commands, in which the speaker does not feel the need to provide rational arguments justifying the proposed action. Thus, the optionality of the hearer (agent) is generally high in the case of advice acts: if he is not convinced by the rational arguments provided by the speaker, he does not have the obligation to follow his advice. However, his freedom may decrease in certain contexts, especially in those where the beneficiary of the piece of advice is not only the hearer but also the speaker or a larger group of people:

(4.127) 'We will need to be careful of our steps and of being seen,' Trey **advised**. 'I will do all I can to help,' Bliss said (iWeb)

In example (4.127) there are two beneficiaries (i.e. speaker and hearer). The freedom of the hearer to opt out is now constrained by the conventions of politeness at work in our society to the effect that not carrying out an act that is also needed by the speaker would be considered socially unacceptable. The preferred conversational turn in these cases, as illustrated by example (4.127), is one of compliance (i.e. *I will do all I can to help*).

Does the speaker attempt to minimise the cost of the action?
Hinkel (1997: 5) points out that 'all advice must be hedged and never given explicitly to avoid offending the hearer'. As shown above, the potential imposition involved is largely softened by the fact that the speaker explicitly justifies his advice act providing rational arguments to highlight its benefits. On the contrary, hedging based on the minimisation of the cost has not been found in our corpus data. This is only to be expected since the action proposed in the act of advising does not seek a cost but rather a benefit for the agent.

Does the speaker attempt to be polite?
The advice acts in our corpus do not prototypically display overt politeness. There are only a few examples in which politeness markers have been used (i.e. adverb *please*). One of them corresponds to a piece of advice which benefits other people apart from the prospective agent:

(4.128) 'Please think back again about your decisions and what you are doing in the next few years because this is not good for your country,' he **advised** (iWeb)

Example (4.128) represents a peripheral instance of advising. In fact, even though it has been categorised as an advice act by the narrator, its categorisation as a request could also have been possible, since the prospective agent does not exclusively coincide with the beneficiary of the action, the latter including other people as well (i.e. the whole country). Hence the possibility of a request interpretation and its compatibility with the use of overt politeness.

Politeness has also been observed in examples like (4.122) above, which is characterised by a small social distance between speaker and hearer. As explained above in relation to this example, the social closeness between the participants prompts the speaker to get emotionally involved and, therefore, eager to get the hearer to comply and benefit from his advice. In this specific sense, the speaker perceives himself as beneficiary from the action (i.e. his goal is to achieve his friend's welfare), which explains the use of politeness to gain the hearer's compliance.

As will be explained below in relation to the power variable, politeness requirements also increase in contexts in which the speaker is less powerful than the hearer.

Is social power relevant to the act of advising?
In his exhaustive study of advice acts, Hinkel (1997: 5) claims that the speaker is presupposed to have the right or the authority to give advice. Advice is normative in the sense that it always entails an evaluation of a future behaviour or a future action as desirable, good, healthy, etc. The one who advises 'describes, recommends or otherwise forwards a preferred course of future action' (Heritage & Sefi, 1992). Therefore, advice giving is prototypically performed in contexts in which participants display an asymmetrical relationship. The advice giver is in the position to propose a certain course of action, because he is more experienced, skilled, or informed than the hearer (Hutchby, 1995; Butler et al., 2010).

The data in our corpus fully confirms previous claims on the existence of a power asymmetry between those participants involved in an act of advising. Nevertheless, the power involved in advising is of a special type and different from the one that characterises speakers uttering more impositive acts, like orders, commands, or threats. Verschueren (1985: 181) refers to this power as *knowledge power* or *authority,* and different authors have later on made use of diverse labels, such as *rational power* (Merin, 1991) or *expert power* (Spencer-Oatey, 1996), to name the same concept. Knowledge power stems from an individual's larger experience (e.g. the knowledge accumulated by elderly people) or greater understanding of a subject or situation (i.e. the one acquired through learning and/or training), as illustrated by example (4.129) where a teacher advises his students:

(4.129) 'Rather, focus on taking incremental steps that keep you learning and growing. It is not only good for your career but also makes life much more interesting,' Cambray **advised** students (iWeb)

Knowledge authority is of a rather weak nature if compared, for example, to the *physical or institutionally-granted* power of a speaker uttering a threat or an order. As pointed out in Pérez-Hernández (2001: 154), this type of knowledge authority 'merely entitles the speaker to attempt to influence the addressee's future actions'. It is a type of power, therefore, that does not restrict the hearer's freedom of action. The distinction between knowledge and institutional power is not inconsequential. The possession of knowledge authority allows a speaker who is institutionally powerless to advice someone who is his equal or who is higher up in the social or institutional ladder. Our data suggests, however, that in those cases in which the speaker has knowledge authority but no institutional power, there is a higher need for politeness. This is the case with example (4.130) in which a blogger advises other bloggers. He has the necessary expertise to issue a piece of advice, but no institutional power to impose on the others, who are his equals on the scale of social power. Consequently, the advice act is expressed more politely and tentatively through the use of a past modal.

(4.130) 'I *would* strongly recommend any bloggers using Google's Blogger platform to host their work should start looking elsewhere before the rug is pulled from under them,' he **advised** any other bloggers out there (iWeb)

Is the social distance between the speakers relevant to the act of advising?
Advice acts can be performed regardless of the degree of intimacy that exists between participants in a conversation. However, the values taken up by the variable of social distance may influence the workings of other attributes of the act of advising. In this respect, it is important to bear in mind, as explained above, that social distance interacts with the speaker's desire that the proposed action is complied with, as well as with politeness (see discussion on example (4.122)). Curiously enough, our corpus also shows that, in the case of unsolicited advice, very large social distances also require higher amounts of indirectness and politeness. Thus, in example (4.131), a conference speaker addresses an unknown audience

(i.e. large social distance). Instead of expressing his advice as an action to be performed by the members of the audience, he simply states it in the form of a non-compelling declarative sentence without an explicit agent.

(4.131) In his talk he implored wide-eyed hopefuls of any 'renaissance' to patiently beware the pitfalls of an overly commercialised path to normalisation. 'Better to value self-attraction over promotion,' he **advised** (iWeb)

Is the formality of the context relevant to the act of advising?
Advising can be performed in all contexts regardless of their formality. EFL students, however, should be aware of the fact that formal contexts ask for more tentative and indirect pieces of advice. See examples (4.132) and (4.133) by means of illustration:

(4.132) 'Employers are encouraged to work with their safety and health committees, worker representatives of workers to prepare a hot weather plan,' the board has **advised** (iWeb)
(4.133) 'I think the key is providing enterprise alternatives that fulfil people's needs,' Lavenda **advised** (iWeb)

In example (4.132), set in the highly formal context of a professional meeting, the board issues its advice for employers by means of a passive sentence, which increases the indirectness of the act (cf. *Work with safety and health committees, You are encouraged to work with safety and health committees*). In example (4.133), again in a professional formal context, the piece of advice is formulated indirectly by means of a declarative sentence which does not make explicit the prospective agent, thus increasing the politeness of the act (see Table 4.17).

4.5.2 The Know-How of Advice Acts

The textbooks analysed in Chapter 3 were shown to include a rather modest inventory of linguistic strategies for the expression of advice acts. Most of them emphasised the use of modal verbs for this task (e.g. YOU SHOULD / OUGHT TO / MUST DO X), and only a couple of textbooks offered alternative constructions such as evaluative declarative sentences (IT'S GOOD TO DO X, DOING X MIGHT BE A GOOD IDEA) or conventional formulae such as IF I WERE YOU, I'D DO X, or YOU'D BETTER DO X. As can be observed in Table 4.18, the data in our corpus

Table 4.17 *The know-what of advice acts*

Advice acts are weak directive speech acts in which a speaker attempts to benefit someone by getting him to perform a certain action. When someone advises someone else to do something, they communicate the following:

'I have the necessary knowledge authority to present you with a course of action that is beneficial to you. I ask you to do it because I know it is beneficial to you. I have no institutional, physical, or social power to impose the action on you, but I expect you to take advantage of my expertise and to follow my advice.'

What you need to bear in mind in order to perform a successful piece of advice:

- The person who is to carry out the action proposed in your piece of advice can be the hearer, the speaker and the hearer, or a third person/group of people. What is important is that the agent of the action is also the one who benefits from it.
- As speaker, you know that your knowledge authority is not enough to impose your will on the hearer and that you should respect his freedom to decide whether or not to carry out the proposed action.
- As speaker, when you give a piece of advice you want the hearer to comply with it, especially when the advice has been solicited by the hearer, or when you are emotionally involved with the agent's well-being.
- Advice acts seek the benefit of the prospective agent; therefore, you do not need to minimise the cost of the action, which is by default beneficial to him.
- Since you need to respect the freedom of the prospective agent, but you also want him to comply because you know that the action will be beneficial to him, you attempt to persuade him into action by presenting him with rational arguments that justify the need to carry out the proposed action.
- When advising, politeness is not necessary by default. It will only be necessary in some cases (see below).
- You can perform advice acts in all contexts regardless of their formality and regardless of the social distance or power that separates you from the person to whom you address your advice, but you need to be aware of some interactions between these social variables and other attributes of the act of advising. See below.

BE AWARE!!

- If the piece of advice benefits not only the hearer but also you and/or a third party, you do not need to respect the freedom of the hearer so much, and it is acceptable to make your advice a bit more compelling through the use of politeness markers that make the hearer aware of the fact that his compliance is socially expected.
- If you are less powerful than the hearer (social/institutional power), you are expected to soften your advice by increasing its indirectness and, ultimately, the politeness of your act.
- If you are socially close to the hearer, you are likely to be more emotionally involved, you will want him to follow your advice, and you will need to make use of politeness to achieve his compliance.
- If you find yourself in a formal context, you are expected to decrease the impositive force of your advice act, preferably by means of indirectness, tentativeness, and impersonal sentences.

Table 4.18 *Base constructions for the act of advising in English*

Base constructions	Occurrences	Percentage
IMPERATIVE	298	59.6
CONDITIONALS IF I WERE YOU, I WOULD DO X	58	11.6
DECLARATIVE (EVALUATIVE) SENTENCE E.G. DOING X IS/CAN BE GOOD, IT WOULD BE GOOD/USEFUL TO DO X, YOU WOULD DO WELL TO DO X, I THINK IT IS IMPORTANT TO DO X	31	6.2
YOU NEED TO DO X	27	5.4
DECLARATIVE SENTENCE (REASON) + CO-ORDINATING CONJUNCTION (SO) E.G. SO YOU SHOULD DO X, SO DOING X IS IMPORTANT, SO IT'S BEST TO DO X	23	4.6
YOU/WE SHOULD DO X	17	3.4
PERFORMATIVE VERBS E.G. YOU ARE ADVISED TO DO X, I RECOMMEND THAT YOU DO X, I ENCOURAGE/URGE YOU TO DO X	14	2.8
YOU HAVE TO DO X	8	1.6
I WANT YOU TO DO X	8	1.6
YOU'D BETTER DO X	6	1.2
YOU/WE MUST DO X	4	0.8
YOU CAN DO X	4	0.8
WHY DON'T YOU DO X?	2	0.4
Total	**500**	**100**

shows a much richer taxonomy of base constructions at use by native speakers (including IMPERATIVE base constructions, DECLARATIVE constructions based on evaluative sentences or used in conjunction with co-ordinated clauses expressing reasons/causes, etc.). In addition, according to our data, those constructions including modal verbs and conventional formulae that are currently being taught to EFL students are not those that are preferred by English speakers. Modal verb constructions yield a low number of occurrences (less than 5 per cent of the total each), and overused conventional formulae like IF I WERE YOU, I'D DO X roughly amount to 11 per cent of the cases. By contrast, native speakers exhibit a marked preference for the use of the IMPERATIVE base construction for communicating their pieces of advice. This construction is largely absent from the textbooks under scrutiny, which again makes it manifest

Table 4.19 *Realisation procedures for the act of advising*

Realisation procedures for advising	Occurrences	Percentage
DECLARATIVE SENTENCE (REASON/CAUSE)	276	55.2
SUBORDINATE CLAUSE (REASON/CAUSE) E.G. BECAUSE …, SINCE …, GIVEN THAT…	40	8
CO-ORDINATE CLAUSE (REASON/CAUSE) E.G. SO …, FOR …	38	7.6
SUBORDINATE CLAUSE (PURPOSE) E.G. TO, IN ORDER TO, SO THAT …	34	6.8
OTHERS (PROMISE, POLITENESS MARKERS, ETC.)	20	4
NO ADDITIONAL REALISATION PROCEDURE	92	18.4
Total	**500**	**100**

that there exists a significant gap between the real use of English and the linguistic strategies presently being taught to EFL students.

Wunderlich (1980) states that some speech acts can only be singled out pragmatically and that advising is one of them, since it cannot be distinguished from other directives in terms of grammatical or formal traits. In fact, most of the strategies used in advice giving (e.g. conditionals (*If I were you* …), modals indicating probability (*It might be better for you to* …), specific formulae (*why don't you* …?), imperatives, declarative sentences with modal verbs of obligation (*should, ought to*), performatives, etc.) are also found at work in the expression of other directives. Are there any formal characteristics that may help to distinguish advice acts from other directives? If the scope of the study is limited to the sentence level and the discourse and conversational dimensions are not observed (as has been reported to be the case in most textbooks, see Alcón & Safont, 2001 and Martínez-Flor, 2003), it is hard to find distinctive features in the linguistic strategies used for advising. However, zooming out on a larger context and considering suprasentential units, it is certainly possible to observe some distinguishing formal traits of advice acts. Table 4.19 captures the realisation procedures that accompany the base constructions used in advising. A significant number of base constructions are combined (either in the same, the previous, or the following conversational turn) with a declarative sentence (55.2 per cent) or clause (subordinate clause: 8 per cent; co-ordinate clause: 7.6 per cent) stating the cause or reason that justifies the proposed action, as illustrated in the following examples:

IF I WERE YOU, I'D DO X Base Construction + DECLARATIVE (Reason)

(4.134) '*They'll stall*,' Jace **advised** him. 'I'd give them a deadline if I were you.' (iWeb)

IMPERATIVE Base Construction + CO-ORDINATE CLAUSE (Reason)

(4.135) 'Spare your ships,' Artemisia **advised**, 'and do not risk a battle; for these people are as much superior to your people in seamanship, as men to women.' (iWeb)

YOU HAVE TO DO X Base Construction + SUBORDINATE CLAUSE (Reason)

(4.136) '… you've got to do what you have to do to make a better life for yourself and certainly if there are children involved *because the pattern repeats itself*,' she **advised** (iWeb)

About 10 per cent of the remaining base constructions highlight their advising nature by combining with subordinate clauses indicating the purpose of the action or promising a benefit for the hearer in case of compliance with it:

EVALUATIVE SENTENCE Base Construction + SUBORDINATE CLAUSE (PURPOSE)

(4.137) As a consequence, Johnson **advised**, 'The best thing marketers can do is to broaden their tactics so that they win back consumer trust and allow influencers to provide authentic buying recommendations to the consumers looking for a trusted opinion on what to buy.' (iWeb)

IMPERATIVE + PROMISE

(4.138) 'Look deep into nature, and then *you will understand everything better*,' **advised** legendary physicist Albert Einstein (1879–1955) (iWeb)

Roughly 18 per cent of the total number of base constructions in our corpus do not combine with any of the realisation procedures described above. It could be argued that these are cases of advising whose interpretation is purely pragmatic and that no formal strategy guides the participants in their interpretation as such. Nevertheless, if the whole conversation is analysed, it becomes obvious that this is not the case. All but twelve of the base constructions that do not combine with further realisation procedures correspond to instances of solicited advice. The hearer has explicitly asked for the speaker's advice, and this somehow frees the latter from adding further justifications. Thus, when the advice has been solicited, a bare imperative, for example, is straightforwardly interpreted as a piece of advice and not as an order or a command.

The statement of the reasons why the speaker points the hearer towards a specific course of action is one of the characteristic semantic attributes of advising (see Section 4.5.1). The specific power held by the speaker (knowledge authority versus institutional/physical power) prevents her from imposing her will on the hearer. This leads her to make use of rational arguments to achieve the latter's compliance and to move him into performing an action that she expects to be beneficial for him. The linguistic strategies described above (i.e. base constructions + reason/purpose clauses/sentences) are, therefore, fully motivated by the semantics of the speech act.

Before ending this description of linguistic strategies for advising, a brief note on the use of the imperative in relation to this directive act is in order, since this is the base construction that displays a higher number of occurrences in the corpus. Tables 4.20 and 4.21 illustrate the use of the imperative in connection with advice acts. As can be observed, nearly 80 per cent of the instances of IMPERATIVE base constructions are used in combination with other realisation strategies (i.e. declarative sentences, subordinate or co-ordinate clauses stating reasons or justifications for the

Table 4.20 *Imperative base construction + realisation procedures for the act of advising*

Imperative constructions for advising	Occurrences	Percentage
BARE IMPERATIVE	68	23.1
IMPERATIVE + DECLARATIVE SENTENCE (REASON)	188	63
IMPERATIVE + SUBORDINATED SENTENCE (REASON)	12	4
IMPERATIVE + SUBORDINATED SENTENCE (PURPOSE)	11	3.7
IMPERATIVE + CONDITIONAL (IF YOU WANT/ NEED)	7	2.3
IMPERATIVE + CO-ORDINATED SENTENCE (REASON)	5	1.6
IMPERATIVE + PROMISE	4	1.3
IMPERATIVE + PLEASE	3	1
Total	**298**	**100**

4.5 Advice Acts

Table 4.21 *Solicited and unsolicited bare imperative advice acts*

Bare imperatives	Occurrences	Percentage
UNSOLICITED	12	17.6
SOLICITED	56	82.4
Total	**68**	**100**

action, etc.). In this respect, IMPERATIVE base constructions function in a similar way to the rest of the base constructions listed in Table 4.18.

Likewise, as expected, Table 4.21 shows that most instances of bare IMPERATIVE base constructions are cases of solicited advice. The formal structure of the conversation, in which the hearer explicitly asks for advice, guides the interpretation of the imperative as a piece of advice rather than as a more impositive act (i.e. order, threat, command). By way of illustration, in example (4.139) the second conversational turn contains the explicit request for advice (i.e. *How do I defend myself?*). Since the person uttering this question is openly asking for directions on how to proceed, the imperative in the next conversational turn cannot be interpreted as anything other than a solicited piece of advice.

(4.139) T1. 'The adult stage of the tick can theoretically cause Lyme disease, but it's big, and people usually find it and remove it before they get sick,' Fish said. 'But if you don't find it, you cannot remove it.'
T2. 'How do I defend myself?'
T3. 'Use tick repellents,' Sood **advised** (iWeb)

Let us now compare the advising linguistic strategies in English with those used by native speakers of Spanish in order to uncover any significant differences or mismatches worth noting for EFL students. Cross-cultural studies on advising are scarce. Among them Hinkel's (1997) study of advice acts performed with native speakers of Chinese and American English hints to some cultural differences in the production of advice acts: Chinese subjects made a wider use of direct advice acts, which suits well the fact that in Chinese, advice acts are considered acts of solidarity. Table 4.22 captures the similarities and differences between the base constructions used in Spanish and in English for the expression of advice acts: those in the white rows are possible in both languages and display a similar frequency of occurrence in our corpora; those in the light grey rows are possible in both languages but more frequent in one of them; and those in the dark grey rows are either not possible or unproductive in one of the two languages under scrutiny.

Table 4.22 *Comparison of base constructions for the act of advising in English and Spanish*

Advising base constructions (English)	Number	Percentage	Number	Percentage	Advising base constructions (Spanish)
IMPERATIVE	298	59.6	242	48.4	IMPERATIVE (2nd person)
Declarative (EVALUATIVE) sentences	31	6.2	52	10.4	Declarative (EVALUATIVE) sentences
E.g. DOING X IS/CAN BE GOOD; IT WOULD BE GOOD/USEFUL TO DO X; YOU WOULD DO WELL TO DO X; I THINK IT IS IMPORTANT TO DO X					E.g. LO MEJOR/ RECOMENDABLE/ IMPORTANTE ES HACER X; ES MEJOR/ESENCIAL/IMPORTANTE/ INDISPENSABLE HACER X; HACER X ES BUENO/BUENA IDEA; NO TE VENDRÍA MAL HACER X
YOU/WE SHOULD DO X	17	3.4	12	2.4	(LO QUE) DEBERÍAS/DEBERÍAMOS HACER ES X
YOU HAVE TO DO X	8	1.6	12	2.4	TIENES/TENEMOS QUE HACER X
YOU CAN DO X	4	0.8	4	0.8	PUEDES/PODEMOS HACER X
WHY DON'T YOU DO X?	2	0.4	4	0.8	¿POR QUÉ NO HACES X?
Performative verbs	14	2.8	136	27.2	Performative verbs
E.g. YOU ARE ADVISED TO DO X, I RECOMMEND THAT YOU DO X, I ENCOURAGE/URGE YOU TO DO X					E.g. TE/OS ACONSEJO QUE HAGAS/ HAGÁIS X
IF I WERE YOU, I WOULD DO X	58	11.6	10	2	TE RECOMIENDO QUE HAGAS X YO EN TÚ/SU LUGAR, HARÍA X YO QUE TÚ/USTED, HARÍA X
YOU NEED TO DO X	27	5.4	2	0.4	NECESITAS HACER X
YOU/WE MUST DO X	4	0.8	12	2.4	DEBES/DEBEMOS HACER X

	DECLARATIVE SENTENCE (REASON) + CO-ORDINATING CONJUNCTION (SO) E.g. SO YOU SHOULD DO X, SO DOING X IS IMPORTANT, SO IT'S BEST TO DO X	I WANT YOU TO DO X	YOU'D BETTER DO X	Possible but not productive	Not possible	
	23	8	6	0	0	Possible but not productive
	4.6	1.6	1.2			
	0	0	0	5	9	Possible but not productive Possible but not productive NO TE VENDRÍA MAL HACER X HAY QUE HACER X
				1	1.8	
Total	500	100	500	100		

Although both English and Spanish make a similar use of the imperative for the expression of advice acts, EFL students should be made aware of some significant differences between the two languages in relation to the illocutionary act of advising. The most striking one is the fact that advice acts based on performative constructions are markedly more frequent in Spanish than in English, amounting to nearly 30 per cent of the occurrences in our corpus of Spanish advice acts. While performative-based advising in English is largely found in formal contexts, in Spanish this type of explicit advice is acceptable in all contexts. As explained by Hernández-Flores (1999), this is only to be expected in a culture in which the act of giving advice is a symbol of high *confianza* or closeness among the interlocutors. By contrast, in English this type of explicit advice is generally felt as a face-threatening act (Brown & Levinson, 1987; Harrison & Barlow, 2009), because it does not allow the interlocutor independence to decide for herself. In fact, according to Locher (2006), direct advice in English can only be tolerated if there are indirect acts of advice that support it. This has been largely confirmed by our constructional analysis of advising which shows that base constructions for advising rarely occur on their own: over 80 per cent of them co-occur with other realisation procedures that justify the act of advising by providing rational arguments about the benefits of the proposed action.

These cultural differences in the conceptualisation of the act of advising also explain that some tentative base constructions used in English (e.g. IF I WERE YOU, I'D DO X, DECLARATIVE (EVALUATIVE) SENTENCE + CO-ORDINATE SENTENCE (SO …), etc.) are not as productive in Spanish, a language that favours a more explicit and direct rendering of advice acts. In contrast to these facts, EFL textbooks give pride of place to conventional formulae like IF I WERE YOU, I'D DO X, and YOU'D BETTER DO X, and to even less frequent constructions based on the use of modal verbs (i.e. YOU SHOULD DO X, YOU HAVE TO DO X) for the teaching of the act of advising to advanced Spanish students of English. Although the imperative is taught as a strategy for advice giving, no mention has been found in the textbooks analysed in Chapter 3 to the realisation procedures that prototypically combine with IMPERATIVE base constructions for the expression of advice acts (see Table 4.20). Additionally, little effort is invested in making Spanish students aware of the fact that advice acts that make use of performative verbs are not as widespread in English as they are in their native language. Under the light of these findings, there is ample room for improvement in the representation of advice acts in present-day EFL textbooks.

4.6 Warnings

Warnings are crucial speech acts in human communication, since they often play a significant role in helping others to avoid costly or negative scenarios (e.g. injuries, fatalities, loses, etc.). Example (4.140) displays a prototypical instance of warning:

(4.140) 'Watch out! Quicksand!' [...] Pickett was in the lead walking along the sandy bank of a small stream when suddenly his feet disappeared into the sand. 'It's soft here! Stay back!' he **warned** his friend (iWeb)

As example (4.140) illustrates, in their most explicit form, warnings are complex speech acts that involve a set of at least three illocutionary acts (Carstens, 2002: 192): an alert (e.g. *Beware!, Careful!, Watch out!*), an informative act (i.e. a statement of the hazard and/or consequences of failure to comply: *Quicksand! ... It's soft here!*), and an instruction about what to do or not to do to avoid the hazard (i.e. *Stay back!*).

The force dynamics of warning combine the insistence of beggings and the appeal to rationality of advising. Figure 4.6 illustrates the force image schema underlying example (4.140). An initial force (F_1) alerts the hearer, a second force (F_2) makes him aware of the specific hazard he is facing (*Watch out! Quicksand! It's soft here!*), and a third one (F_3) attempts to push the rational hearer into action in a such a way that he can avoid the danger. By combining declarative and directive forces (i.e. *Watch out! It's soft here! Stay back!*) the speaker attempts to prompt a physical action by the hearer. In contrast to orders and threats, this action is not imposed but reasoned.

Figure 4.6 illustrates a prototypical instance of warning where the different components of the aforementioned scenario can be clearly observed. As shall be further argued in Section 4.6.2, in most instances of warning, F_1 and F_2 fuse into one single force, where the alert element of the scenario is often realised by means of suprasegmental features (e.g. intonation).

The rich conceptual structure of warnings led some authors (Searle, 1969, 1976; Leech, 1983) to reflect on their hybrid nature. In informing about the hazard, they come close to representative acts. However, in

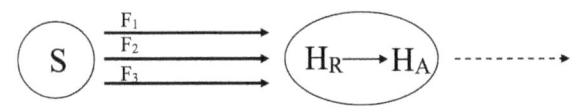

Figure 4.6 Force schema underlying the conceptualisation of warnings

instructing the hearer to follow a particular course of action to avoid a harm, they also display a directive flavour. It is therefore possible to find instances of warning that combine both illocutionary forces within a highly conventionalised formula (e.g. *Watch out* (directive), because there is a bull in the field! (representative); Hengeveld, 2017: 23). However, as pointed out by Leech (1983: 208) there are also instances of warning that are exclusively representative (e.g. *I warn you that the food is expensive*) or fully directive (e.g. *I warn you to take enough money*). Since the focus of this study is on directive speech acts and their related constructions, the data collected in our corpus has been selected to include instances of warnings that display an overt directive meaning, either in isolation or in combination with a representative act. Wholly representative warnings can also be interpreted as directives through inferential means, but the account of these processes exceeds the constructional scope of this work. In addition, in Section 4.6.2, it will be argued that the representative element present in some warnings functions as a type of linguistic strategy that helps to activate key semantic variables of the warning illocutionary ICM and to distinguish this speech act from other directives. In fact, warnings are complex speech acts that combine directive and representative forces, where the latter are subservient to the former. As has been shown to be the case with the act of advising in the previous section, a suprasentential and conversational approach to their study is, therefore, essential in order to capture their formal and constructional nature.

Within the category of directive illocutions, warnings are also easily confused with other speech acts. In their study on Iraqi EFL students' recognition of warnings, Abbas and Saad (2018: 22ff.) found out that over 23 per cent of the students overlapped the speech act of warning with those of threatening and advising, and around 5 per cent of them did so with requests and commands. A fine-grained description of the semantics of warnings is, therefore, essential to guide EFL students.

4.6.1 The Know-What of Warnings

Who is to do the action expressed in a warning?
Warnings prototypically display the hearer as the agent of the proposed action (example (4.141)), but the speaker can also be included as co-agent, as in example (4.142).

(4.141) 'Don't pout, Peabody,' Eve **warned** as they climbed back into the car. 'It's not attractive.' (iWeb)

4.6 Warnings

(4.142) 'I think there is no doubt that when any foreign government tries to impact the integrity of our elections ... we need to take action,' Obama **warned**. 'And we will at a time and place of our own choosing.' (iWeb)

The fact that the speaker is included in the action that is recommended to avoid a potential negative/harmful scenario has an influence on other aspects of the act of warning. Since the speaker is also to benefit from the action, his willingness that the action is carried out increases. The resulting warning, which aims to guarantee compliance by the hearer, tends to be more direct and impositive, cutting down on the hearers' freedom to opt out (e.g. *we need to take action* and we will ...). Notice that in the case of advising, when the speaker and a third party were included as beneficiaries of the action, compliance was sought by means of politeness. Since warnings are aimed at avoiding a cost/harm, which is more essential to a person's well-being than achieving a benefit, politeness is not felt as an effective enough strategy of persuasion, and it is, therefore, substituted by more impositive tactics (see below).

Who will benefit from the action expressed in a warning?
Warnings are mostly aimed at helping the hearer to avoid a potentially negative or harmful situation. However, in some cases, the speaker and/or a third party may also benefit from the action. Examples (4.141) and (4.142) illustrate instances of warnings in which the hearer or the hearer and the speaker together, respectively, benefit from the action. In example (4.143) a third party appears as the only beneficiary of the warning. Thus, if the hearer complies with the speaker's instructions (i.e. by not going outside a specific number), he will prevent some others from an undesirable negative situation:

(4.143) 'If you go outside that number,' he **warned**, 'you strike people who are either not at ease in a ballroom or else make other people not at ease.' (iWeb)

Can the hearer do the action expressed in the warning?
The hearer is expected to be able to carry out the action expressed in the warning. This motivates some warning constructions, such as the YOU CAN (ONLY) DO X construction (e.g. *'You can only push this balloon so far,'* Allbaugh **warned** the panel during the presentation. *'Something is going to pop.'* (see Section 4.6.2)).

Do speaker and hearer want the action to be carried out?
Since the action is in his benefit, the hearer is usually willing to take the warning into consideration and to do as told. Agreement is the usual conversational turn following a warning and compliance the expected move by the hearer. The fact that the person(s) chosen as agents in a warning are generally expected to comply serves as motivation for some warning constructions:

(4.144) '*You want to* stay away from bones. By pressing hard over a bone, you're going to cause pain, not pleasure,' she **warned** (iWeb)

On the contrary, the speaker's wanting the action to be carried out is not as relevant for the act of warning. Our corpus does not yield many instances of warning based on the speaker's willingness that the proposed action takes place. Expressions of speaker's wanting (e.g. *I'd like you to …, I want you to …*), which were so common in the performance of requests and beggings, for instance, are not deemed as efficient strategies for achieving the hearer's compliance when the illocutionary point is that of a warning. The only exceptions correspond to those cases in which the speaker is also the agent and the beneficiary of the action together with the hearer. Example (4.145) illustrates this.

(4.145) 'We know that plastics with BPA have been linked to cancer, poor brain health, and poor heart health, so *we really want* to be careful and get everything with BPA out of our kitchen. And *we certainly don't want* to microwave with it. When you microwave your food in plastic, the high heat really increases the release of those chemicals,' Glassman **warned** (iWeb)

Is the action expressed in the warning necessary?
Since warnings are aimed at helping someone avoid a cost or negative scenario, the proposed action is deemed necessary by the speaker and prototypically taken as such by the potential agent. Many warnings in our corpus exploit this semantic variable in their constructional layout (i.e. YOU NEED TO DO X construction):

(4.146) 'If your company doesn't have a data management policy that you can pick up and look at and you don't know how long you're supposed to be keeping things, *you need to* fix that,' he **warned** (iWeb)

4.6 Warnings

How much freedom does a warning allow the hearer?

Warnings are not impositive speech acts. They allow the agent of the proposed action freedom to do as indicated or to opt out. In this regard, Crystal (2010) argues that warnings belong to a category of negotiable directives (i.e. warnings, advice acts, suggestions, etc.), where instructions are not imposed, and the hearer has optionality to heed or not. This semantic characteristic explains why virtually all warnings in our corpus are generally softened by means of juxtaposed or subordinated clauses that explain the reason for the action (see examples (4.141)–(4.146)). Modals of tentativeness are also fairly common in the acts of warning (e.g. *You* might *want to stop eating junk food*) and also help to distinguish warnings from more impositive speech acts like orders or threats (e.g. *You want to stop eating junk food at once!*).

The inherent optionality that characterises warnings may decrease on some occasions. One of them is when the speaker and a third party are also beneficiaries of the proposed action, as in example (4.142), where the warning is expressed in a more impositive and non-negotiable fashion (i.e. *… we need to take action **and we will** at a time and place of our own choosing*). Warnings also cut down on the agent's optionality when the amount of the cost or harm to be avoided increases. Thus, the higher the cost, the greater the need to reduce the agent's freedom to disregard the instructions that will help her avoid it. In fact, when there is an imminent or especially negative scenario ahead, the warnings in our corpus are realised mainly by sheer imperatives, in the absence of the softening declaratives that characterise less costly scenarios. Examples (4.147) and (4.148) illustrate two situations that require non-negotiable warnings:

(4.147) Two more dogs charged Butcher, drove her back. 'Stop,' I **warned** Rachel (iWeb)
(4.148) 'Everyone, jump!' Mario **warned** as the dragon came near. They all jumped onto Hacktail's body successfully (iWeb)

Does the speaker attempt to minimise the cost of the action?

As explained above, warnings are often softened by means of explicative declarative sentences or modals of tentativeness. This should not, however, be taken as a sign that warnings favour minimisation of the cost of the proposed action. Since warnings are directed to avoid a cost or potentially negative scenario, which is essential to the well-being of the agent, the proposed action is meant to be carried out in full so that its effectiveness is not diminished. Thus, while requests, for instance, used minimisation of cost to increase their politeness (e.g. *Can you **just** wait **a little** more?*), this type of cost reduction would feel odd if used when trying to help someone to avoid a cost (e.g. *Just **watch out** a little! **A car is coming!***). Warnings are not generally mitigated.

As pointed out by Pérez-Hernández (2001: 189), however, there is a particular situation in which the performance of warnings asks for an increase in mitigation. This is so when the speaker himself is causing the potential cost or negative scenario that he wants the hearer to avoid. In these contexts, if the act is not conveniently mitigated, it may come across as a threat. Mitigation helps to favour a warning reading. Consider the following example:

(4.149) 'If you pull out a brochure,' I **warned**, 'I will make you eat it.' (iWeb)

The utterance in example (4.149) has been categorised as a warning. However, it could also be interpreted as a threat. The use of mitigation could favour a warning reading (e.g. ***Just** don't pull out a brochure, or I **may** have to make you eat it*). All things being equal, and no irony intended, the mitigated example activates the non-impositive nature of warnings and makes a threatening interpretation less likely.

Does the speaker attempt to be polite?
Warnings are beneficial to the intended agents because they are aimed at helping them to avoid a cost or a negative event. Because of this, they do not need to resort to politeness as a persuasive strategy, as has been shown to be the case with other directives which do result in a cost to the agent (i.e. requests, beggings) and which, therefore, require of face redress in order to soften their face-threatening nature (Brown & Levinson, 1987). The use of politeness markers in the expression of warnings is only required in formal situations in which politeness is mandatory regardless of the type of speech act that is at stake. This is the case with warnings that are included in instructions. The formal context and the large social distance between the speaker and the intended agent ask for the use of politeness, as in the following example:

(4.150) **WARNING:** *Please* make sure you have or obtain your license activation information before running this procedure if you're using the paid PRO or PREMIUM version as this tool will remove all of the Malwarebytes Anti-Malware program files, logs, and licensing information from your computer. (iWeb)

4.6 Warnings

Is social power relevant to the act of warning?
Like advising, warning requires knowledge authority, whether this originates in first-hand life experience, training, education, or expertise in a particular field. Pérez-Hernández (2001: 190) argues that other types of power (i.e. social, physical, institutional) may interfere in the production of warnings to the extent that, if they are present in a particular situation (i.e. there is a physically or institutionally powerful speaker), an increase in mitigation or politeness may be needed to prevent the act of warning from being interpreted as an order or a threat. This is precisely the case with example (4.151), where the speaker has the power granted by an asymmetrical social relationship (i.e. mother–daughter).

(4.151) 'Never touch a mushroom without Mommy,' I **warned** sternly, 'not for the first time.' (iWeb)

Thus, in the absence of the necessary mitigation and/or politeness, the interpretation of the act as either a warning or an order may be a hard choice.

Is the social distance between the speakers relevant to the act of warning?
The social distance between speakers interplays with other variables like the degree of speaker's willingness, mitigation, and politeness. The more intimate the participants are, the higher the emotional involvement of the speaker, and the higher his desire for the addressee to follow his warning and to avoid a potentially negative scenario. This increase in speaker's willingness is often paired with a decrease in mitigation and politeness. In these contexts, warnings are thus more impositive and aimed at cutting down the risk of non-compliance. Forceful warnings of this kind (see example (4.151) above) represent peripheral instances of the category which may resemble other directives like orders.

On the contrary, larger social distances correlate with higher levels of politeness and mitigation, as illustrated by example (4.150) above. Warnings addressed at strangers make extensive use of overt verbal politeness (i.e. use of adverb *please*).

Is the formality of the context relevant to the act of warning?
Warnings can be performed in all contexts regardless of their formality. As pointed above, however, the EFL student should be aware of the fact that the more formal the context, the more polite the warning is expected to be (see example (4.150)). Table 4.23 summarises the conceptual layout of the act of warning.

Table 4.23 *The know-what of warnings*

Warnings are directive speech acts in which a speaker tells someone to do or not to do an action so that he can avoid a dangerous, unpleasant, or simply unwanted state of affairs. When someone warns someone else, they communicate the following:

'I have the necessary knowledge authority to present you with a course of action that will prevent you from suffering a cost. I ask you to do it because I know it is in your best interest to do it. I have no institutional, physical, or social power to impose the action on you, but I expect you take advantage of my knowledge/expertise and follow my warning.'

What you need to bear in mind in order to perform a successful warning:

- The person who is to carry out the action proposed in a warning can be the hearer, the speaker and the hearer, or a third person/group of people. What is important is that the agent of the action is also the one who will avoid a cost by following it.
- As speaker, you know you that your knowledge authority is not enough to impose your will on the hearer, and that you should respect his freedom to decide whether or not to carry out the proposed action.
- Warnings seek a benefit for the prospective agent (=avoidance of cost); therefore, you do not need to minimise the cost of the action, which is by default beneficial to him. There is an exception to this, though: if the potential cost is caused by you, then you do need to mitigate you act in order to prevent it from being interpreted as a threat.
- Since you need to respect the freedom of the prospective agent, but you also want him to comply, because you know that the action will be beneficial to him, you attempt to persuade him into action by presenting him with rational arguments that justify the need to carry out the proposed action.
- When warning, politeness is not necessary by default. It will only be necessary in some cases (see below).
- You can perform warnings in all contexts regardless of their formality and of the social distance or power that separates you from the hearer, but you need to be aware of some interactions between these social variables and other attributes of the act of warning (see below).

BE AWARE!!

- If the warning benefits not only the hearer but also you and/or a third party, you do not need to respect the freedom of the hearer so much, and it is acceptable to make your warning a bit more compelling through the use of directness and impositive strategies that make the hearer aware of the fact that his compliance is expected.
- If you are more powerful than the hearer (social/institutional power), you are expected to soften your warning by increasing the politeness of your act. Otherwise, it can be understood as an order or a threat.
- If you are socially close to the hearer, you are likely to be more emotionally involved, you will want him to follow your warning, and you will need to make use of imposition (i.e. reducing mitigation and politeness) to achieve his compliance. On the contrary, if the social distance with the hearer is larger, you will need to increase the politeness of your warning to make it socially acceptable.
- If you find yourself in a formal context, you are expected to increase the politeness of your warning, preferably by means of overt verbal politeness markers (e.g. adverb *please*).

4.6 Warnings 177

4.6.2 The Know-How of Warnings

In his foundational work on speech acts, Searle (1969: 67) suggests that most warnings are essentially hypothetical 'if –then' statements: IF YOU DO NOT DO X, THEN Y WILL HAPPEN. Abbas and Saad (2018) provide a richer inventory of the linguistic strategies for the expression of warnings that have been described to date in the literature. They distinguish between direct strategies (i.e. performatives and conventional expressions like *watch out, be careful, mind,* or *look out*; Austin, 1962; Griffiths, 2006; Goddard & Wierzbicka, 2013) and indirect procedures (declarative sentences, imperative and negative imperatives, if-conditionals, interrogative structures, modal constructions; Sadock, 1974; Wierzbicka, 1987; Goddard, 2011; Goddard & Wierzbicka, 2013; Radden, 2014). There is, however, no quantitative account to date about which of these strategies are preferred by native speakers of English. This information is relevant for the design of EFL textbooks, so that professionals can choose the more frequently used warning constructions and/or schedule their teaching throughout the different proficiency levels, leaving the more complex or less frequent strategies for the higher levels of instruction. The analysis of the warning constructions in our corpus offers the following information in this regard.

As was the case with other directives, IMPERATIVE constructions take pride of place in the production of warnings, amounting to 50 per cent of the total number of occurrences. They are followed by conditional constructions (over 19 per cent) which, as already pointed out by Searle (1969), are fairly productive for the expression of warnings. The use of modal constructions (i.e. YOU MUST / CAN / NEED / HAVE TO DO X) adds up to around 10 per cent of the total. Performatives are used in slightly over 5 per cent of the interactions, and DOING X and YOU WANT / DON'T WANT TO DO X constructions represent a bare 3 per cent of the total each.

Base constructions for warning, like those listed in Table 4.24, do not generally occur on their own. Only one hundred and forty-eight instances of bare base constructions have been identified in our corpus (i.e. 29 per cent of the total number of constructions). Most of them are instances of warnings in which the potential cost to be avoided is already clear from the context, which makes it unnecessary to make it explicit. In these cases, a sheer imperative, for instance, is capable of activating the warning illocutionary act as a whole in the absence of further explicit information. Example (4.152), where the danger of looking up at a broken bulb is obvious, illustrates this:

(4.152) Pop! – A bulb broke as its string slid down a cable. 'Don't look up! Don't look up!' **warned** Johnny Robertson, who was winding the string of lights into a circle on the sidewalk (iWeb)

Table 4.24 *Base constructions for the act of warning in English*

Base constructions	Occurrences	Percentage
IMPERATIVE (DO X/DON'T DO X)	250	50
CONDITIONAL IF YOU DO/DON'T DO X, THEN Y	98	19.6
PERFORMATIVES		
BE WARNED	26	5.2
BE CAREFUL/CAUTIOUS TO/NO TO DO X	20	4
DOING X CONSTRUCTIONS	16	3.2
YOU SHOULD DO X	16	3.2
YOU WANT/DON'T WANT TO DO X	14	2.8
YOU'D BETTER DO X	14	2.8
YOU MUST DO X	14	2.8
YOU CAN DO X	12	2.4
PASSIVES	12	2.4
YOU HAVE TO DO X	6	1.2
YOU NEED TO DO X	2	0.4
Total	**500**	**100**

Bare base constructions for warning also correspond to situations in which the social distance between participants is very short. As explained in Section 4.6.1, a short social distance triggers a higher emotional involvement on the part of the speaker, who wants the hearer to avoid the potential harm at all costs. In order to achieve his goal, the speaker needs to maximise the impositive power of his act. This motivates the use of bare IMPERATIVE constructions which resemble orders rather closely. For similar reasons, bare base imperatives displaying an impositive intonation and including forceful modals (i.e. YOU HAVE TO DO X) are also used in contexts in which there is a high urgency to avoid a cost, and/or when the cost to be avoided is very high. In example (4.153), the vocative (i.e. Talia) makes explicit the intimacy between the speakers who use their first names to address each other. In addition, the situation requires a prompt reaction, and hence the use of the bare IMPERATIVE base construction effectively communicates the warning reading.

(4.153) Something or someone was near. 'Talia, do not move,' he **warned** (iWeb)

Finally, base constructions that consist in a main sentence plus a subordinate clause also tend to occur on their own. This is the case with conditional warning constructions (i.e. IF YOU DO / DON'T DO X, THEN Y), in

4.6 Warnings

which the subordinate clause specifies the action that the hearer should carry out, and the main clause states the cost that he will be able to avoid by doing so:

(4.154) 'Beware!' they **warned** the boy constantly. 'If you but touch the water, a hand will rise up and drag you down.' (iWeb)

Similarly, in the absence of other linguistic strategies, DOING X base constructions also manage to communicate both the proposed action and the cost that can be avoided if it is taken into consideration:

(4.155) 'Scrolling through song lists on a cell phone, or texting while driving is not just irresponsible, it can have tragic consequences,' Foxx **warned** (iWeb)

Finally, performative constructions make the warning interpretation clear by virtue of the meaning of the performative verb that they include:

(4.156) 'Be **warned** that using ELMO can lead to many small fuzzy red creatures appearing in your work area.' (iWeb)

All base constructions involved in the production of warnings and listed in Table 4.24 have been previously found to be at work in the expression of other directives. This may lead to the wrong conclusion that their ultimate interpretation as warnings lies on inferential processes. Nevertheless, zooming out beyond the sentence level and looking at the way in which the above base constructions combine with other linguistic strategies, it is possible to offer a constructional account of warnings that leaves little or no space left to inferential calculations. Table 4.25 summarises the main realisation procedures that combine with the base constructions in Table 4.24 to render a warning reading.

Over two-thirds of the base constructions in Table 4.24 combine with one or more of the linguistic strategies in Table 4.25 to render a clear warning reading. As can be observed in the following examples, the base construction generally communicates the action suggested by the speaker in order to avoid a negative scenario, and the linguistic realisation procedure states the reason for doing it, and/or the cost that will be avoided through compliance:

(4.157) YOU'D BETTER DO / NOT DO X CONSTRUCTION + DECLARATIVE SENTENCE:

'You better not hold out money like that when you know I won't take it,' he **warned**, taking a step back. 'Someone might run up and snatch it right out of your hand.' (iWeb)

Table 4.25 *Realisation procedures of the act of warning*

Realisation procedures for warning	Occurrences	Percentage
DECLARATIVE SENTENCE (REASON/CAUSE)	202	40.4
DISJUNCTIVE CLAUSE (E.G. OR Y)	74	14.8
SUBORDINATE CLAUSE (REASON/CAUSE) (E.G. BECAUSE Y, SINCE Y, GIVEN THAT Y)	47	9.4
CO-ORDINATE CLAUSE (E.G. AND Y)	21	4.2
OTHERS (POLITENESS MARKERS, ETC.)	6	1.2
SUBORDINATE CLAUSE (PURPOSE; E.G. TO, IN ORDER TO, SO THAT…)	2	0.4
NO ADDITIONAL REALISATION PROCEDURE	148	29.6
Total	**500**	**100**

(4.158) IMPERATIVE BASE CONSTRUCTION + DISJUNCTIVE CLAUSE:

'You must never sleep facing a mirror,' she **warned** me, '*or* your soul will go into the mirror and live in it.' (iWeb)

(4.159) IMPERATIVE BASE CONSTRUCTION + CO-ORDINATE CLAUSE:

'Get those negotiations wrong *and* the consequences will be dire,' she **warned** Wednesday (iWeb)

(4.160) YOU SHOULD DO X CONSTRUCTION + REASON CLAUSE:

'You should register with the province *because* the DA won't interact and associate with you legally and having a deed only as you profess is not enough, but you should give credentials to the relevant authorities and not ignore protocol,' she **warned** (iWeb)

As examples (4.157)–(4.160) illustrate, the combination of any base construction (i.e. IMPERATIVE, MODAL, etc.) with one of the aforementioned linguistic strategies makes the central attributes of the warning ICM explicit (i.e. the cost to be avoided and the action that should be taken to avoid it) and its interpretation unambiguous. The number of potential combinations is high, but once EFL students have learned the pool of base constructions and linguistic strategies at work for this specific directive act, they are set to perform the act of warning in a fairly flexible, creative, and at the same time, simple and communicatively safe way. Whichever combination they choose to use, they will be able to put across their warning message to their interlocutors.

4.6 Warnings

Learning how to perform warnings correctly in a second language is also facilitated by the explicit teaching of the differences between the warning constructions used in the target and native languages. Studies on the interlanguage pragmatic and constructional nature of warnings are scarce. Bataineh and Aljamal (2009) dealt with the differences in the use of the speech act of warning between American speakers and Jordanian undergraduate learners of English. They concluded that the IMPERATIVE construction was the most widely used by both groups.

A comparison between the warning constructions used by English and Spanish speakers yields similar results. Half the occurrences of warnings in both corpora make use of the IMPERATIVE construction, in either its affirmative (i.e. DO X / HAZ X) or negative form (i.e. DON'T DO X / NO HAGAS X). Spanish students of English will also find it easy to learn CONDITIONAL warning constructions and MODAL constructions (YOU MUST DO X / DEBES HACER X), because they are used in similar contexts and with a similar frequency of occurrence in their native language. However, the data in Table 4.26 also shows some areas of divergence between both languages, which need to be taken into account in the teaching of this directive act. It is essential to make Spanish students aware of the fact that performatives (i.e. TE LO ADVIERTO / BE WARNED) are much more frequent in Spanish than in English. This is connected to the fact that the acts of warning (like those of advising) are considered acts of *confianza* and social closeness in Spanish. Hence, the directness of a performative is not perceived as an imposition in the Spanish culture. English, on the contrary, has been shown to have a preference for indirectness and to disfavour the use of this type of explicit warnings, except in cases in which the urgency of the situation or the potential high cost of inaction justifies their use. This preference for indirectness also explains the fact that constructions based on the use of modal verbs (i.e. YOU CAN DO X, YOU NEED TO DO X), expressions of willingness (i.e. YOU WANT / DON'T WANT TO DO X), or passive constructions (i.e. X SHOULD BE DONE) abound in the English corpus, while they are not as productive in the Spanish one. Table 4.26 shows those constructions that are similar in both languages in the white rows, those that are preferred by one of the languages under scrutiny in the light grey rows, and those that are not productive in one of the languages in the dark grey rows. This traffic light of warning constructions should ideally guide the choice of strategies to be included in textbooks and also help EFL teachers and textbook designers to schedule the learning of the different constructions throughout the curriculum, leaving those which show mismatches for the higher levels of instruction.

Table 4.26 *Comparison of base constructions for the act of warning in English and Spanish*

Warning base constructions (English)	Number	Percentage	Number	Percentage	Warning base constructions (Spanish)
IMPERATIVE (DO/DON'T DO X)	250	50	224	44.8	IMPERATIVE (HAZ/NO HAGAS X)
CONDITIONAL (IF YOU DO/ DON'T DO X, THEN Y)	98	19.6	63	12.6	CONDITIONAL (Si haces/no haces x, entonces y)
YOU MUST DO X	14	2.8	11	2.2	DEBES HACER X
PERFORMATIVES	26	5.2	112	22.4	PERFORMATIVES
BE WARNED					TE LO ADVIERTO
BE CAREFUL (NOT) TO DO X	20	4	40	8	CUIDADO/OJO CON HACER X
YOU HAVE TO DO X	6	1.2	16	3.2	TIENES QUE HACER X
YOU SHOULD DO X	16	3.2	6	1.2	DEBERÍAS HACER X
YOU'D BETTER DO X	14	2.8	4	0.8	MÁS TE VALE/VALDRÍA HACER X
Possible but not productive	0		12	2.4	DECLARATIVE SENTENCES E.g. La razón por la que no debes hacer eso es….
Not possible			12	2.4	HAY QUE HACER X
YOU NEED TO DO X	2	0.4	0		Possible but not productive
DOING X CONSTRUCTIONS	16	3.2	0		Possible but not productive
YOU CAN DO X	12	2.4	0		Possible but not productive
PASSIVES	12	2.4	0		Possible but not productive
YOU WANT/DON'T WANT TO DO X	14	2.8	0		Possible but not productive
TOTAL	500	100	500	100	

5

A Cognitive Pedagogical Grammar of Directive Speech Acts II: Activities and Practice Materials

Contemporary research suggests that an effective approach to teaching speech acts involves providing explicit instruction on the acts (Tateyama et al., 1997) and opportunities to practise them (Bialystok, 1993; Morrow, 1995). This chapter offers a sample of activities for teaching directive speech acts to Spanish advanced EFL students. The teaching and practice materials have been designed in accordance with the tenets of cognitive pedagogical grammar (Dirven, 1985, 1990, 2001; Taylor 2008, Ruiz de Mendoza & Agustin, 2016), which, as explained in detail in Chapter 1, advocates an explicit instruction approach to L2 teaching.

Explicit instruction is particularly fitted for teaching advanced EFL students, who already have the necessary command of the English language to understand the explanations of subtle nuances about a new topic (Rose & Ng, 2001; Takahashi, 2001, Tateyama, 2001; Rajabia, Azizifara & Gowhary, 2015a, 2015b). A similar approach could also be used in lower levels of instruction, although in these cases, using the students' native language in the instruction may be required. The use of the students' first language in the EFL classroom has been a matter of debate, but its usefulness in explicit instruction approaches to teaching has also been widely attested (Auerbach, 1993; Hall & Cook, 2013; Blooth, Azman & Ismail, 2014; Alshehri & Abdulaziz, 2017).

All in all, there is a vast body of research that has provided evidence of the positive effects of explicit pedagogical intervention in facilitating the development of EFL students' pragmatic competence, in general, and their ability to perform speech acts appropriately in a second and/or foreign language, in particular (House, 1996; Kasper & Rose, 2002; Bacelar da Silva, 2003; Martínez-Flor & Fukuya, 2005; Gu, 2011; Rajabia, Azizifara & Gowhary, 2015a, 2015b). According to Schmidt (1990: 132–134), the conscious understanding of a certain aspect of language makes it possible for the learner to analyse it and compare it to what he has learned before, which, in turn, results in memorising and language acquisition. This conscious process can be considerably assisted through the use of explicit instruction in EFL teaching. Noticing and deliberately paying attention to language phenomena has been reported to facilitate language learning and to be a special prerequisite for adult learners (Schmidt, 1990: 149).

However, as was shown in Chapter 3, EFL textbooks hardly attempt to teach directive speech acts in an explicit and systematic fashion, most of them limiting the teaching of speech acts to that of several formulaic linguistic strategies in isolation from the contextual, social, and interactional factors that license their use (see also Diepenbroek & Derwing (2013) and Pérez-Hernández (2019) on the limitations of EFL textbooks in the teaching of pragmatics and speech acts). This has a bearing on EFL learners, for many of whom their main sources of pragmatic input are most likely their EFL textbooks and English language teachers. As a result, their pragmatic competence is often less advanced than their grammatical knowledge (Bardovi-Harlig & Dönyei, 1998).

In this connection, Matsumura (2001) claims that living in an EFL setting had a positive impact on students' production of advice acts, which suggests that EFL learners, who do not enjoy the advantages of living in an EFL environment, may benefit from some pedagogical intervention in the form of explicit instruction to acquire the necessary pragmatic competence.

In addition, given the limited number and formulaic character of the linguistic strategies for speech act production included in EFL textbooks, students are also generally not provided with the necessary knowledge about illocutionary constructions to be able to produce flexible directives adapted to particular contextual and situational needs.

Explicit instruction requires directly explaining the pragmatic, semantic, socio-cultural, and linguistic knowledge related to the target language (Rose, 2005; Ishihara, 2010; Bu, 2012; Taguchi, 2015). These explanations should be carried out in plain, jargon-free language and include a rich collection of real language examples to help students understand them. The pedagogical cognitive grammar of directive speech acts developed in Chapter 4 offers the necessary pragmatic and constructional/linguistic information for the appropriate production of directive speech acts in English. The basic information about each directive speech act under consideration has been summarised in the corresponding know-what and know-how tables. The former includes the pragmatic, social, and contextual variables that characterise each directive, and the latter the linguistic constructions and realisation procedures that the language system offers in order to express the variables and attributes that conform to each directive speech act. In the ensuing sections, the information provided in this pedagogical grammar of directive speech acts will be implemented into a set of instructional activities that is organised in three categories, depending on whether they highlight the teaching of the semantics/pragmatics (i.e. know-what), linguistic strategies and constructions (i.e. know-how), or cross-linguistic/cultural issues of the directive acts under scrutiny.

The proposed activities encourage learners to carefully observe salient pragmatic and cognitive phenomena connected with the production and understanding of directives. By pointing learners towards relevant features of the input, such observation tasks can help them make connections between linguistic forms, pragmatic functions, their occurrence in different social contexts, and their cultural meanings. Some of the activities are specifically designed to make the most of the cross-linguistic information included in the cognitive pedagogical grammar of directive speech acts, thus leading students to notice specific constructions that are only possible in either L1 or L2, as well as those that are more frequent in L2. Students are thus guided to learn the information they need in order to develop their pragmatic competence and their knowledge of those linguistic constructions and strategies that characterise directive speech acts in English. In accordance with previous explicit instruction proposals (Fujimori & Houck, 2004), the type of activities offered include consciousness-raising, knowledge-development, comprehension, and production-development tasks.

One of the main criticisms that has been made of the representation of speech acts in current EFL textbooks is the lack of real, authentic language examples. This means that the speech acts included in teaching materials are often isolated sentences deprived of a context and presented outside their naturally occurring discourse (Bardovi-Harlig, 1992). In turn, this limits the socio-pragmatic information available to the students and invalidates those materials for teaching purposes at least from a pragmatic stance. As Judd (1999: 158) remarks in relation to the teaching of apologies, 'to provide learners with only one apology formula to apply on the many occasions when apologies are necessary in English is a misrepresentation of the complexity of this speech act'. The use of authentic instances of speech acts within their actual discourse environment has, therefore, been advocated recently by a growing number of scholars. Koike (1996) and Martínez-Flor (2005), among others, concluded that learners of a foreign language need to be exposed to contextualised language in order to recognise speech acts at both grammatical and pragmatic levels of use. This includes the use of media materials (audio-visual shows, recorded conversations, etc. (Judd, 1999)), as well as of written and spoken corpora (Bardovi-Harlig, Mossman & Vellenga, 2014a). In line with this stance, the activities proposed in the following sections make use of real language examples, except in those cases in which it is necessary to manipulate them in order to highlight specific aspects of the nature of speech acts for teaching purposes.

5.1 Teaching the Know-What of Directives

The know-what of directive speech acts included in the cognitive pedagogical grammar expounded in Chapter 4 shows that each of these illocutionary acts is a complex conglomerate of interactional, transactional, and social features. Nevertheless, they all share the fact that they act as forces that attempt to move the hearer into action. It is, therefore, important to make students aware of this forceful nature of directives. It is also essential to make them realise that the intensity of the force is different in each case, and that this has a bearing on the face-threatening nature of each particular directive and will also influence other variables, such as the degree of politeness that is necessary to perform the act correctly or the optionality that the act grants to the hearer to comply or to refuse to do as told. Activities 1, 2, and 3 are designed to raise students' awareness about these issues. They take the form of consciousness-raising tasks by means of which learners are exposed to real language examples with attention directed to the target pragmatic features and sociolinguistic variables of particular speech events (e.g. participants, power/social distance relationships, formal/informal contexts).

Activity 1

Observe Figures 5.1 and 5.2. They represent the types of force that can be exerted by means of two different directive speech acts (i.e. orders and requests). Then, answer the questions a–e below.

a. *Which force is stronger? The intensity of the force is represented by the thickness of the force vector (F).*
b. *Which force does not encounter any obstacles in its way to the hearer (H)?*
c. *Which of the two forces is more likely to have an effect on the hearer (H) and move him into action?*
d. *Considering the strength of these two forces, which speaker do you think is more powerful?*
e. *Considering the strength of these two forces, which hearer do you think has more freedom to refuse to comply with what he is told to do?*

5.1 Teaching the Know-What of Directives

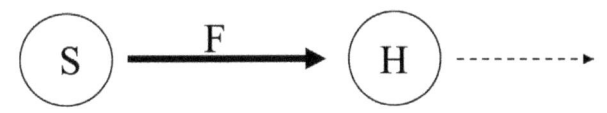

Figure 5.1 Force dynamics of orders: S = speaker; F = force; H = hearer

This activity helps students to visualise the differences in force dynamics between orders and requests. The visual aid provided by Figures 5.1 and 5.2 should lead them to conceptualise orders as a more forceful directive than requests: a compulsion force that does not envisage any obstacles in its way towards the hearer and can, therefore, exert its causative power over him easily. The answers to the questions and the ensuing discussion offer the EFL teacher an opportunity to explain some of the defining attributes of orders (i.e. they are produced by powerful speakers who do not expect any obstacles in their attempt to move the hearer into action, and they are received by hearers who have little freedom to refuse to do as told) and requests (i.e. they are produced by speakers who do not have the necessary power to impose their will on the hearer, and they need to overcome some impediments before succeeding in moving him into action). The teacher can then further explain which type of obstacles or impediments can get in the way of a successful request: the lack of willingness of the hearer to comply, his lack of ability to do as told, or the fact that the requested action is too costly, for example, could get in the way and prevent the requestive force from moving the hearer into action. Eventually, the discussion about the obstacles that prevent a request from succeeding gives the EFL teacher an opportunity to introduce the notion of politeness, as a persuasive strategy that may help the speaker to overcome some of those obstacles and to secure the hearer's compliance.

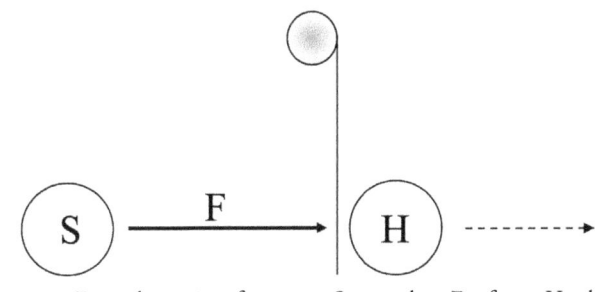

Figure 5.2 Force dynamics of requests: S = speaker; F = force; H = hearer

Activity 2

Observe Figure 5.3. It represents the force dynamics of the act of begging. Compare the intensity and nature of the force(s) involved with those of orders and requests in Activity 1. Then answer the following questions:

a. *Are the force vectors involved in the act of begging as strong as those found in the acts of ordering and requesting?*
b. *According to what you see in Figure 5.3, does the speaker uttering a begging achieve his goal the first time, or does he need to keep trying several times until he succeeds?*
c. *From your answers to the two previous questions, what can you conclude about the power of the speaker uttering a begging? Does he have the necessary power to impose his will on the hearer?*
d. *From the fact that the speaker keeps trying to achieve his goal by exerting several forces, what can you infer about his desire that the hearer carries out the proposed action? Does the speaker have a strong desire that the action is carried out?*
e. *As indicated in Figure 5.3, the forces exerted by the speaker need to act on the rationality and the social nature of the hearer ($H_{R/S}$) to eventually move him into action (H_A). Look at the following three examples of begging and decide whether the speech act is acting on the rationality, the social conscience of the hearer, or both in order to persuade him to comply with the proposed action:*

(5.1) He then reached out at him. Attempting to grab him and the mother pulled her son away. # – # The mother shouted at him crying 'You leave him alone! He is just a child! I'll go! Just don't hurt him! Please!!' # She then begged at him (iWeb)

(5.2) # His heart cried out ... No! This isn't right ... where is she going?! his mind raced frantically, trying to make sense of what she was saying. # 'I don't *want* to be apart, April. Don't go ... please,' he futilely begged, his eyes moistening again. 'I want to be with you ... forever ... have a family with you ... you *can't* go!' He was on the

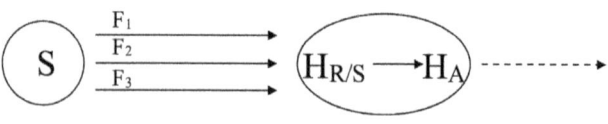

Figure 5.3 Force dynamics of beggings: S = speaker; F = force; $H_{R/S}$ = hearer as rational/social being; H_A = hearer as agent

5.1 Teaching the Know-What of Directives

verge of breaking down, again. # April turned to face Nathan and her hair blew in her face. She gently brushed it over her ear and smiled. 'I have to go now ...' # (iWeb)

(5.3) # Then one day in the laundry, in the spring of 1943, she was approached by a small Jewish man who told her he needed women to work in the factory. Oscar Schindler's factory. 'I don't know why I was chosen that day,' she later said, 'It's a question I've asked myself hundreds and hundreds of times. Why me? Why was I chosen to live?' # At first, Anna did not want to go and leave her sister Erna. *'But she begged me. Go. With Schindler, there is life. You must go',* Anna later said # (iWeb)

After completing this activity, students will have become aware of the main features of the act of begging: the fact that the speaker has a strong desire that the action is carried out by the hearer, the fact that the speaker is not powerful enough to impose her will, and the fact that she needs to act on the rationality and/or the social conscience of the hearer to persuade her into action.

Activity 3

Compare the type of force (intensity/nature) used in suggestions (Figure 5.4) with those that characterise orders, requests, and beggings (see Figures 5.1, 5.2, and 5.3 in activities 1 and 2) and make a list of the main differences between them. How would you describe the force involved in the act of suggesting? Is it a strong or a weak force? Is it iterative like that involved in the act of begging?

Then, read the information about the act of suggesting included in the related know-what table (Table 5.1) and answer the following questions:

a. *Which pieces of information included in the know-what of suggestions explain the nature of the type of force involved in the act of suggesting?*

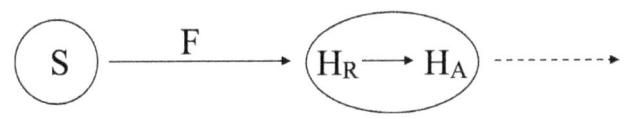

Figure 5.4 Force dynamics of suggestions: S = speaker; F = force; H_R = hearer as rational being; H_A = hearer as agent

Table 5.1 *The know-what of suggestions*

Suggestions are weak directive speech acts by means of which a speaker asks the hearer(s) to consider the merits or benefits of a potential course of action. When someone suggests someone else to do something, he communicates the following:

'I believe that a particular course of action may be positive for you, for both of us, or for someone else. You could consider doing it. I have no particular interest in you carrying out that action, neither do I have the social, institutional, or experiential power to impose the action on you, but I share it with you for your consideration.'

What you need to bear in mind in order to perform a successful suggestion:

- The beneficiary of the action may be the speaker, the hearer, both of them, or a third person.
- Regardless of who is to benefit from the action, the speaker shows no special desire or interest in its materialisation. He merely presents it for the hearer's consideration.
- Whether or not the hearer wants to do as told is unknown or irrelevant for the speaker, who respects the hearer's freedom to comply or refuse to do as suggested.
- In order to respect the optionality of the hearer, the speaker makes no overt attempt to minimise the cost of the action or to persuade the hearer to comply through insistence, imposition, or the use of politeness.

BE AWARE!!!

You can make suggestions in all contexts, regardless of their formality and of the power relationship or social distance that separates you from the hearer(s). However, if there are power asymmetries between the speakers, if the social distance between them is large, or if the context is formal, your suggestions will need to include attempts to minimise their cost and/or exhibit a higher use of tentativeness.

b. *Does the interest/attitude of the speaker towards the materialisation of the action and his respect towards the freedom of the hearer explain the type and intensity of force that characterises beggings?*
c. *Why are suggestions not insistent, like beggings?*
   Reason your answers.

This activity leads students to an understanding of the force dynamics of suggestions and their connection with the semantic features that define this directive speech act. It is designed to raise their awareness about the fact that speakers uttering suggestions are not as eager to achieve compliance as those uttering beggings, requests, or orders, for example. Students are also informed about the fact that suggestions respect the optionality/freedom of the hearer to decide upon his future course of action by avoiding the insistence and the imposition of beggings and orders, respectively.

As explained in depth in Chapter 4, the know-what of each directive speech act includes the knowledge of their characterising transactional and social attributes and variables, as well as the interactions that may exist between them. Activities 4–7 are designed to help students learn these essential semantic and pragmatic keystones of each directive speech act. They are also aimed at helping EFL learners to reflect on the potential interactions between attributes and variables, and on how these may affect the final form of the directive. These activities include knowledge-development tasks, which expose learners to pragmatic input and also have them act on this input by writing a reflection about it, evaluating the appropriateness of the target pragmatic forms, or selecting appropriate answers from a list of options.

Activity 4

Read the following examples of warnings and answer the questions below. With the answers to all the questions try to write a brief description about the act of warning, highlighting who is to be the agent of the action, who is to benefit from it, how much power and which type of power do speakers need to carry out this speech act successfully, how imposing the act is, and how much freedom does the hearer has to comply or to opt out.

(5.4) I remembered how as a little kid Mom would tell me an old Chinese superstition. 'You must never sleep facing a mirror,' she **warned** me, 'or your soul will go into the mirror and live in it.' A part of me dismissed her words as a chunk of nonsense, but another part of me believed her and hence there were no mirrors in my bedroom. # (iWeb)

(5.5) After an identical Obama threat, US cyber-soldiers shut down the entire North Korean internet. 'I think there is no doubt that when any foreign government tries to impact the integrity of our elections… we need to take action,' Obama **warned**. 'And we will at a time and place of our own choosing.' # (iWeb)

(5.6) # Transport for London, which oversees public transport in the capital, posted a picture from a traffic camera showing large numbers of the insects collecting on a traffic light, and warned drivers that a pedestrian crossing was partially obstructed by bees. It **warned**: 'Please approach with caution.' # (iWeb)

Questions:

a. Who will be performing the proposed action? The speaker, the hearer, both of them?

b. Who will benefit from doing as warned? The speaker, the hearer, both of them?
c. Does the speaker have any type of power that licenses him to utter the warning? Social power? Institutional power? Knowledge power?
d. What do you think the hearer will do? Will he follow the warning and do as told? How free is he to decide about his future course of action? Which factors may limit his freedom?

The answers to questions a–d will lead students to consider some of the main features that characterise the act of warning, as summarised in the know-what of warnings (see Chapter 4, Section 4.6.1, Table 4.23).

Activity 5

Read carefully the following examples of directives and say which of them make use of politeness as a strategy to persuade the hearer into action (e.g. adverb please, question tags, hedges like just, kindly, formulaic expressions like WOULD YOU MIND DOING X?, etc.):

(5.7) The commander was consumed by fury and the terrorists were dumbfounded. 'Shoot at the sky!' the command ordered. The five directed their rifles upward, and all five rifles shot. *'Now shoot him!'* he **ordered**. The five rifles wouldn't budge # (iWeb)

(5.8) # 'We were just having a little fun, Barbie,' Abby said. 'You're just so fun to tease!' # *'Well, could you please stop?'* she **requested**. 'I am in charge here, and I don't ask for a lot of respect, but …' # (iWeb)

(5.9) # 'You know, I should really tell your mother about this?' # *'Oh, please don't Aunt Lucy! I promise I won't do it again. I'll give you everything I have on you. Just please don't tell Mum'*, he **begged** # (iWeb)

(5.10) # *'So, do you want to go swimming Sam? Afterwards we can play a little volleyball to help dry us off,'* Michael **suggested** as he took off his sandals # (iWeb)

(5.11) # An engaging presentation might help a good article reach more audience, but if there is no story 'all data skills in the world will mean nothing,' said Tom Felle, Acting Director, Interactive and Newspaper Journalism at City University. # *'Have a nose for stories. Data is a great way of finding a story. Go and get trained. Journalism is still king, and it has to be,'* he **advised** aspiring journalists # (iWeb)

(5.12) # Conservative Prime Minister Theresa May called the snap election three years early in a bid to boost the Conservative majority in Parliament, which she says will strengthen Britain's hand in divorce talks with the European Union. # *'Get those negotiations wrong and the consequences will be dire,'* she **warned** Wednesday # (iWeb)

Now, look at the following modified versions of some of the directive speech acts above:

(5.7, modified order):   Now shoot him! Please! He ordered.
(5.10, modified suggestion):   So, do you want to go swimming Sam? Afterwards, can we please play a little volleyball to help dry us off?
(5.11, modified advice):   Please, have a nose for stories. Data is a great way of finding a story. Please, go and get trained. Journalism is still king, and it has to be.
(5.12, modified warning):   Get those negotiations wrong, please, and the consequences will be dire.

We have added a politeness marker (i.e. please) to those directive speech acts that do not generally exhibit politeness as one of their prototypical features. Some of these modified versions do not sound natural in English, others have changed their illocutionary force, and one of them is no longer acceptable in English. Discuss with you classmates which one of them falls into which of these categories.

Directive speech acts have traditionally been considered face-threatening acts because they try to influence the hearer's future course of action to a greater or lesser extent, thus imposing on his freedom. Because of this they have also traditionally been connected with the need to use politeness strategies to minimise the imposition. However, this activity is designed to show students that politeness is more central to some directives than to others. It also reveals that for some directives, politeness is not a valid strategy, as is the case with orders and suggestions (see detail explanations in the know-what tables for these directive speech acts in Chapter 4).

Activity 6

In activity 5 you have learned how some directive speech acts are more likely to make use of politeness than others. Thus, while requests and beggings make an extensive use of this strategy, other directives like suggestions and orders are characterised by their lack of deference, and yet others, like advice acts and warnings make use of politeness only in some specific situations. Read the following examples of warnings and advice acts and try to think of reasons why they have been produced in a polite fashion. In your answer, you should consider potential interactions with social variables like power, social distance, and the formality of the context. If necessary, read the know-what tables (see Chapter 4) for each of these speech acts before doing the activity.

(5.13)   # Then they all heard Bloom's voice. # 'What's going on here? Where am I?' She got up slowly # *'Bloom, **please** you'd better lie down.' Flora **advised** #* 'No, I'm fine.' # (iWeb)

(5.14)   # Iraqi Abdallah al Hillali warned the president that the ban would put the US in jeopardy. # '**Please** think back again about your decisions and what you are doing in the next few years because this is not good for your country,' he **advised** #

(5.15)   # **WARNING: Please** make sure you have or obtain your license activation information before running this procedure if you're using the paid PRO or PREMIUM version as this tool will remove all of the Malwarebytes Anti-Malware program files, logs, and licensing information from your computer. You will need to reactivate the program using the license you were sent via email. #

By commenting on examples (5.13–5.15), students will become aware of how different social variables interact with the amount of politeness used in the expression of warnings and advice acts. Thus, they will realise that small social distances (i.e. relations between friends, relatives, etc.) favour the use of polite advice acts, since in these situations the speaker gets emotionally involved and, therefore, is eager to get the hearer to comply and benefit from his advice. In this specific sense, the speaker perceives himself as beneficiary from the action. In example (5.13), for instance, the speaker's goal is to achieve her friend's welfare. Hence the use of politeness to gain the hearer's compliance. Politeness is also used in advice acts when the proposed action benefits not just the hearer but also other people, as is the case in example (5.14). In these situations, appealing to the hearer's social consciousness through politeness strategies is used as a means to make the advice act more compelling and to secure compliance. Finally, example (5.15) illustrates a polite warning. EFL students need to be taught that in formal contexts, like that of a manual of instructions, in which there is also a large social distance between the speaker and the hearer, warnings conventionally include politeness markers.

5.1 Teaching the Know-What of Directives

Activity 7

Read the following examples of directive speech acts and fill in the gaps with the performative verb (i.e. ordered or requested) that you think best describes the act. Justify your answer by commenting on the power of the speaker and the freedom of the hearer to comply or to refuse to do as told. Remember that orders are impositive acts uttered by powerful speakers, and that they offer little freedom of action to the hearer, while requests are polite acts produced by speakers who do not have the power to impose on the hearer and, therefore, the latter is free to decide whether to do as told or not. Some of the examples are peripheral instances of the directive categories under consideration (i.e. polite orders, impolite requests). Can you explain what makes them appear as less central examples of their categories?

(5.16) # 'I wrote it up myself,' Harpers secretary replied. # 'Do you happen to have her address out there, by any chance?' # 'I don't know,' Mollie said, 'but it would be on the mailing list.' # 'Dig it out for me and bring it in here, please,' Harper _____ (ordered/ requested) # (iWeb)

(5.17) # 'Go down to Thomas and get me some more' his father _____ (ordered/requested), but it was more of an _____ (order/request) than anything. 'And be quick this time' # (iWeb)

(5.18) ## 'Toruos would you mind holding my ankles, so I don't fall.' Sajin _____ (ordered/requested) # 'of course milord' the rhino replied as he walked up behind Sajin and firmly grasped his ankles # (iWeb)

(5.19) # Back aboard Trafalgar, de Bicardi once again heard, 'torpedo in the water! Its right above us sir!' # 'All stop!' the captain _____ (ordered/requested), some stress finally creeping into his voice. Trafalgars pump jet propulsion ceased, and the sub glided through the water, a shadow in the deep. 'Sonar, a report if you please.' # (iWeb)

(5.20) # 'Could you teach me how to dance, Misty?' He _____ (ordered/requested). # 'What?' # 'You heard me. I don't know how to dance.' # Misty gave this some thought for a second before coming to a decision. # 'Ok. I'll do it.' # (iWeb)

This activity seeks to make students familiar with the prototypical nature of speech act categories, and how there can be better or worse instances of a particular speech act. It is also designed to lead students to reflect on which are the most essential semantic/pragmatic elements that define each directive category. Thus, if there is a powerful speaker capable of imposing his will on the hearer, so that the latter lacks the freedom to refuse to do as told, the overt use of politeness (which is a characteristic of requests) may turn the utterance into a fake request or a camouflaged order. This is the case with examples (5.16), (5.17), and (5.18) in the activity, which are peripheral instances of orders, displaying the politeness typical of requests without losing the impositive force that emerges from the powerful status of the people who utter them (i.e. a boss, a father, a lord).

5.2 Teaching the Know-How of Directives

Directive speech act constructions consist in pairings of linguistic forms and functions. As explained in Chapter 4, these constructions are more fluid than those found at the argument-structure level of linguistic description. Speech acts are complex, dynamic concepts whose essential transactional attributes interact with several social and contextual variables in such a way that the final conceptual make-up of a directive speech act will vary in different contexts. For this reason, directive speech act constructions are also necessarily fluid. They consist, as shown in Chapter 4, of base constructions that combine with linguistic strategies that help tune the former for the needs of different contexts by activating the necessary attributes and variables of the corresponding speech acts. In Chapter 4, it was shown how, even though the same base constructions may be found in the expression of different directives, their combination with diverse linguistic strategies allows speakers to further specify them in order to communicate a particular directive meaning. The corpus-based study of directive speech acts reported in the previous chapter revealed clear tendencies for each directive to favour different configurations of base constructions and linguistic strategies, thus paving the way for a constructional account of speech acts and also providing useful information for the purpose of teaching directives to EFL learners. The following activities illustrate possible ways in which the know-how of directives included in our cognitive pedagogical grammar can be implemented in the teaching practice and in the design of EFL textbooks. Activities 8–14 include consciousness-raising, knowledge-development, and productive-skills tasks in a variety of formats, including role-playing activities, structured conversations, and discourse-completion tests, among others (see Bardovi-Harlig & Mahan-Taylor (2003,) Ishihara & Cohen (2010), Ishihara & Maeda (2010) and Tatsuki & Houck (2010) for applications of this type of activities to the teaching of pragmatics).

5.2 Teaching the Know-How of Directives

One relevant aspect of speech act constructions, as revealed in Chapter 2 (Section 2.5.5), is their metonymic nature. Directive speech acts are multifaceted, complex concepts. This makes it difficult, hardly economical, and often communicatively unnecessary for their linguistic forms to reflect all the attributes and variables that conform to their semantics. Base constructions and linguistic strategies, therefore, often activate the most central and/or contextually relevant elements of the directive speech act that needs to be communicated. Activity 8 aims at raising the students' awareness of this fact.

Activity 8

Read the following examples of requests. Each of them makes use of a base construction and several linguistic strategies that metonymically activate some key elements of the act of requesting. For each of the examples, note down which pieces of knowledge included in the know-what of requests (short version included in Table 5.2) are being metonymically activated. The underlined words are hints that can help you find the answers.

Table 5.2 *The know-what of requests (short version)*

Requests are directive speech acts in which a speaker asks the hearer(s) to carry out an action. When someone requests someone else to do something, they communicate the following:
'I want you to do something because it is beneficial to me or to someone that I also want to benefit from the action. I know it is costly to you, and I do not have the necessary power to impose the action on you. I acknowledge your freedom to comply or to opt out.'
What you need to bear in mind in order to perform a successful request:
- Prototypically, the requested action benefits the speaker, but more peripheral instances of requests may be intended to benefit the hearer, a third party, or a combination of the former.
- Requests stem from a need or a desire on the part of the speaker, who does not have the necessary social power to impose his will on the hearer and who is, therefore, aware of the fact that he may need to overcome some obstacles in order to get the hearer to comply with his wish.
- Among the obstacles to overcome, there is the willingness and ability of the hearer to carry out the proposed action, the cost of the action, and the freedom of the hearer to carry out the action or not.
- To overcome the aforementioned obstacles, prototypical requests are polite, they attempt to minimise the cost of the proposed action, and they offer freedom to the hearer to refuse to do as told.

(5.21) # After such a wholesome adventure, Denali and I agreed to postpone work till Saturday (when we would for sure do it, seriously). '**Can you** wake **me** up early tomorrow when you head to the dining hall?' she **requested**. # 'If I can wake up, sure,' I promised, 'And will you wake me up if I don't wake you up?' # (iWeb)

(5.22) # I create the weekly newsletters for his website and also help him increase his subscribers. He **requested** today '**I want** you to **please** come up with a way to encourage subscribers to cancel, within the first three sentences of the newsletter.' (iWeb)

(5.23) # 'So Bella, **tell us a little bit** about yourself.' He **requested** politely. I pulled my face out of Edward's chest and shrugged. # 'What is there to tell?' I questioned # (iWeb)

(5.24) # '**Will you** do **me** the favour, Octavie,' **requested** the judge **in the courteous tone** which he never abandoned, 'to remove that veil which you wear. It seems out of harmony, someway, with the beauty and promise of the day.' # (iWeb)

Activity 8 will make students cognizant of the fact that the base constructions used in the examples correspond to key elements of the semantics of requests. The IMPERATIVE base construction selects the hearer as the agent of the proposed action, the CAN YOU DO X? and WILL YOU DO X? constructions refer to some of the obstacles that may prevent the requestive force from moving the hearer into action (i.e. the hearer's lack of ability or willingness to comply), and the I WANT YOU TO DO X base construction reflects the fact that the speaker has a strong desire that the proposed action is carried out. In addition, several linguistic strategies combine with these base strategies to metonymically activate further elements of the semantics of requests. Thus, in example (5.21), the pronoun *me* and the interrogative intonation activate the beneficiary of the action (i.e. the speaker) and the optionality (i.e. freedom) that requests offer hearers to decide whether to comply with the action or not, respectively. In example (5.22), the adverb *please* makes explicit one of the central features of requesting: the use of politeness as a persuasive strategy to avoid imposition and to gain the hearer's compliance. In example (5.23), the pronoun *us* makes manifest who is to be the beneficiary of the action, and the hedging expression *a little bit* minimises the cost of the action. Finally, in example (5.24), the courteous tone activates the lack of imposition and politeness characterises prototypical requests. By making

5.2 Teaching the Know-How of Directives

explicit some of the central semantic aspects of requesting through the flexible combination of base constructions and linguistic strategies, the expressions in examples (5.21)–(5.24) manage to metonymically activate the act of requesting as a whole.

The metonymical nature of speech acts also offers speakers the possibility of producing directives with different degrees of explicitness, as required by the context and their communicative intentions. Activity 9 illustrates this.

Activity 9

Example (5.25) makes use of the IMPERATIVE base construction, which presents the hearer(s) as the agent of the proposed action. This makes it compatible with any type of directive (e.g. order, request, advice, begging, suggestion, warning), since they all share the aforementioned goal. Can you think of a context in which example (5.25) would be understood straightforwardly as an order? Think of the type of person who is licensed to give orders and of the people who are likely to receive them. Then, fill in the gaps below to create a context in which the IMPERATIVE base construction can be understood as an order.

(5.25) […] When all men see it, the whole world will be at peace. # '*Go ahead!*' the _____ ordered loudly to his _____. # They did not have long to wait. A great golden cauldron, big enough to boil an ox, was set outside the court. (iWeb)

In the absence of a rich informative context like the one you have created above, the IMPERATIVE base construction could have been understood as any other directive act. Is it possible to activate linguistically the semantic features that were activated contextually in example (5.25) (i.e. the existence of a powerful speaker who can impose his will on the hearer(s))? Look at the following examples, which have been isolated from their context, and choose the ones that can be straightforwardly understood as orders. Which one is a better example of an order? Can you rate the examples from (5.26) to (5.30) according to how good an instance of order they are (1 = worst instance of order, 5 = best instance of order)?. Then reflect on the linguistic strategies that allow their interpretation as such and explain which aspects of the semantics of ordering they activate explicitly (e.g. powerful speaker, lack of optionality for the hearer, imposition, etc.).

(5.26) Go ahead, if you please.
(5.27) Go ahead!!! NOW!
(5.28) Private Johnson, go ahead at once!!!

(5.29) Go ahead, and you'll eventually find what you are looking for.
(5.30) Go ahead, you moron!

The aim of this activity is to make students aware of the fact that illocutionary constructions are fluid. Their base constructions can be combined with a varied number of linguistic strategies to metonymically activate a smaller or larger number of semantic attributes of the directive speech act that needs to be communicated, thus rendering instances of speech acts with different levels of explicitness. If the context is rich and provides the necessary information about participants, as is the case with example (5.25), then a bare base construction is enough to convey the order message. In the absence of a context (examples (5.26)–(5.30)), speakers will rely for their interpretation on the linguistic strategies that accompany the base construction. Students will realise that example (5.28) is a highly explicit instance of order, because the vocative makes explicit the power asymmetry between the participants, and the expression of immediateness (i.e. *at once*) and the impositive intonation activate the lack of freedom of the hearer to refuse to do as told. A powerful speaker, an impositive nature, and the lack of optionality on the part of the hearer are central features of ordering, hence the explicitness of example (5.28). Example (5.27) does not make explicit the asymmetrical power of the participants, but this can be inferred from the impositive tone and the use of the expression of immediateness (i.e. *Now!*), since these are generally used by powerful speakers. The degree of explicitness of this example as an order is still fairly high. Likewise, example (5.30) makes use of a vocative that downgrades the hearer, which helps to present the speaker as somehow (at least psychologically) more powerful than the hearer. Together with the impositive intonation, this example manages to convey an order interpretation fairly easily but to a lesser extent than the two previous examples. Examples (5.26) and (5.29), on the contrary, do not make any of the features of ordering explicit. Example (5.26) increases the optionality of the hearer (i.e. *if you please*), which favours a request interpretation. Example (5.29) adds an explanation of the benefit that the hearer will gain by complying with the imperative, which points to its interpretation as a piece of advice.

Activity 10 represents a knowledge-development activity connected to the versatility of base constructions to communicate different directive speech acts unambiguously when combined with the right linguistic strategies.

Activity 10

The base construction YOU HAVE TO DO X has traditionally been connected with orders. A corpus-based study of directives (see Chapter 4) has shown that it is also used to convey some other directives, in which a certain degree of imposition is necessary and compatible with the goal of the act. Look at the following examples and decide which directive speech act is being communicated. Fill in the gaps with the appropriate performative verb (e.g. warned, advised, ordered, requested, etc.). The linguistic strategies that guide the interpretation have been underlined to serve as hints.

(5.31) # 'You know, I didn't like sweet, Woman.' He replied her with annoyed look. # *'You have to taste before complain. Eat!* **Now!***'* she _____ him. # 'Bossy witch!' he complained but opened his mouth (iWeb)

(5.32) # *'***PLEASE. Promise** *me, Gabriel,'* Corrine had _____ him in the hospice, thin and wasted from the cancer that was killing her. *'You have to* ***promise****.'* # (iWeb)

(5.33) # Here is Grey's _____ on how **to get the best deal on your next new car.** # [...] 1. Know what you want. It will take some time to research which new car fits your buying checklist and your budget. *'You have to know what you want and be smart about it,'* Grey _____ (iWeb)

(5.34) # 'Everything is viral ... immediate ... and real-time.' # 'It's an extraordinary way to become a global business and have a global relevance and voice. *But you have to be cautious and thoughtful about it,'* he _____. *'***People don't always read things the way they are intended.***'* # '**Starbucks recently found itself defending and then abandoning a campaign to bring awareness to promote discussion of racial issues. Baristas were encouraged to write 'Race Together' on cups.**' # (iWeb)

After completing this activity, students will realise that the impositive flavour of the YOU HAVE TO DO X base construction fares well with orders (example (5.31)), beggings (example (5.32)), advice acts (example (5.33)), and warnings (example (5.34)). The impositive nature of orders emerges from a power asymmetry between the participants. Beggings also make use of imposition in combination with politeness and insistence. As shown in Chapter 4 (Section 4.3.1) this is due to the fact that speakers uttering a begging have a high desire to achieve their goal, which explains their use of impositive formulae that may be effective in moving the hearer into action. The imposition, however, is simultaneously softened with politeness strategies due to the fact that speakers uttering beggings do not have the necessary power to actually impose on the hearer. In this case, the use of impositive base constructions is just a means of letting the hearer know how important it is for the speaker that the action is carried out. As regards advice acts and warnings, the use of impositive formulae is licensed by the fact that these acts seek a benefit for the hearer. Therefore, imposition is not perceived as face-threatening, but rather as an expression of concern for the hearer, whom the speaker wants to benefit from his knowledge and from carrying out the proposed action.

This activity could be complemented with the following question to help students develop their knowledge about this construction further:

> *It is an interesting fact that the YOU HAVE TO DO X base construction has not been found at work in the expression of requests and suggestions. Can you think of which aspects of the semantics (i.e. know-what) of these two directives make this base construction not useful in these cases? To reason your answers, compare the know-what of requests and suggestions with that of beggings in relation to the speaker's degree of willingness that the proposed action is carried out. Also compare requests and suggestions with advice acts and warnings regarding the attribute of cost–benefit (i.e. who is to benefit from the proposed action). The know-what tables of each of these directives can be found in Chapter 4.*

By comparing the attributes of speaker's willingness and cost–benefit in the directives under consideration, students will realise that speakers uttering requests and suggestions do not have such a high degree of willingness for the action to be performed as is the case with beggings. Also, they will see that requests and suggestions seek the benefit of the speaker, while advice acts and warnings aim to benefit the hearer. When the goal is to benefit some else, the use of imposition is not felt as impolite as when the benefit is for oneself. Hence the aforementioned compatibility of beggings, advice acts, and warnings with the notion of imposition communicated by the YOU HAVE TO DO X base construction is not shared by requests and suggestions.

Once the metonymic and fluid nature of directive constructions has been learned, students can be asked to practise the recognition and production of directive speech acts adapted to a variety of contexts. For this purpose, they should have at hand the know-what descriptions and the sets of base constructions and linguistic strategies for each directive speech act reported in Chapter 4. EFL teachers and textbook designers can choose whether to use full versions of them or to divide them into modified shorter versions

5.2 Teaching the Know-How of Directives

that focus on different constructions or fit the needs of particular contexts. Activities 11 and 12 illustrate how this can be done.

Activity 11

All directives are sensitive to contextual and social factors, and their forms may change accordingly. Requests are one type of directive that is specially affected by these variables. Read the section of the know-what of requests that summarises possible interactions with contextual and social dimensions of their realisation (see Table 5.3; full version in Chapter 4, Section 4.2.1).

After reading and commenting on the interactions included in the know-what of requests, look at the contexts below and choose the most appropriate realisation of the CAN YOU DO X? base construction. Underline and comment on the linguistic strategies that have been added to the base construction. Afterwards, say which interactions between the attributes of requesting and the contextual/social variables are being highlighted by them.

Context 1. *You are with your brother or sister and need to borrow a dictionary to do your homework. How would you request it from your sibling using the CAN YOU DO X? base construction. Choose one of the following options:*

a. *Can you lend me your dictionary?*
b. *If you don't mind, could you please lend me your dictionary?*

Context 2. *You want to take your father's car to take your boyfriend to the prom. This is quite a costly favour to ask since your father is very keen on his car and systematically refuses to let other people drive it. Which of the two versions of the CAN YOU DO X? base construction below do you think could be more successful in helping you achieve your goal?*

Table 5.3 *The know-what of requests (interactions between attributes and variables)*

Interactions between cost of the action, politeness, optionality, and minimisation of cost.
The higher the cost of the action, the higher the need to be polite, to acknowledge the freedom of the hearer to refuse, and/or to minimise the cost of the action.

Interactions between politeness, formality, and social distance.
You can perform requests in all contexts regardless of their formality, and they can be directed to hearers regardless of the social distance that separates them from the speaker. Nevertheless, you should be aware that the higher the formality of the context or the larger the social distance between the participants, the politer the request will need to be to secure compliance. Remember that politeness can also be achieved indirectly by means of minimising the cost of the action and/or increasing the optionality of the hearer to do as told.

---

a. *Dad, could you lend me your car to take Paul to the prom? Just once, just tonight?*
b. *Can you please lend me your car to take Paul to the prom?*

Context 3. *You ask a stranger for the time. Which realisation of the CAN YOU DO X? base construction seems more appropriate:*

a. *Sir, can you tell me the time?*
b. *Sir, could you tell me the time, please?*

Activity 11 teaches students that small social distances do not require high amounts of politeness (context 1), except when the cost of the requested action is high (context 2), which asks for higher politeness (i.e. modal in the past) and minimisation of cost (i.e. *Just once? Just tonight?*) strategies. On the contrary, large social distances (context 3) demand higher doses of politeness (i.e. vocative signalling the hearer's superiority, modal in the past, explicit politeness marker *please*), independently of the cost of the proposed action, to secure compliance.

Activity 12

Use the linguistic realisation procedures included in Table 5.4 to adapt the IMPERATIVE base construction for requests to the communicative needs of the different contexts given below.

Context 1. *You are sitting next to your classmate in the library. The book you need is by his side. Request the book of him. Take into account the social distance variable in your choice of linguistic strategies.*

Context 2. *You are talking to the mayor of your city during an informal meeting between local politicians and citizens. You want to ask her to devote more resources to keeping the city clean. How would you request it using the IMPERATIVE base construction? Take into account the power asymmetry between you and your interlocutor, but also bear in mind that the meeting is an informal one.*

Context 3. *You need to ask your best friend to babysit your kids on Friday night so that you can go out with your new date. This is a big and costly favour to ask from your friend, since your kids are rather naughty, and your friend does not like kids so much. Which linguistic strategies would you add to the IMPERATIVE base construction taking into account the costly nature of this request?*

5.2 Teaching the Know-How of Directives

Table 5.4 *Linguistic realisation procedures for combination with request base constructions*

EXPRESSIONS OF POLITENESS	*please, kindly, use of modals in past tense*
EXPRESSIONS OF OPTIONALITY	*if you please, if you will, if possible, if you can, question tags (can you?, will you?)*
EXPRESSIONS OF SOCIAL CLOSENESS	*diminutives, endearment terms, vocatives signalling social closeness*
EXPRESSIONS OF MINIMISATION OF COST	*a (little) bit, just, a second, a moment*
EXPRESSIONS PRAISING THE HEARER or SIGNALLING HIS SUPERIORITY	*vocatives (sir, madam, etc.)*

Activity 12 is a production-development task that prompts students to experiment with the different linguistic strategies that can be combined with the IMPERATIVE base construction to render requests with varied degrees of politeness, optionality, and/or minimisation of cost as required by contextual needs. Thus, context 1, which displays a small social distance between participants, does not ask for higher dose of politeness and a bare imperative or an imperative with a vocative signalling the social closeness between participants suits the context well (e.g. *Buddy, pass the book*). In context 2, the informal context licenses the use of the IMPERATIVE base construction, but the power asymmetry between the participants asks for some markers of optionality and politeness (e.g. *If possible, devote some more resources to keep the city clean, please*). Finally, in context 3, the costly nature of the request requires of minimisation of cost and the use of politeness to gain the hearer's compliance (e.g. *Please, babysit for me on Friday. Just this once!*).

As detailed in Chapter 4, while some directives like orders, and to a lesser extent requests and suggestions, display constructions whose scope does not generally go beyond the sentence level; others, like beggings, advice acts, and warnings often make use of suprasentential configurations in their expression. Their base constructions are thus combined with one or more clauses or sentences, either in the same or different conversational turns, in order to activate the relevant semantic features of the directive act. Activity 13 offers practice on this issue in relation to the act of begging.

Activity 13

The linguistic realisation of the act of begging often involves the combination of a base construction (e.g. IMPERATIVE, CAN YOU DO X?, etc.) and several other linguistic strategies, which involve the use of additional clauses (e.g. reason, purpose) and sentences realising further speech acts (e.g. promising, negotiating). Look at the examples of begging below and identify for each of them the base construction and the additional linguistic strategies. Then, explain which aspects of the meaning of beggings do each of them help to activate.

(5.35) # Given Jacob's history with hobbies, it was no surprise that Jacob's father was reluctant to buy him a magician's kit for his birthday. 'Geez, Jacob … You sure you wouldn't rather I got you more guitar lessons?' He suggested. Jacob was insistent. *'Dad, you've got to get me the magician's kit. This time I'll stick with it for real. I promise! Come on, Dad,'* Jacob **begged**. Jacob's father sighed and then replied, 'Oh, I don't know, Jacob. Things are awfully tight right now.' (iWeb)

(5.36) I took the game out of my pocket and tried to give it back to him, but he wouldn't even look at me. […] I didn't know how bad it was going to be, but I knew it was going to be really bad. *'Please don't call the police!'* I **begged**. *'It was only one little thing and I promise I'll never ever do it again!'* (iWeb)

(5.37) # 'Will you come tomorrow and pick me up? Bring Theo so he can see my mum?' I asked hopefully. My mum would be upset if she didn't get to see her grandson too. # He groaned loudly. *'Can't you just buy a return ticket?'* # *'Finn, please?'* I begged. *'My mum would love to see you two.'* That wasn't strictly true, she would probably rather not see Finn. *'Please?'* (iWeb)

After completing this activity, students will realise that the base constructions (i.e. YOU'VE GOT TO DO X, IMPERATIVE, and CAN'T YOU DO X?, respectively) are used to specify the actions that the speakers want the hearers to carry out. Additionally, reason clauses/sentences (i.e. *My mum would love to see you two, It was only a little thing*) and promise acts (i.e. *I'll promise I'll never do it again*) are strategies aimed at insisting and negotiating with the hearer to gain his compliance. Both of them are motivated by some of the key semantic features of beggings. The use of insistence reveals the high degree to which speakers uttering beggings want the proposed action to be carried out. The need for negotiation strategies, in turn, shows that the speaker does not have the necessary power to impose his will, which leads him to find other ways to achieve his goal.

Advice and warning acts also make use of suprasentential units to put across their message. In Activity 14, students are asked to put this specific aspect of the production of directive constructions into practice within the setting of a role play game. More specifically, students are asked to practise the production of warnings by taking specific roles in hypothetical scenarios and interacting with their peers.

Activity 14

Look at the following example of warning:

'*Watch out! Quicksand!*' [...] Pickett was in the lead walking along the sandy bank of a small stream when suddenly his feet disappeared into the sand. '*It's soft here! Stay back!*' he **warned** his friend (iWeb)

As the example illustrates, warnings are complex speech acts that involve a set of at least three illocutionary acts (Carstens, 2002: 192): an alert (e.g. Beware!, Careful!, Watch out!), an informative act (i.e. a statement of the hazard and/ or consequences of failure to comply: Quicksand! ... It's soft here!), and an instruction about what to do or not to do to avoid the hazard (i.e. Stay back!). The order in which these elements of warning are expressed in real situations need not be the one in the example above. If the harm or danger is imminent, the instruction may be given before the informative act. They may even appear in different conversational turns. Also take into account that the informative act may be omitted if the negative state of affairs menacing the hearer is obvious from the context.

Practise giving explicit warnings like the one above in the following situations. For each of them consider carefully whether your warning should include an alert, an informative act, and an instruction, or whether some of these elements of warning can/should be omitted in the context under consideration. Also think about which should be the correct order of these elements in each context.

Context 1. *You are strolling with your friend. He is crossing the street without noticing that a car is coming at full speed towards him.*

Context 2. *You are a member of the advisory board of an important business company. You are discussing the course of actions to be taken to help improve the results of the company. You have confidential information that attempting* *to expand exports to other countries at this moment is too risky. You express this information in the form of a warning to the rest of the members of the advisory board. Would the alert element be necessary in this particular interaction? Would you start you warning with an informative act or with the instruction?*

Students should come to the conclusion that the imminent danger in context 1, and the fact that such danger and its consequences are already obvious from the context, make the informative act unnecessary. The speaker uttering a warning in this context would most probably just give an alert (i.e. *Watch out!!*) and/or an instruction (i.e. *Stop!!*).

Context 2 represents a more formal context, and the danger involved is not imminent. An alert would probably feel too informal in this situation, and it would be more appropriate to simply offer an informative act justifying the subsequent instruction.

5.3 Teaching Cross-Cultural and Cross-Linguistic Issues of Directives

Different languages have developed different constructions for the expression of directive speech acts, and sometimes, even when the same constructions exist in L1 and L2, each of them favours the use of particular linguistic configurations for the production of the same act. As argued in contemporary contrastive studies this is a potential source of difficulties for learners of a second language (Hijazo-Gascón, Cadierno & Ibarretxe-Antuñano, 2016; Ruiz de Mendoza & Agustin, 2016). As Holme (2009) has noted, lack of awareness of these constructional mismatches may result in transfer effects and faulty representations, leading the EFL learner to make errors based on the use of L1 forms and meanings in L2.

Taking a contrastive approach to the teaching of constructions to EFL students has, therefore, been recently advocated by researchers within the cognitive linguistics paradigm (Römer, O'Donnell & Ellis, 2014, Ruiz de Mendoza & Agustin, 2016). As De Knop and De Rycker (2008: 2) rightly argue, this contrastive approach may serve 'the purpose of preparing teaching materials and exploiting these in L2/FL instruction' with the aim of helping students avoid mistakes stemming from mismatches between the semantics, pragmatics, and formal features between two languages. Recent experimental studies have also provided evidence on the psychological validity of constructions for EFL students, as well as the benefits that can be obtained from teaching practices and materials based on the explicit instruction of constructional aspects of language (Holme, 2010; Baicchi, 2016; Sung & Yang, 2016).

The cognitive pedagogical grammar of directive speech acts offered in Chapter 4 provides corpus-based information on the constructional mismatches that exist in the production of directive speech acts in Spanish and English. Activities 15–21 exploit the aforementioned data for teaching purposes.

Activity 15

Consider the contexts of situation in Table 5.5 and carry out the following fieldwork. First read the contexts to at least ten people of your choice, who should be speakers of your native language, and ask them to complete the gaps with a directive speech act (e.g. order, request, suggestion, warning, begging, or advice act).

Then compare the Spanish constructions provided by your informants to the ones that would be used in English in the same contexts (helping yourselves with the information included in the know-what and know-how tables for suggestions in Chapter 4, Sections 4.4.1 and 4.4.2) and discuss the similarities and differences.

Comparing the L1 and L2 directive constructions that are used to fill in the gaps in Activity 15 will lead students to realise that there are L1 constructions that are not possible in L2, such as the use of questions in the present tense as means of suggestions (e.g. ¿Vamos a la discoteca? *Do we go to the disco?). The activity will also offer students a chance to reflect on the fact that unsolicited advice to people who have a higher social status (context 2) is considered a face-threatening act in English and therefore requires of more indirect constructions than in Spanish. Context 3 will

Table 5.5 *Fieldwork, comparison, and discussion task*

Context 1. You are with your friends planning what to do on Friday night. You suggest going to the disco: _____

Context 2. Your boss is going through a rough phase in his life. You would like to give him a good piece of advice that helps him solve his problems. You say: _____

Context 3. Your see that your best friend is going to make a big mistake at work. You want to warn him and say: _____

most probably be filled in with performative expressions in Spanish (e.g. *Be warned that ...; I warn you that ...*), but not in English. Students will be taught that this is connected to the fact that the act of warning (like that of advising) is considered an act of *confianza* and social closeness in Spanish. Hence, the directness of a performative is not perceived as an imposition in the Spanish culture.

Activity 16

¿ME HACES X?, as in ¿Me pasas la sal? (*Do you pass me the salt?), is one of the most productive request constructions in Spanish. However, direct translation of this construction into English (*DO YOU DO ME X?) is not acceptable. Choose those English request constructions in Table 5.6 that can

Table 5.6 *Base constructions for requests in English*

IMPERATIVE
CAN YOU DO X?
COULD YOU DO X?
I WOULD LIKE X
I WOULD LIKE YOU TO DO X
I WISH X
I WISH YOU TO DO X
IF YOU WILL DO X
WILL YOU DO X?
WOULD YOU DO X?
DO YOU HAVE X?
HAVE YOU GOT X?
CAN WE NOT DO X?
COULD WE NOT DO X?
MAY YOU DO X?
I WANT YOU TO DO X
I NEED YOU TO DO X
IT'S TIME FOR YOU TO DO X
IT WOULD BE GOOD IF YOU COULD DO X
YOU THINK YOU COULD DO X
WOULD YOU MIND DOING X?
ANY CHANCE YOU COULD DO X?
I DIRECT THAT YOU SHALL DO X
I ASK YOU TO DO X
I ASK THAT YOU DO X
YOU ARE REQUESTED TO DO X

5.3 Teaching Cross-Linguistic Issues of Directives

be used to convey a similar requestive meaning in English. Take into account that the constructions that you choose should be similar in terms of politeness, optionality, etc., and appropriate to be used in similar contexts.

After considering the politeness and optionality offered by the ¿ME HACES X? construction in Spanish, EFL students should come to the conclusion that the most similar English constructions would be CAN YOU DO X (FOR ME)? and WILL YOU DO X (FOR ME)?

Activity 17 encourages the use of free online corpora to involve students in consciousness-raising tasks about constructional differences in the production of requests between English and Spanish. The use of corpus-based real language data for developing EFL teaching materials has been strongly advocated as a means of avoiding the already amply documented mismatches between real language and the one used in textbooks (Cohen & Ishihara, 2013; Bardovi-Harlig, Mossman & Vellenga, 2014a). This activity goes one step further, teaching advanced EFL students how to look for real language data in free online corpora and then guiding them in the analysis of those data to assess the productivity of a particular construction in L1 and L2.

Activity 17

The CAN YOU DO X (FOR ME)? base construction for requests in English has a counterpart in Spanish (i.e. ¿(ME)PUEDES HACER X?). However, this construction is much more frequent and productive in one of these two languages. Use the iWeb and the Corpes XXI free online corpora for English and Spanish, respectively, to make a simple search for these two constructions in collocation with the performative verbs 'requested' and 'pidió', respectively. Which of the two languages makes a more extensive use of this construction? Confirm your findings by checking the know-how section on requests in the cognitive pedagogical grammar (Chapter 4, Section 4.2.2).

Follow-up question: Which other similar constructions can be used in Spanish instead of ¿ME PUEDES HACER X? to convey a similar meaning? Look at Table 5.7, which lists the most common request base constructions in Spanish, and choose those that may be used in similar contexts.

The students' searches in the suggested corpora will make them realise that the CAN YOU DO X? base construction is much more productive

Table 5.7 *Base constructions for requests in Spanish*

¿(ME) PODRÍAS HACER X?
¿TIENES X?
(YO) TE PIDO QUE HAGAS X
(LO QUE) YO NECESITO ES QUE HAGAS X
¿NO PODRÍAS/PODRÍAMOS HACER X?
IMPERATIVE
¿(ME) PUEDES HACER X?
ME GUSTARÍA X
ME GUSTARÍA QUE TÚ HAGAS X
ESPERO X
ESPERO QUE HAGAS X
QUIERO QUE HAGAS X
¿ME HACES X?
¿ME HARÍAS X?

than its Spanish counterpart ¿ME PUEDES HACER X? With the help of their teachers they should also come to the conclusion that Spanish has alternative constructions that can be used in similar contexts (e.g. ¿ME HACES/HARÍAS X?).

As noted by Taguchi (2011), together with corpus-based activities, technology has brought exciting new venues for materials and formats used in pragmatic teaching. When dealing with speech acts, multimedia teaching materials offer an ideal context in which to learn key pragmatic issues, since they provide students with the rich socio-cultural setting that surrounds the act in a natural, catching, and entertaining manner (for a review of Web sites on the use of multimedia in L2 pragmatics, see Cohen (2008)). This is especially useful in teaching contrastive aspects of speech acts. Textbook designers can create specific multimedia materials, but EFL teachers can also use clips of real movies and TV series for these purposes. Activity 18 suggests a simple way of taking advantage of real multimedia materials to create a consciousness-raising exercise that focuses on the differences between the constructional realisations of speech acts in L1 and L2.

Activity 18

Watch an episode of the well-known TV series Friends *and note down all instances of directives produced by their protagonists. Then translate the directives literally into your own native language. Would you use the same constructions in your native language? Are there any constructions that do not exist in your own language? Which ones would you use to make those acts sound natural in your language and in the contexts in which they have been used in the TV show?*

5.3 Teaching Cross-Linguistic Issues of Directives

Activity 18 provides students with real contexts and real L2 constructions for the expression of directive acts. The task of translating them into their own native language will help them become aware of possible mismatches both in the form and function of those speech acts. They will realise, for example, that in Spanish it is more common to use direct, unmitigated advice acts, while English favours more indirect forms to avoid imposition. As noted in Chapter 4 (Section 4.5.1), advice acts in Spanish are considered acts of *confianza,* and this licenses the use of more direct formulae in their expression. Activity 19 puts forward a sample exercise that allows students to put this knowledge into practice in a production-development task.

Activity 19

Consider the contexts described below and decide which linguistic formulae you would use to give advice in your own language. Then, think of which constructions and linguistic strategies would be appropriate in English. You can choose them from Table 5.8, which includes some of the most common advice constructions in English. Before doing the exercise and in order to make the appropriate choices, read again the information included in the know-what

Table 5.8 *Base constructions for advice acts in English*

IMPERATIVE
CONDITIONALS
IF I WERE YOU, I WOULD DO X
DECLARATIVE (EVALUATIVE) SENTENCE
E.G. DOING X IS/CAN BE GOOD, IT WOULD BE GOOD/USEFUL TO DO X, YOU WOULD DO WELL TO DO X, I THINK IT IS IMPORTANT TO DO X
YOU NEED TO DO X
DECLARATIVE SENTENCE (REASON) + CO-ORDINATING CONJUNCTION (SO)
E.G. SO YOU SHOULD DO X, SO DOING X IS IMPORTANT, SO IT'S BEST TO DO X
YOU/WE SHOULD DO X
PERFORMATIVE VERBS
E.G. YOU ARE ADVISED TO DO X, I RECOMMEND THAT YOU DO X, I ENCOURAGE/URGE YOU TO DO X
YOU HAVE TO DO X
I WANT YOU TO DO X
YOU'D BETTER DO X
YOU/WE MUST DO X
YOU CAN DO X
WHY DON'T YOU DO X?

Table 5.9 *The know-what of advice acts (interactions with socio-contextual variables)*

- If the piece of advice benefits not only the hearer but also you and/or a third party, you do not need to respect the freedom of the hearer so much, and it is acceptable to make your advice a bit more compelling through the use of politeness markers that make the hearer aware of the fact that his compliance is socially expected.
- If you are less powerful than the hearer (social/institutional power), you are expected to soften your advice by increasing its indirectness and ultimately the politeness of your act.
- If you are socially close to the hearer, you are likely to be more emotionally involved, you will want him to follow your advice, and you will need to make use of politeness to achieve his compliance.

of advice acts (a modified short version is provided in Table 5.9). You should also take into account the fact that while advice acts are considered acts of high confianza *and social closeness within the Spanish culture, English users tend to understand them as potentially face-threatening acts. This favours the use of direct explicit advising in Spanish (i.e. imperatives, performatives), as opposed to the use of more indirect constructions in English (i.e. IF I WERE YOU, I WOULD DO X).*

Context 1. *Your child starts acting up in the middle of the street. He is throwing a tantrum and screaming. A stranger stops by and tries to help by giving advice on how to handle the situation.*

Context 2. *Your child starts acting up in the middle of the street. He is throwing a tantrum and screaming. Your mother is with you and tries to help by giving advice on how to handle the situation.*

Context 3. *Your child starts acting up in the middle of the rehearsal of a school performance. He is throwing a tantrum and screaming and he is spoiling the rehearsal. Your child's teacher tries to help by giving advice on how to handle the situation.*

By completing this activity students will learn that Spanish speakers could use a direct advice in the three situations without risking threatening the hearers' social face (e.g. IMPERATIVE base construction, performative verbs). It should also become apparent that in English context 1 would require a more tentative advice construction due to the social distance that exists between the participants (i.e. IF I WERE YOU, I'D DO X, YOU'D

5.3 Teaching Cross-Linguistic Issues of Directives

BETTER DO X, etc.). The speaker in context 2 (i.e. the hearer's mother) is expected to be more emotionally involved because of her social closeness with the hearer, and this will lead her to make use of polite realisation procedures as a strategy to get the hearer to comply with her advice (e.g. Honey, please, DO X, YOU HAVE TO DO X, YOU NEED TO DO X). Finally, in context 3, the social distance between the speakers asks for the use of indirect advice constructions. Additionally, since the beneficiary of the advice is not just the hearer but also the teacher himself and the rest of the children taking part in the rehearsal, the teacher is likely to make use of politeness strategies to inform the hearer that compliance is socially expected (e.g. IT WOULD BE GOOD / USEFUL TO DO X, PLEASE, I THINK IT'S IMPORTANT TO DO X).

Discourse-completion tasks can also be a useful classroom activity to develop students' ability to produce context-appropriate speech acts (Eslami-Rasekh, 2005; Limberg, 2015). In this connection, Activity 20 prompts students to elicit responses that include suggestions and beggings.

Activity 20

Form small groups of three or four students and work on the discourse-completion task provided in Table 5.10. Work together to complete the missing directive(s). In doing this, help yourselves by checking the information included in the know-what and know-how of the directives involves (see the corresponding tables in Chapter 4). Share your answers with the rest of the groups and discuss their appropriateness. Your discussion should make use of arguments that reflect an understanding of the information provided in the know-what and know-how of suggestions and beggings, respectively. Finally, choose the most appropriate

Table 5.10 *Discourse-completion task*

SUGGESTIONS & BEGGINGS: DISCOURSE-COMPLETION TASK
Context and instructions: You are making plans for the weekend with your friends. You would like to attend a new arts exhibition in London. Make a suggestion to visit the exhibition. You: _____
Your friends start suggesting other activities. They do not seem to be very excited about the exhibition. However, you really want to visit it because you brother's paintings are part of it. Let your friends know how badly you want to attend the exhibition by begging them to go. You: _____

proposals and act them out for the class. Debate whether the same constructions would have been used by native speakers of English. Do you think that your choices have been influenced by your L1 knowledge about these particular speech acts?

This activity asks students to produce suggestions and beggings that are adjusted to a specific informal context and that are uttered by participants who are socially close to each other. The production-development task is guided by the information included in the cognitive pedagogical grammar (know-what and know-how) of the directive acts involved. The ensuing discussion serves the purpose of making students reflect on the adequacy of the different constructions chosen by each group. By comparing their proposals and discussing and assessing their appropriateness in the context under consideration, students should become aware of negative pragmatic transfers they may be making from their own L1 (Limberg, 2015). The same objective of developing the students' L2 pragmatic competence can be achieved by offering them activities that ask them to analyse and repair errors in the expression of speech acts within a given context. Activity 21 illustrates this.

Activity 21

Read and analyse the directives in Table 5.11. Then decide whether (1) the directive chosen by the speaker is the one that best fits the situation, and (2) if it has been carried out appropriately in the context under consideration. If not, provide an alternative. If needed, check out the information included in the know-what and know-how for each directive in Chapter 4.

Discuss your corrections with the rest of the class and act out the pragmatically appropriate version(s).

Follow-up question: compare the directives chosen to what you would say in your own language. Would you use the same amount of politeness? Would you be more or less direct than the speakers in the above contexts? Discuss and explain the differences that you perceive between the constructions used in English and those that would be used in your native language.

Repairing activities of this kind (adapted from Limberg, 2015) help to develop students' awareness of key semantic, socio-cultural, and linguistic/

5.3 Teaching Cross-Linguistic Issues of Directives

Table 5.11 *Repair and comparison task*

DIRECTIVES: ANALYSE, REPAIR, AND COMPARE TASK
Context 1. Two friends have been playing together the whole afternoon. It is time to go home, and Pete's mother has asked them to put things away before leaving. Pete orders his friend to put things away for him: 'Dave, put the PlayStation away in its shelf. Now!'
Context 2. You need a kidney transplant. Your sister is the only person compatible with you. You need to ask her to donate one of her kidneys to you. You say: 'Ann, you know I need a transplant. You are the only compatible relative. Would it be possible for you to consider donating a kidney to me?'
Context 3. You are walking along the street with one of your colleagues. You see a pot about to fall from one window in the building ahead of you that may fall right on your colleague's head. You warn him of the danger: 'John, stop! That pot is about to fall.'
Context 4. You are attending the first board meeting in your new company. There is an ongoing discussing about the new measures that need to be taken to improve revenues. You want to share a suggestion with the rest of the board members: 'Cut down the prices, and the sales will go up. That's what needs to be done, mates!'.
Context 5. Your daughter is about to break a long-term relationship with her boyfriend and comes to you for advice on what to do. She specifically asks for your advice, and you tell her the following: 'Honey, the sooner the better. Do it today and be straightforward!'

constructional aspects of directive speech acts. They also lead them to put the acquired knowledge into practice by having to propose correct alternatives, thus developing their competence in the production of L2 directives. The follow-up question leads them to reflect on potential mismatches with the realisation of those directives in their native language.

6
Conclusions

> However well-equipped our language, it can never be forearmed against all possible cases that may arise and call for description: fact is richer than diction.
>
> Austin (1979: 195)

There is probably a substantial degree of truth in Austin's pessimistic quote about the scope to which language can faithfully describe reality and help us interact with others smoothly. This is especially true as regards speech acts. As has been made apparent in the previous chapters, their kaleidoscopic nature, which involves the mastering of a complex and dynamic interplay among cultural, pragmatic, transactional, and interactional variables, turns their learning and appropriate use into a challenge, especially for foreign language students. This has also taken a toll on EFL textbooks, whose treatment of speech acts is undisputedly far from satisfactory at present.

Despite the inherent difficulty involved in the use of illocutionary acts and the ever-present risk of miscommunication, language is to date our main and most highly developed tool of communication, and understanding how it works is central to our conceptualisation of reality, to our ability to convey thoughts, and to meeting our needs to interact with others and get them to act in our benefit. Bearing this in mind, the present book has focused on the description of a specific subgroup of directive speech acts in order to unveil their conceptual nature and to offer an inventory of the most frequent constructions and linguistic realisation procedures for their expression in English. This has been done in the form of a cognitive pedagogical grammar of directive speech acts, which has also been translated into practical teaching activities, thus offering examples that can be used for textbook design and serve as a guide for EFL teachers interested in creating their own teaching materials.

This book is motivated by the attested underrepresentation and unsystematic treatment of directive speech acts in current EFL textbooks

(Nguyen, 2011; Ulum, 2015; Ren & Han, 2016; Pérez-Hernández, 2019). The reasons for this poor handling of directives in contemporary teaching materials may be varied but, as has emerged in the course of this investigation, there are two main factors that clearly contribute to this situation. The first is related to the disconnection that exists between the research carried out in the field of speech acts and its implementation in teaching materials. Speech acts have been a thriving field of investigation ever since Austin's and Searle's foundational contributions in the 1960s and 1970s, and speech acts have been approached from a myriad of diverse, sometimes even contradictory, theoretical perspectives. Research advancements on speech acts have mounted up over the years, but their transfer to the teaching practice has not been quite as dynamic. Textbook designers have often found themselves facing different proposals on the nature of speech acts with no tools and/or criteria to choose the best suited for teaching purposes and, in many cases, the pragmatic approach being an exception to this, with little or no illustration or sample materials to achieve this. It should come as no surprise, therefore, that the treatment of speech acts in EFL textbook series is often anecdotal, highly formulaic, and unsystematic.

The second reason behind the underrepresentation of directive speech acts in current EFL textbooks is undoubtedly the complexity of the task involved. The multifaceted nature of illocutionary acts and the rich amount of interactional, transactional, social, and cultural variables that need to be mastered to produce speech acts appropriately in specific contexts make their teaching difficult and their learning by EFL students arduous. This may also explain, at least partially, why EFL textbooks have not yet approached the teaching of speech acts in a systematic and detailed manner, limiting their intervention to a small number of highly formulaic directive expressions, which are not always faithful to the actual constructions favoured by native speakers. The difficulty of the task, however, should not prevent teaching professionals from attempting to at least provide their students with the knowledge of the most frequent directive constructions in English, the tools to know which of those constructions best fit a particular context, and the resources to be able to modify them to serve different interactional and social needs.

This book challenges the current state of the art in the teaching of directives to advanced EFL students and offers EFL teachers and textbook designers the necessary information to improve their teaching throughout the curriculum. To achieve this aim, a revision of current theoretical approaches on this matter has been carried out, leading to the formulation of a comprehensive theory of speech acts that brings together attested findings from each of the former approaches. The resulting account of directive speech acts is based on the evidence drawn from a corpus analysis of real language data and is compatible with current psycholinguistic experimental knowledge on speech act production and understanding. To bridge the gap between theory and practice, this theoretical account of directives has been offered in the form of a cognitive pedagogical grammar of directive speech acts that avoids excessive specialised jargon and provides ample exemplification to make its understanding easier for non-specialists. Finally, a set of practical implementations has been provided to illustrate how the knowledge about the meaning and form of directives included in the *cognitive pedagogical grammar* can be implemented in real teaching materials. By offering a comprehensive account of speech acts, compatible with current research and experimental evidence, in an accessible manner, this book has tackled the main factors that have so far prevented a comprehensive and systematic treatment of speech acts in EFL textbooks. It has taken attested advancements from the different contemporary approaches to illocution to build a unified psychologically adequate framework of speech acts; it has spelled out the complexity of their semantics, their rich interactions with social and contextual variables, their formal, constructional nature, and their cognitive basis in a reader-friendly manner; and finally, it has bridged the gap between theory and practice by showing how to implement the former into the latter. This final section summarises the main contributions made in each of the chapters of this book, connects them to current trends, and specifies potential future research.

Chapter 1 established the relevance of directive speech acts for human relationships. In a world in which social interaction is central to personal and professional relations, learning how to produce directives appropriately in different contexts is proven to be crucial. It was also argued that the difficulties associated with their learning and the social risks involved in their use represent an especial challenge for EFL learners and teachers alike, thus focusing on the treatment of directive speech acts in EFL textbooks and highlighting their present underrepresentation as an issue of concern.

Chapter 1 asked whether there is still room for improvement in the teaching of directive speech acts, and it was attested that on the basis of the existing literature there are at least three areas (i.e. cross-linguistic, cognitive, and constructional aspects of illocutionary performance) in which the portrayal of directives in EFL textbooks falls short of taking advantage of current research advancements. This led to the formulation of the

Conclusions

main objectives guiding the investigation reported in this book: (1) revising current research on illocutionary acts to establish a comprehensive theoretical framework that is compatible with current experimental knowledge on this issue, and that integrates already attested facts about speech act performance with further advancements stemming from a cognitive/constructional analysis of the subject matter (Chapter 2); (2) identifying those aspects of directive speech acts that are still underdeveloped or poorly treated in contemporary EFL textbooks (Chapter 3); (3) offering a cognitive pedagogical grammar of directive speech acts that supports the theoretical framework described in Chapter 2 (Chapter 4); and (4) providing a rich collection of practice materials exploiting the cognitive pedagogical grammar of directive speech acts in order to enable teachers and textbook designers to take advantage of the theoretical proposals that are currently missing in EFL textbooks (Chapter 5). In so doing, this book applies the tenets of cognitive linguistics to the teaching of directive speech acts, thus opening a new, currently little explored path to further applications of this theoretical approach to language within the realm of higher levels of linguistic description.

Chapter 2 revealed that contemporary theories on speech acts are often skewed towards one of the many aspects at work in this multifaceted phenomenon: either towards their pragmatic and interactional nature (Leech, 1983; Brown & Levinson, 1987), their conversational structure (Schegloff, 1979, 2007; Levinson, 1983; Mey, 1993; Kasper, 2006), or their cognitive grounding (Pérez-Hernández, 1996, 2001, 2012, 2013, 2019; Panther & Thornburg, 1998, 2003; Ruiz de Mendoza & Baicchi, 2007; Vassilaki, 2017), thus running short of offering a comprehensive account of the various factors involved in illocutionary performance. Additionally, most theories were shown to fall within one of three main categories depending on their acceptance or rejection of the Literal Force Hypothesis, and consequently to give pride of place to codification (Ross, 1970; Sadock, 1974; Halliday, 1978, 1994; Dik, 1989, 1997), convention (Searle, 1975, 1979; Morgan, 1978), or inference (Bach & Harnish, 1979; Levinson, 1983; Leech, 1983, 2014; Sperber & Wilson, 1995) in the production and understanding of speech acts. As a result, many of those theories display an unbalanced tendency towards either the over-grammaticalisation or over-pragmatisation of illocutionary phenomena. Despite their attested limitations, Chapter 2 explored the advancement and insight into the nature of illocutionary acts provided by each of the theories under revision. Thus, functionalists and pragmatists were credited for revealing the pivotal role of politeness and the interactional/social dimensions of illocutionary performance. Conversationalists brought to the fore the advantages of using real language data and of considering larger chunks of language beyond the sentence level. Cognitivists placed the focus on the cognitive mechanisms that underlie the production and understanding of speech acts. Bringing together the advancements provided by each of these theoretical threads into a single unified framework was argued to be not only desirable but also necessary in order to have a full understanding of this linguistic phenomenon.

No matter how linguists will attempt to overcome the limitations of these partial accounts of illocution, what seems uncontroversial at this stage is that new proposals need to be compatible with the existing experimental evidence on the psychology of speech acts (Coulson & Lovett, 2010; Van Ackeren et al., 2012; Gisladottir, Chwilla & Levinson, 2015; Tromp, Hagoort & Meyer, 2016; Trott, 2016; Ruytenbeek, 2017). For this reason, Chapter 2 also included a revision of current psycholinguistic works on the cognition of directives. At first sight, the experiments carried out to date seemed to yield inconclusive results. Some of them, based on reaction times (Clark & Lucy, 1975) and eye tracking tests (Yin & Kuo, 2013), suggested that speakers need to decodify the literal meaning before calculating the indirect one, thus confirming the validity of the Literal Force Hypothesis. A second group of reaction time tests (Ervin-Tripp et al., 1987; Gibbs & Gerrig, 1989; Gibbs, 1994, 2002) and electroencephalography experiments (Coulson & Lovett, 2010) revealed that indirect speech acts do not take longer to be understood than literal expressions, thus refuting the need for the Literal Force Hypothesis. A third group of experiments proved the psychological reality of conventional speech acts, based on the lower reaction times needed for the interpretation of this type of conventional forms (Clark, 1979; Abbeduto, Furman & Davies, 1989). As recently pointed out by Ruytenbeek (2017: 15), this seemingly contradictory finding is most probably due to the fact that different experiments provide differing amounts of linguistic versus contextual information in their design. Despite their scarcity and apparent inconclusiveness, most contemporary experimental studies were found to converge in one point: the fact that there exist differences in the way direct and indirect speech acts are processed. Experiments are conclusive that indirect speech acts involve a higher amount of memory retrieval, an extra activation of the Theory of Mind areas, and also result in larger pupil diameters, which points to a higher processing cost than that of direct speech acts (Coulson & Lovett, 2010). These findings directed us to consider the cognitive mechanisms that underlie speech act production and understanding with a view to proposing a theory of speech act performance that actually accounts for the differences in the processing of direct, indirect, and conventional speech acts as revealed by contemporary experimental studies.

Evidence was also provided about the need to adhere to a weaker version of the Literal Force Hypothesis (Risselada, 1993), which was redefined in terms of sentence type/speech act compatibility, as opposed to the original formulation involving a univocal association between the form and the illocutionary force of a sentence. The weaker version of the Literal Force Hypothesis advocated in Chapter 2 was shown to still be compatible with the typological evidence about the existence of three major universal sentence types. It was also found to be useful in wiring the speakers' interpretation processes towards a default set of meanings, restricting the potential targets to those compatible with each sentence type. More importantly, it was also shown that, unlike the original Literal Force Hypothesis, this weaker version does not impose a two-step interpretation pattern of indirect speech acts, where the literal meaning needs to be accessed before the indirect one is derived, thus directly leading to higher processing times for indirect speech acts, a fact that experimental studies had not been able to confirm. A weak Literal Force Hypothesis in terms of compatibility, on the contrary, was found to be capable of accommodating the differences in processing among direct and indirect (conventional and non-conventional, or fully inferred) acts, as well as of accounting for the prototypical nature of the category of conventional speech acts, without necessarily singling one of them out as more time-consuming than the others. It was further hypothesised that the amount of time that it takes speakers to interpret the meaning of a speech act is rather a function of the degree of linguistic specification of the utterance used for the expression of a particular illocutionary act and the amount of contextual information available to fill in the information missing in the linguistic form. If the context is rich, an unspecified utterance could be interpreted as fast as one that is linguistically explicit. This hypothesis fits some of the experimental data available to date, which points to equally low processing times for direct, conventional speech acts (i.e. linguistically specified) and indirect, non-conventional speech acts, as long as sufficient contextual information is provided for the latter (Section 2.5.1).

The acceptance of a revised weaker version of the Literal Force Hypothesis, together with the fact that the traditional distinction between direct and indirect speech acts is not paralleled by different processing times in experimental studies, led to a redefinition of the notions of direct and indirect speech acts. It was concluded that an act is *direct* when the addressee has enough available information to be able to recognise its illocutionary force effortlessly, regardless of whether this information is provided linguistically or contextually. On the contrary, an act would be considered *indirect* if the information available is not rich enough to reach the intended interpretation unequivocally. This lack of information, either contextual or linguistic, was also argued to be responsible for higher response times, a higher cognitive cost in terms of memory retrieval, and a greater risk of misinterpretation.

In addition, Chapter 2 showcased the importance of the notions of *conceptual metonymy* and *illocutionary construction* as key analytical categories in the explanation of the process of interpretation of both direct and indirect speech acts. Hearers need to identify the illocutionary force intended by the speaker as being compatible with the sentence type used for its expression. In this process, they are guided by linguistic and/or contextual cues, which activate one or more of the characteristic attributes of the intended speech act. As already argued, speech acts are highly complex concepts, involving a high number of attributes (i.e. optionality, willingness, capability, mitigation, politeness, etc.) together with the interplays between them and with other social variables (i.e. formality, social power, and distance). Full linguistic rendering of these attributes and variables is not always desirable (i.e. speakers may prefer to formulate their speech acts in a more indirect way in order to increase their optionality and politeness and to decrease their impositive flavour), is rarely necessary (because the context often fills in the missing information), and is hardly economical, since full explicitation would result in rather long-winded, cumbersome utterances. Hearers, therefore, make use of metonymic processes to infer the intended illocutionary meaning on the basis of the cues provided by the linguistic expression and the contextual information available (Gibbs, 1994; Panther & Thornburg, 1998; Pérez-Hernández, 2013). In Chapter 2, it was argued that these metonymic projections are possible thanks to the fact that speakers have systematised the necessary knowledge about each speech act category in the form of *idealised illocutionary cognitive models* that are available in their long-term memory. It was further noted that the metonymic exploitation of these illocutionary ICMs involves a special type of mapping where one or more elements in the source domain are mapped onto the target domain (i.e. *(multiple source)-in-target metonymies*). The number and centrality of the attributes of the illocutionary ICMs that are mapped onto the target domain is, therefore, flexible, thus allowing for a continuum of explicitness in the expression of speech acts.

Chapter 2 also addressed the question of whether a constructional account of directive speech acts is possible. Building such a constructional

Conclusions

account faces difficulties stemming from the complex and fluid nature of speech acts, whose forms are constantly reshaped as needed by the ever-changing transactional, interactional, and contextual situations in which the speech act is to be uttered. For this reason, pairing full linguistic forms with illocutionary meanings has long failed to describe speech act constructions (e.g. Searle's *IFIDs*; Dik's *illocutionary conversors*, etc.). Chapter 2 provided arguments to the effect that dealing with constructions at higher levels of linguistic description (i.e. pragmatics, discourse) requires a somewhat different and more flexible approach. In line with Goldberg and Suttle's (2010: 469–470) recent definition of constructions as form-meaning pairings that display a high frequency of use, evidence was provided about the existence of sets of *illocutionary base constructions* for each directive speech act under investigation. It has also been shown how these base constructions can be further specified by means of *linguistic realisation procedures* to communicate a specific directive meaning with diverse degrees of explicitness. The combination of base constructions and realisation procedures gives way to *families of speech act constructions* with varying degrees of conventionality, as determined by their frequency of use. In this regard, the present account differs from other contemporary proposals on illocutionary constructions (see Stefanowitsch, 2003; Ruiz de Mendoza & Baicchi, 2007; Brdar-Szabó, 2009; Del Campo, 2013).

Chapter 3 reported the results of an analysis of ten advanced EFL textbooks in relation to their representation of directive speech acts and the extent to which they have engaged with the theoretical advancements on illocution described in Chapter 2. In providing an informed answer to the question of whether current EFL textbooks offer a quantitatively accurate and qualitatively up-to-date portrayal of directive speech acts, Chapter 3 justifies the need for the present book. The exploration of the collection of EFL textbooks under analysis has revealed that their quantitative representation of directives is weak and inconsistent. While most textbooks include some popular directive acts like requests, suggestions, and advice acts; other illocutionary acts like beggings and warnings are absent from the vast majority of textbooks. In addition, it was also observed that the number of activities/exercises devoted to each speech act was generally low (i.e. one activity per act), with again the exception of the acts of requesting, suggesting, and advising, which would feature up to five activities in some of the textbooks.

In connection with qualitative aspects of the representation of directive speech acts in EFL textbooks, Chapter 3 concluded that most of them overlook the teaching of the essential pieces of information students need to gain a clear understanding of the workings of these speech acts. Thus, instructional material on the semantic attributes that conform to each directive act (i.e. agent, beneficiary, cost/benefit, optionality, politeness, etc.), or about their interconnections and synergies with other pragmatic and social variables (i.e. social distance and power, formality) was absent from the vast majority of the EFL textbooks under scrutiny. The only interactional attribute that was found to receive some consideration was that of politeness, but no systematic explanation was offered about the type of contexts and/or situations that make its use necessary. Regarding the effects of social variables on the performance of directives, only three of the textbooks dealt with those of social distance and formality. Social power was overlooked in all of them. Still these variables were considered only in relation to the act of requesting, the rest of directives lacking analogous explanations.

Regarding the formal and constructional aspects of speech acts, the exploration of the textbooks revealed that their approach to the teaching of directives is limited to offering students random lists of expressions and that, in addition, the formulae chosen as teaching targets are far from representative of those actually used by native speakers. Students are not taught the motivation of those forms, or the mental mechanisms (i.e. metonymy) that enable the use of largely unspecified forms to activate a particular directive meaning. Neither are they informed about the possibility of modulating the degree of explicitness, imposition, politeness, etc. of their acts by means of combining realisation procedures with the base constructions associated with each directive act. As Boers and Lindstromberg (2008), Holme (2009), and Tyler (2012), among others, have pointed out making students aware of the constructional nature of language and the semantic motivation underlying linguistic forms helps them wed form to meaning and facilitates learning and memorisation.

Chapter 3 also revealed that the use of real language data in instructional materials is not widespread, with only half the textbooks under analysis committed to this practice. In the absence of real examples within their context of use, it comes as no surprise that most EFL textbooks also overlook conversational aspects of illocutionary performance, including the fact that some acts are produced through more than one conversational turn and are beyond the scope of single sentences. Much in the same vein and as previously attested in the contemporary studies of Neddar's (2010, 2012) and Luomala's (2010), the EFL textbooks under consideration were found to neglect cross-linguistic and cross-cultural issues of directive speech acts performance.

Conclusions 227

As Neddar (2012: 5691) rightly remarks, the omission of cross-cultural/linguistic issues of illocutionary performance in EFL textbooks has to do more with a lack of knowledge in its methodological implementation than with a denial of its effectiveness in inducing learning. Similarly, the attested exclusion of conversational, constructional, and pragmatic key aspects of illocution in EFL textbooks may stem from the lack of co-operation between speech act theoreticians, on the one hand, and teaching professionals and textbook designers, on the other, as well as to the shortage of works providing the latter with the necessary information, together with rich sample materials about how it can be implemented.

Having attested the fact that EFL textbooks rarely make use of the theoretical advancements described in Chapter 2, Chapters 4 and 5 set out to fight this unproductive disconnection between theory and practice, as well as the underlying idea that teaching speech acts properly and in an effective manner is too complex a task to be systematically tackled in EFL textbooks. It was argued that this endeavour would, in fact, be possible if teachers and textbook designers had at their disposal the necessary information about the semantics and formal nature of speech acts to endow their teaching with an explicit instruction approach. To this end, Chapter 4 offered a corpus-based cognitive pedagogical grammar of directive speech acts based on the theoretical postulates spelled out in Chapter 2. Both the semantic/pragmatic knowledge associated with each directive under consideration (i.e. their know-what) and the base constructions and realisation procedures offered by the English language for their expression (i.e. their know-how) were described and extensively exemplified with real language data from the iWeb corpus. Cross-linguistic comparisons of the constructions used in English and Spanish for each directive speech act under consideration were also included with the aim of providing the necessary information about potential learning difficulties stemming from mismatches between the two languages. Additionally, suprasentential and conversational aspects of illocutionary performance were considered when relevant to the workings of the speech acts (e.g. advice acts, warnings).

Chapter 5 presented activities that show how the information in Chapter 4 can be implemented in EFL textbooks and in the classroom practice. They tackled semantic/pragmatic (i.e. know-what), linguistic and constructional (i.e. know-how), and cross-linguistic/cultural issues, thus offering practice on the three pivotal aspects of directives included in their associated *cognitive pedagogical grammar* proposed in Chapter 4. The type of activities chosen included consciousness-raising, knowledge-development, comprehension, and production-development tasks. In the design of these activities, real language data from several corpora was used whenever teaching purposes allowed it, thus offering rich contexts in order to grant students access to pragmatic, conversational, and situational aspects of the directives involved.

In contrast to Chapters 2 and 3, which were addressed to a more specialised readership, with expert knowledge on the topic of speech acts, Chapters 4 and 5 kept the terminological jargon to a minimum to facilitate their use by EFL teachers and textbook designers, as well as by graduate and postgraduate students wanting to explore the field of directive speech acts. These two chapters provide evidence of the potential pedagogical applications of cognitive linguistics to EFL teaching. Although beyond the scope of this book, further experimental evaluation of the effectiveness of these pedagogical applications will be essential for assessing the theoretical plausibility of the cognitive framework itself (Langacker, 2008: 66).

This book had two major aims. First, to offer a unified model of illocution that integrates contemporary theoretical advancements and that is compatible with current experimental findings on the workings of speech acts and, second, to translate this model into a cognitive pedagogical grammar of directive speech acts and a collection of practice materials that help to enable their efficient teaching to advanced EFL students. Throughout the chapters, linguistic evidence has been provided to support the argumentation, formulated on the basis of real language examples and tested against alternative hypotheses when needed. For practical reasons, the scope of the investigation has been limited to directive speech acts. Future research will need to be carried out to assess the possibility of extending the same theoretical framework to other speech act types, like expressives, commmissives, or assertives. Further empirical validation from other disciplines and from experimental analyses, both in the fields of psycholinguistics and foreign language learning/teaching, will also be needed to lend stronger support to the claims presented in these pages. This book thus opens up new complementary lines of investigation in the field of empirical testing that go beyond the scope of the present research. In the meantime, it is this author's hope that the information provided here can contribute to setting the grounds for a more comprehensive approach to the illocutionary phenomenon, as well as for a more efficient teaching of this complex but communicatively essential and powerful dimension of language.

References

Abbas, L. H. & Saad, Q. K. (2018). Iraqi EFL students' linguistic strategies in approaching warning and prohibition. *English Language Teaching*, 11(12), 11–37.

Abbeduto, L., Furman, L. & Davies, B. (1989). Identifying speech acts from contextual and linguistic information. *Language and Speech*, 32(3), 189–203.

Achard, M. (2018). Teaching usage and concepts: toward a cognitive pedagogical grammar. In A. Tyler, L. Huang & H. Jan, eds., *What Is Applied Cognitive Linguistics? Answers from Current SLA Research*. Berlin: Mouton de Gruyter.

Achard, M. & Niemeier, S., eds. (2004). *Cognitive Linguistics, Second Language Acquisition, and Foreign Language Teaching*. Berlin: Mouton de Gruyter.

Aijmer, K. (1996). *Conversational Routines in English: Convention and Creativity*. London: Longman.

Akbari K. A. & Sharifzadeh, A. (2013). An evaluation of Top Notch series. *International Journal of Language Learning and Applied Linguistics World*, 4(4), 60–73.

Aksoyalp, Y. & Toprak, T. E. (2015). Incorporating pragmatics in English language teaching: to what extent do EFL course book address speech acts? *International Journal of Applied Linguistics and English Literature*, 4(2), 125–133.

Alcón, E. (2005). Does instruction work for learning pragmatics in the EFL context? *System*, 33(3), 417–435.

Alcón, E. & Safont, P. (2001). Occurrence of exhortative speech acts in ELT materials and natural speech data: a focus on request, suggestion and advice realisation strategies. *SELL: Studies in English Language and Linguistics*, 3, 5–22.

Alshehri, E. & Abdulaziz, K. (2017). Using learners' first language in the EFL classroom. *IAFOR Journal of Language Learning*, 3(1), 20–33.

Alston, W. P. (2000). *Illocutionary Acts and Sentence Meaning*. Ithaca, NY: Cornell University Press.

Atay, D., Kurt, G., Çamlibel, Z., Ersin, P. & Kaslioglu, O. (2009). The role of intercultural competence in foreign language teaching. *Inonu University Journal of the Faculty of Education*, 10(3), 123–135.

Auerbach, E. (1993). Re-examining English only in the ESL classroom. *TESOL Quarterly*, 27(1), 9–32.

Austin, J. L. (1962). *How to Do Things with Words*. Oxford: Clarendon Press.
Austin, J. (1979). *Philosophical Papers*, 2nd ed. Oxford: Oxford University Press.
Bacelar da Silva, A. J. (2003). The effect of instruction on pragmatic development: teaching polite refusal in English. *Second Language Studies*, 22(1), 55–106.
Bach, K. (1998). Standardisation revisited. In A. Kasher, ed., *Pragmatics: Critical Assessment*. London: Routledge, pp. 712–722.
Bach, K. & Harnish, R. M. (1979). *Linguistic Communication and Speech Acts*. Cambridge, MA: The MIT Press.
Baicchi, A. (2016). The role of syntax and semantics in constructional priming: experimental evidence from Italian university learners of English through a sentence-elicitation task. In S. De Knop and G. Gaëtanelle, eds., *Applied Construction Grammar*. Berlin: Mouton de Gruyter, pp. 211–236.
Banerjee, J. & Carrell, P. L. (1988). Tuck in your shirt, you squid: suggestions in ESL. *Language and Learning*, 38(3), 313–364.
Bardovi-Harlig, K. (1992). The relationship of form and meaning: a cross-sectional study of tense and aspect in the interlanguage of learners of English as a second language. Applied Psycholinguistics, 13, 253–278.
Bardovi-Harlig, K. (2001). Evaluating the empirical evidence: grounds for instruction in pragmatics? In K. Rose and G. Kasper, eds., *Pragmatics in Language Teaching*. Cambridge: Cambridge University Press, pp. 13–32.
Bardovi-Harlig, K. & Dörnyei, Z. (1998). Do language learners recognise pragmatic violations? Pragmatic versus grammatical awareness in instructed L2 learning. *TESOL Quarterly*, 32(2), 233–259.
Bardovi-Harlig, K. & Hartford, B. S. (1996). Input in an institutional setting. *Studies in Second Language Acquisition*, 18, 171–188.
Bardovi-Harlig, K. & Mahan-Taylor, R. (2003). *Teaching Pragmatics*. Washington, DC: United States Department of State.
Bardovi-Harlig, K. & Mossman, S. (2016). Corpus-based materials development for teaching and learning pragmatic routines. In B. Tomlinson, ed., *SLA Research and Materials Development for Language Learning*. New York: Routledge, pp. 250–267.
Bardovi-Harlig, K., Mossman, S. & Su, Y. (2017). The effect of corpus-based instruction on pragmatic routine. *Language Learning & Technology*, 21(3), 76–103.
Bardovi-Harlig, K., Mossman, S. & Vellenga, H. E. (2014a). Developing corpus-based materials to teach pragmatic routines. *TESOL Journal*, 6(3), 499–526.
Bardovi-Harlig, K., Mossman, S. & Vellenga, H. E. (2014b). The effect of instruction on pragmatic routines in academic discussion. *Language Teaching Research*, 19(3), 324–350.
Barron, A. (2007). 'Can you take the other bed, please?' An appraisal of request presentation in EFL textbooks. Paper presented at the 22nd Congress of the German Society for Foreign (and Second) Language Research, Justus Liebig University, Giessen, Germany.
Bataineh, R. F. & Aljamal, M. A. (2009). *Jordanian EFL and American Students' Use of Warning in English: A Contrastive Study*. Saarbrücken: VDM Verlag.

Bataller, R. (2013). Making a request for a service in Spanish: pragmatic development in the study abroad setting. *Foreign Language Annals*, 43(1), 160–175.
Bertolet, R. (1994). Are there indirect speech acts? In S. L. Tsohatzidis, ed., *Foundations of Speech Act Theory. Philosophical and Linguistic Perspective*. London: Routledge, pp. 335–349.
Bialystok, E. (1993). Symbolic representation and attentional control in pragmatic competence. In G. Kasper & S. Blum-Kulka, eds., *Interlanguage Pragmatics*. Oxford: Oxford University Press, pp. 43–57.
Blooth, A., Azman, H. & Ismail, K. (2014). The role of the L1 as a scaffolding tool in the EFL reading classroom. *Procedia. Social and Behavioural Sciences*, 118, 76–84.
Blum-Kulka, S. (1982). Learning how to say what you mean in a second language: a study of the speech act performance of learners of Hebrew as a second language. *Applied Linguistics*, 3, 29–59.
Blum-Kulka, S. (1987). Indirectness and politeness: same or different? *Journal of Pragmatics*, 11, 145–160.
Blum-Kulka, S. (1991). Interlanguage pragmatics: the case of requests. In R. Phillipson, E. Kellerman, L. Selinker, M. Sharwood Smith & M. Swain, eds., *Foreign/Second Language Pedagogy*. Clevedon: Multilingual Matters, pp. 255–272.
Blum-Kulka, S. & House, J. (1989). Cross-cultural and situational variation in requesting behaviour. In S. Blum-Kulka, J. House and G. Kasper, eds., *Cross-Cultural Pragmatics: Requests and Apologies*. Norwood, NJ: Ablex, pp. 123–154.
Blum-Kulka, S., House, J. & Kasper, G. (1989). *Cross-Cultural Pragmatics: Requests and Apologies*. Norwood, NJ: Ablex.
Boers, F. & Demecheleer, M. (1998). A cognitive semantic approach to teaching prepositions. *English Language Teaching Journal*, 52(3), 197–204.
Boers, F. & Lindstromberg, S. (2008). *Cognitive Linguistic Approaches to Teaching Vocabulary and Phraseology*. Berlin: Mouton de Gruyter.
Borer, B. (2018). Teaching and learning pragmatics and speech acts: an instructional pragmatics curriculum development project for EFL learners. *School of Education Student Capstone Projects*. Available at https://digitalcommons.hamline.edu/hse_cp/176.
Bouton, L. (1996). *Pragmatics and Language Learning*. Urbana-Champaign, IL: University of Illinois.
Boxer, D & Pickering, L. (1995). Problems in the presentation of speech acts in ELT materials: the case of complaints. *ELT Journal*, 49(1), 44–58.
Brdar-Szabó, R. (2009). Metonymy in indirect directives: stand-alone conditionals in English, German, Hungarian, and Croatian. In K. U. Panther, L. Thornburg & A. Barcelona, eds., *Metonymy and Metaphor in Grammar*. Amsterdam: John Benjamins, pp. 323–336.
Brown, P. & Levinson, S. C. (1987). *Politeness: Some Universals in Language Usage*, 2nd ed. Cambridge: Cambridge University Press.

Bu, J. (2012). A study of the effects of explicit and implicit teachings on developing Chinese EFL learners' pragmatic competence. *International Journal of Language Studies*, 6(3), 57–80.
Burkhardt, A. (1990). Speech at theory. The decline of a paradigm. In A. Bukhardt, ed., *Speech Acts, Meaning, and Intentions. Critical Approaches to the Philosophy of John R. Searle*. New York: Walter de Gruyter, pp. 91–128.
Butler, C. W., Potter, J., Danby, S., Emmison, M. & Hepburn, A. (2010). Advice-implicative interrogatives: building 'client-centred' support in a children's helpline. *Social Psychology Quarterly*, 73(3), 265–287.
Byram, M. S. & Risager, K. (1999). *Language Teachers, Politics and Cultures*. Bristol: Multilingual Matters.
Carroll, D. (2011). Teaching preference organisation: learning how not to say 'no'. In N. Houck and D. Tatsuki, eds., *Pragmatics: Teaching Natural Conversation*. Alexandria: TESOL, pp. 105–118.
Carstens, A. (2002). Speech act theory in support of idealised warning models. *Southern African Linguistics and Applied Language Studies*, 20(4), 191–200.
Carter, R., Hughes, R. & McCarthy, M. (2000). *Exploring Grammar in Context: Upper-Intermediate and Advanced*. Cambridge: Cambridge University Press.
Castro, P. (1999). La dimensión europea en la enseñanza/aprendizaje de lenguas extranjeras: la competencia intercultural. *Lenguaje y Textos*, 13, 41–53.
Castro, P., Sercu, L. & Garcia, M. C. M. (2004). Integrating language-and-culture teaching: an investigation of Spanish teachers' perceptions of the objectives of foreign language education. *Intercultural Education*, 15(1), 91–104.
Cenoz, J. & Valencia, J. F. (1996). Cross-cultural communication and interlanguage pragmatics: American vs. European requests. In L. F. Bouton, ed., *Pragmatics and Language Learning*. Champaign, IL: University of Illinois at Urbana-Champaign, pp. 47–53.
Chen, L. & Oller, J. W. (2008). The use of passives and alternatives in English by Chinese speakers. In S. De Knop and T. De Rycker, eds., *Cognitive Approaches to Pedagogical Grammar*. Berlin: Mouton de Gruyter, pp. 385–415.
Chomsky, N. (1964). *Current Issues in Linguistic Theory*. The Hague: Mouton.
Chomsky, N. (1965). *Aspects of the Theory of Syntax*. Cambridge, MA: MIT Press.
Clark, H. H. (1979). Responding to indirect speech acts. *Cognitive Psychology*, 11(4), 430–477.
Clark, H. H. & Lucy, P. (1975). Understanding what is meant from what is said: a study in conversationally conveyed requests. *Journal of Verbal Learning and Verbal Behaviour*, 14, 56–72.
Cohen, A. (2008). Teaching and assessing L2 pragmatics: what can we expect from learners? *Language Teaching*, 41, 213–235.
Cohen, A. D. & Ishihara, N. (2013). Pragmatics. In B. Tomlinson, ed., *Applied Linguistics and Material Development*. London: Bloomsbury, pp. 113–126.
Coulson, S. & Lovett, C. (2010). Comprehension of non-conventional indirect requests: an event-related brain potential study. *Italian Journal of Linguistics*, 22(1), 107–124.

Crandall, E. & Basturkmen, H. (2004). Evaluating pragmatics-focused materials. *English Language Teaching Journal*, 58(1), 38–49.
Crystal, D. (2010). *The Cambridge Encyclopaedia of Language*, 3rd ed. Cambridge: Cambridge University Press.
Dascal, M. (1989). On the roles of context and literal meaning in understanding. *Cognitive Science*, 13, 253–257.
De Knop, S. & De Rycker, T. (2008). *Cognitive Approaches to Pedagogical Grammar*. Berlin: Mouton de Gruyter.
De Knop, S. & Gilquin, G. (2016). *Applied Construction Grammar*. Berlin: Mouton De Gruyter.
Del Campo, N. (2013). *Illocutionary Constructions in English: Cognitive Motivation and Linguistic Realisation*. Berlin: Peter Lang.
Delen, B. & Tevil, Z. M. (2010). Evaluation of four coursebooks in terms of three speech acts: requests, refusals and complaints. *Procedia-Social and Behavioral Sciences*, 9, 692–697.
Diepenbroek, L. G. & Derwing, T. (2013). To what extent do popular ESL textbooks incorporate oral fluency and pragmatic development? *TESL Canada Journal*, 30(7), 1–20.
Dik, S. C. (1989). *The Theory of Functional Grammar: Part I: The Structure of the Clause*. Dordrecht: Foris Publications.
Dik, S. C. (1997). *The Theory of Functional Grammar: Part II: Complex and Derived Constructions*. Berlin: Mouton de Gruyter.
Dirven, R. (1985). Definition of a pedagogical grammar (seen from a linguist's point of view). *ITL: Review of Applied Linguistics*, 67(1), 43–67.
Dirven, R. (1990). Pedagogical grammar. *Language Teaching*, 23(1), 1–18.
Dirven, R. (2001). English phrasal verbs: theory and didactic application. In M. Putz, S. Niemeier & R. Dirven, eds., *Applied Cognitive Linguistics II: Language Pedagogy*. Berlin: Mouton de Gruyter, pp. 3–28.
Dobrovie-Sorin, C. (1985). *Actes de Langage et Théorie de L'énonciation*. Collection ERA 642 (UA 04 1028). Paris: University of Paris 7 Press.
Edelhoff, C. (1993). English among the other European languages. *English Language Learning in Europe: Issues, Tasks and Problems*. Best of ELTECS Conference, Bratislava, pp. 27–38.
Edmondson, W. & J. House. (1981). *Let's Talk and Talk About It*. Munich: Urban and Schwarzenberg.
Ekin, M. T. Y. (2013). Do current EFL coursebooks work for the development of L2 pragmatic competence? The case of suggestions. *Procedia-Social and Behavioral Sciences*, 93, 1306–1310.
Ellis, N. (2001). *Form-Focus Instruction and Second Language Learning*. Oxford: Blackwell.
Ellis, N. (2002). Frequency effects in language processing: a review with implications for theories of implicit and explicit language acquisition. *Studies in Second Language Acquisition*, 24, 143–188.
Ervin-Tripp, S., Strage, A., Lampert, M. & Bell, N. (1987). Understanding requests. *Linguistics*, 25, 107–143.

Escandell, M. V. (1993). *Introducción a la Pragmática*. Barcelona: Anthropos.
Eslami-Rasekh, Z. (2005). Raising the pragmatic awareness of language learners. *English Language Teaching Journal*, 59(3), 199–208.
Faerch, C. & Kasper, G. (1989). Interlanguage request modification. In S. Blum-Kulka, J. House & G. Kasper, eds., *Cross-Cultural Pragmatics: Requests and Apologies*. Norwood, NJ: Ablex, pp. 221–247.
Farashaiyan, A. & Muthusamy, P. (2017). The linguistic presentation of speech acts in Top-Notch Intermediate textbooks. *International Journal of Linguistics*, 9(3), 1–20.
Farashaiyan, A., Tan, K. H. & Shahragard, R. (2018). An evaluation of the pragmatics in the Cutting Edge Intermediate textbooks. *3L: Language, Linguistics and Literature: The Southeast Asian Journal of English Language Studies*, 24(4), 158–170.
Fraser, B. (1974). An analysis of vernacular performative verbs. In R. Shuy & C. J. Bailey, eds., *Towards Tomorrow's Linguistics*. Washington, DC: Georgetown University Press, pp. 139–158.
Fujimori, J. & Houck, N. (2004). Practical criteria for teaching speech acts. *The Language Teacher*, 28(4), 3–9.
Fukushima, S. (2000). *Requests and Culture: Politeness in British English and Japanese*. Bern: Peter Lang.
Geis, M. (1995). *Speech Acts and Conversational Interaction*. Cambridge: Cambridge University Press.
Gibbs, R. W. (1979). Contextual effects in understanding indirect requests. *Discourse Processes*, 2, 1–10.
Gibbs, R. W. (1984). Literal meaning and psychological theory. *Cognitive Science*, 8, 265–304.
Gibbs, R. W. (1994). *The Poetics of Mind: Figurative Thought, Language, and Understanding*. Cambridge, MA: Cambridge University Press.
Gibbs, R. W. (2002). A new look at literal meaning in understanding what is said and implicated. *Journal of Pragmatics*, 34(4), 457–486.
Gibbs, R. W. & Gerrig, R. (1989). How context makes metaphor comprehension seem 'special'. *Metaphor and Symbolic Activity*, 4, 154–158.
Gisladottir, R. S., Chwilla, D. J. & Levinson, S. C. (2015). Conversation electrified: ERP correlates of speech act recognition in underspecified utterances. *PLoS ONE*, 10(3), 1–24.
Givon, T. (1989). *Mind, Code, and Context. Essays in Pragmatics*. Hillsdale, NJ: Lawrence Erlbaum.
Glaser, K. (2009). Acquiring pragmatic competence in a foreign language: mastering dispreferred speech acts. *Topics in Linguistics*, 4, 50–57.
Goddard, C. (2011). *Semantic Analysis: A Practical Introduction*, 2nd ed. Oxford: Oxford University Press.
Goddard, C. & Wierzbicka, A. (2013). *Words and Meanings: Lexical Semantics Across Domains, Languages, and Cultures*. Oxford: Oxford University Press.
Goldberg, A. E. (1995). *Constructions: A Construction Grammar Approach to Argument Structure*. Chicago, IL: University of Chicago Press.

Goldberg, A. E. (2006). *Constructions at Work. The Nature of Generalisations in Language.* Oxford: Oxford University Press.
Goldberg, A. E. & Suttle, L. (2010). Construction grammar. *WIREs Cognitive Science*, 1(4), 468–477.
Gonzálvez-García, F. (2019). Exploring the pedagogical potential of vertical and horizontal relations in the construction: the case of the family of subjective-transitive constructions with *decir* in Spanish. In R. Llopis-García & A. Hijazo-Gascón, eds., *Applied Cognitive Linguistics to L2 Acquisition and Learning: Research and Convergence. International Review of Applied Linguistics in Language Teaching*, 57(1), 121–145.
Gordon, D. & Lakoff, G. (1975). Conversational postulates. In P. Cole & J. Morgan, eds., *Syntax and Semantics. Vol. 3. Speech Acts.* New York: Academic Press, pp. 83–106.
Grant, L. & Starks, D. (2001). Screening appropriate teaching materials: closing from textbooks and television soap operas. *International Review of Applied Linguistics in Language Teaching*, 39(1), 39–50.
Grice, H. P. (1975). Logic and conversation. In P. Cole & J. Morgan, eds., *Syntax and Semantics. Vol. 3. Speech Acts.* New York: Academic Press, pp. 41–58.
Griffiths, P. (2006). *An Introduction to English Semantics and Pragmatics.* Edinburgh: Edinburgh University Press.
Grossi, V. (2009). Teaching pragmatic competence: compliments and compliment responses in the ESL classroom. *Macquarie University*, 24(2), 53–62.
Gu, X. (2011). The effect of explicit and implicit instructions of request strategies. *Intercultural Communication Studies*, 20(1), 104–123.
Hall, G. & Cook, G. (2013). Own-language use in ELT: exploring global practices and attitudes. ELT Research Paper, British Council, London.
Halliday, M. A. K. (1973). *Explorations in the Functions of Language.* London: Edward Arnold.
Halliday, M. A. K. (1978). *Language as Social Semiotics: The Social Interpretation of Language and Meaning.* London: Edward Arnold.
Halliday, M. A. K. (1994). *An Introduction to Functional Grammar*, 2nd ed. London: Edward Arnold.
Halliday, M. A. K. & Matthiessen, C. (1999). *Construing Experience Through Meaning.* London: Cassell.
Harrison, S. & Barlow, J. (2009). Politeness strategies and advice-giving in an online arthritis workshop. *Journal of Politeness Research Language Behaviour Culture*, 5(1), 93–111.
Harwood, N. (2014). Content, consumption, and production: three levels of textbook research. In N. Harwood, ed., *English Language Teaching Textbooks: Content, Consumption, Production.* Basingstoke: Palgrave MacMillan, pp. 1–41.
Haverkate, H. (1984). *Speech Acts, Speakers, and Hearers: Reference and Referential Strategies in Spanish.* Amsterdam: John Benjamins.
Hayakawa, S. I. (1969). *Modern Guide to Synonyms and Related Words.* Darmstadt: Verlag.

Hengeveld, K. (2017). A hierarchical approach to grammaticalisation. In K. Hengeveld, H. Narrog & H. Olbertz, eds., *The Grammaticalisation of Tense, Aspect, Modality and Evidentiality*. Berlin: Walter de Gruyter, pp. 13–39.

Heritage, J. & Sefi, S. (1992). Dilemmas of advice: aspects of the delivery and reception of advice in interactions between health visitors and first-time mothers. In P. Drew & J. Heritage, eds., *Talk at Work: Interaction in Institutional Settings*. Cambridge: Cambridge University Press, pp. 359–417.

Hernández-Flores, N. (1999). Politeness ideology in Spanish colloquial conversation. The case of advice. *Pragmatics*, 9(1), 37–49.

Hijazo-Gascón, A., Cadierno, T. & Ibarretxe-Antuñano, I. (2016). Learning the placement caused motion construction in L2 Spanish. In S. De Knop & G. Gilquin, eds., *Applied Construction Grammar*. Berlin: Mouton de Gruyter, pp. 185–210.

Hinkel, E. (1997). Appropriateness of advice: DCT and multiple-choice data. *Applied Linguistics*, 18(1), 1–26.

Holdcroft, D. (1994). Indirect speech acts and propositional content. In S. L. Tsohatzidis, ed., *Foundations of Speech Act Theory. Philosophical and Linguistic Perspective*. London: Routledge, pp. 350–364.

Holme, R. (2009). *Cognitive Linguistics and Language Teaching*. London: Palgrave MacMillan.

Holme, R. (2010). A construction grammar for the classroom. *International Review of Applied Linguistics in Language Teaching*, 48, 355–377.

Holmes, J. (1983). The structure of teachers' directives. In J. C. Richards & R. W. Schmidt, eds., *Language and Communication*. Cambridge: Cambridge University Press, pp. 87–115.

Holtgraves, T. (1994). Communication in context: effects of speaker status on the comprehension of indirect requests. *Journal of Experimental Psychology: Learning, Memory, and Cognition*, 20(5), 1205–1218.

House, J. (1996). Developing pragmatic fluency in English as a foreign language: routines and metapragmatic awareness. *Studies in Second Language Acquisition*, 19, 225–252.

House, M. & Kasper, G. (1981). Politeness markers in English and German. In F. Coulmas, ed., *Conversational Routine*. The Hague: Mouton de Gruyter, pp. 157–185.

Huddleston, R. & Pullum, G. K. (2002). *The Cambridge Grammar of the English Language*. Cambridge: Cambridge University Press.

Hutchby, I. (1995). Aspects of recipient design in expert advice giving on call-in radio. *Discourse Processes*, 19, 219–223.

Ibarretxe-Antuñano, I. & Cheikh-Khamis, F. (2019). 'How to become a woman without turning into a Barbie': change-of-state verb constructions and their role in Spanish as a foreign language. In R. Llopis-García & A. Hijazo-Gascón, eds., *Applied Cognitive Linguistics to L2 Acquisition and Learning: Research and Convergence. International Review of Applied Linguistics in Language Teaching*, 57(1), 97–120.

Ishihara, N. (2010). Adapting textbooks for teaching pragmatics. In N. Ishihara & A. D. Cohen, eds., *Teaching and Learning Pragmatics: Where Language and Culture Meet*. Harlow: Longman, pp. 145–165.
Ishihara, N. & Cohen, A. D. (2010). *Teaching and Learning Pragmatics: Where Language and Culture Meet*. London: Routledge.
Ishihara, N. & Maeda, M. (2010). *Advanced Japanese: Communication in Context*. London: Routledge.
Jacobsen, N. D. (2012). Applying cognitive linguistics and task-supported language teaching to instruction of English conditional phrases. PhD thesis. Washington, DC: Georgetown University.
Jacobsen, N. (2015). A cognitive linguistic analysis of English conditionals in English for Academic Purposes (EAP) instruction: implications from sociocultural theory. In K. Masuda, C. Arnett & A. Labarca, eds., *Cognitive Linguistics and Sociocultural Theory: Applications for Second and Foreign Language Teaching*. Mouton de Gruyter, pp. 103–129.
Jacobsen, N. (2018). The best of both worlds: combining Cognitive Linguistics and pedagogic tasks to teach English conditionals. *Applied Linguistics*, 39(5), 668–693.
Jiang, X. (2006). Suggestions: what should ESL students know? *System*, 34(1), 36–54.
Johnson, M. (1987). *The Body in the Mind: The Bodily Basis of Meaning, Imagination and Reason*. Chicago, IL: University of Chicago Press.
Judd, E. L. (1999). Some issues in the teaching of pragmatic competence. In E. Hinkel & M. H. Long, eds. *Culture in Second Language Teaching and Learning*. Cambridge: Cambridge University Press, pp. 152–167.
Kachru, Y. (1994). Cross-cultural speech act research and the classroom. *Pragmatics and Language Learning*, 5, 39–51.
Kasper, G. (1989). Variation in interlanguage speech act realisation. In S. Gass, C. Madden, D. Preston & L. Selinker, eds., *Variation in Second Language Acquisition: Discourse and Pragmatics*. Clevedon: Multilingual Matters, pp. 37–58.
Kasper, G. (2006). Speech acts in interaction: towards discursive pragmatics. In K. Bardovi-Harlig, C. Félix-Brasdefer & A. S. Omar, eds., *Pragmatics and Language Learning*, Vol. 11, pp. 281–314.
Kasper, G. & Rose, K. R. (2002). *Pragmatic Development in a Second Language*. Oxford: Blackwell.
Katz, J. J. (1990). Literal meaning and logical theory. In A. Bukhardt, ed., *Speech Acts, Meaning, and Intentions. Critical Approaches to the Philosophy of John R. Searle*. New York: Walter de Gruyter, pp. 229–258.
Kaufmann, M. (2012). *Interpreting Imperatives*. Dordrecht: Springer.
Kempson, R. M. (1975). *Presupposition and the Delimitation of Semantics*. Cambridge: Cambridge University Press.
Kissine, M. (2011). Misleading appearances: Searle, assertion, and meaning. *Erkenntnis*, 74, 115–129.

Kissine, M. (2012). Sentences, utterances, and speech acts. In K. Allan & K. M. Jaszczolt, eds., *Cambridge Handbook of Pragmatics*. Cambridge: Cambridge University Press, pp. 160–190.
Kissine, M. (2014). *From Utterances to Speech Acts*. Cambridge: Cambridge University Press.
Kissine, M. & Jary, M. (2014). *Imperatives*. Cambridge: Cambridge University Press.
Koester, J. (2002). The performance of speech acts in workplace conversations and the teaching of communicative functions. *System*, 30(2), 167–184.
Koike, D. (1994). Negation in Spanish and English suggestions and requests: mitigating effects? *Journal of Pragmatics*, 21, 513–526.
Koike, D. (1996). Transfer of pragmatic competence and suggestions in Spanish foreign language learning. In S. M. Gass & J. Neu, eds., *Speech Acts across Cultures*. Berlin: Mouton de Gruyter, pp. 257–281.
Koosha, B. & Vahid Dastjerdi, H. V. (2012). Investigating pragmatic competence: the case of requests in Interchange Series. *Asian Social Science*, 8(1), 54–61.
Lakoff, G. (1987). *Women, Fire, and Dangerous Things. What Categories Reveal about the Mind*. Chicago, IL: Chicago University Press.
Langacker, R. W. (2008). Cognitive grammar as a basis for language instruction. In P. Robinson & N. Ellis, eds., *Handbook of Cognitive Linguistics and Second Language Acquisition*. London: Routledge.
Leech, G. (1983). *Principles of Pragmatics*. New York: Longman.
Leech, G. (2014). *The Pragmatics of Politeness*. Oxford: Oxford University Press.
Levinson, S. C. (1983). *Pragmatics*. Cambridge: Cambridge University Press.
Limberg, H. (2015). Principles for pragmatics teaching: apologies in the EFL classroom. *English Language Teaching Journal*, 69(3), 275–285.
Lindstromberg, S. (1996). Prepositions: meaning and method. *English Language Teaching Journal*, 50, 225–36.
Lindstromberg, S. & Boers, F. (2005). From movement to metaphor with manner-of-movement verbs. *Applied Linguistics*, 26, 241–61.
Littlemore, J. & Low G. (2006). Metaphoric competence, second language learning, and communicative language ability. *Applied Linguistics*, 27, 268–94.
Liu, D. (2010). Going beyond patterns: involving cognitive analysis in the learning of collocations. *TESOL Quarterly*, 44, 4–30.
LoCastro, V. (2012). *Pragmatics for Language Educators*. New York: Routledge.
Locher, M. A. (2006). *Advice-Giving in an American Internet Health Column*. Amsterdam: John Benjamins.
Luomala, P. (2010). Pragmatics exercises and pragmatic metalanguage in English United textbooks series for Finnish upper secondary school. Master's thesis. University of Jyväskylä.
Mandala, S. (1999). Exiting advice. *Pragmatics and Language Learning*, 9, 89–111.
Marcondes, D. (1984). *Language and Action. A Reassessment of Speech Act Theory*. Amsterdam: John Benjamins.
Márquez-Reiter, R. (2002). A contrastive study of conventional indirectness in Spanish pragmatics. *Quarterly Publication of The International Pragmatics Association*, 12(2), 135–151.

Martínez-Flor, A. (2003). Non-native speakers' production of advice acts: the effects of proficiency. *Spanish Journal of Applied Linguistics*, 16, 139–153.

Martínez-Flor, A. (2005). A theoretical review of the speech act of suggesting: towards a taxonomy for its use in FLT. *Revista Alicantina de Estudios Ingleses*, 18, 167–187.

Martínez-Flor, A. & Fukuya, Y. (2005). The effects of instruction on learners' production of appropriate and accurate suggestions. *System*, 33(3), 463–480.

Masuda, K. (2018). *Cognitive Linguistics and Japanese Pedagogy. A Usage-Based Approach to Language Learning and Instruction*. Berlin: Walter de Gruyter.

Matsumura, S. (2001). Learning the rules for offering advice: a quantitative approach to second language socialisation. *Language Learning*, 51, 635–679.

Matsumura, S. (2003). Modelling the relationships among interlanguage pragmatic development, L2 proficiency, and exposure to L2. *Applied Linguistics*, 24(4), 465–491.

Mauri, C. & Sansò, A. (2011). How directive constructions emerge: grammaticalisation, constructionalisation, cooptation. *Journal of Pragmatics*, 43, 3489–3521.

McConachy, T. & Hata, K. (2013). Addressing textbook representations of pragmatics and culture. *ELT Journal*, 67(3), 294–301.

McGrath, I. (2002). *Materials Evaluation and Design for Language Teaching*. Edinburgh: Edinburgh University Press.

Merin, A. (1991). Imperative vs. philosophy. *Linguistics*, 29, 669–702.

Meunier, F. (2008). Corpora, cognition and pedagogical grammars: an account of convergences and divergences. In S. De Knop & T. D. de Rycker, eds., *Cognitive Approaches to Pedagogical Grammar: A Volume in Honour of Rene Dirven*. Mouton de Gruyter, pp. 91–121.

Mey, J. (1993). *Pragmatics: An Introduction*. Oxford: Blackwell.

Moradi, A., Karbalaei, A. R. & Afraz, S. (2013). A textbook evaluation of speech acts and language functions in high school English textbooks (I, II, and III) and Interchange series, books I, II, and III. *European Online Journal of Natural and Social Sciences*, 2(2), 323–335.

Morgan, J.L. (1978). Two types of convention in indirect speech acts. In P. Cole, ed., *Syntax and Semantics. Vol. 9. Pragmatics*. London: Academic Press, pp. 261–280.

Morrow, C. (1995). The pragmatic effects of instruction on ESL learners' production of complaint and refusal speech acts. Doctoral dissertation, State University of New York at Buffalo, NY.

Neddar, B. A. (2010). Cross-cultural pragmatic information in Algerian textbooks. A paper presented as a web poster in the 4th International Conference on Intercultural Pragmatics. Madrid.

Neddar, B. A. (2012). Short notes on discourse, interlanguage pragmatics and EFL teaching: where do we stand? *Procedia-Social and Behavioral Sciences*, 46, 5687–5692.

Nguyen, M. Th. Th. (2011). Learning to communicate in a globalised world: to what extent do school textbooks facilitate the development of intercultural pragmatic competence? *RELC Journal*, 42(1), 17–30.

Niemeier, S. & Reif, M. (2008). Making progress simpler? Applying cognitive grammar to tense-aspect teaching. In S. de Knop & T. de Rycker, eds., *Cognitive Approaches to Pedagogical Grammar: A Volume in Honour of Rene Dirven*. Mouton de Gruyter, pp. 325–356.

Norris, J. & Ortega L. (2000). Effectiveness of L2 instruction: a research synthesis and quantitative meta-analysis. *Language Learning*, 50, 417–528.

Nourdad, N. & Roshani Khiabani, L. (2015). Pragmatic content analysis of newly developed Iranian EFL English textbooks. *International Journal of Language Learning and Applied Linguistics World*, 10(1), 24–39.

Panther, K. U. & Thornburg, L. (1998). A cognitive approach to inferencing in conversation. *Journal of Pragmatics*, 30, 755–769.

Panther, K. U. & Thornburg, L. (2003). Metonymies as natural inference and activation schemas: the case of dependent clauses as independent speech acts. In K. U. Panther & L. Thornburg, eds., *Metonymy and Pragmatic Inferencing (Pragmatics & Beyond New Series 113)*. Amsterdam: John Benjamins, pp. 127–147.

Panther, K. U. & Thornburg, L. (2005). Motivation and convention in some speech act constructions: a cognitive-linguistic approach. In S. Marmaridou, K. Nikiforidou, & E. Antonopoulou, eds., *Reviewing Linguistic Thought: Converging Trends for the 21st Century*. Berlin: Mouton de Gruyter, pp. 53–76.

Pérez-Hernández, L. (1996). The cognition of requests. *Estudios Ingleses de la Universidad Complutense*, 4, 189–208.

Pérez-Hernández, L. (1999). Grounding politeness. *Journal of English Studies*, 1, 209–236.

Pérez-Hernández, L. (2001). *Illocution and Cognition: A Constructional Approach*. Logroño: University of La Rioja Press.

Pérez-Hernández, L. (2012). Saying something for a particular purpose: constructional compatibility and constructional families. *Spanish Journal of Applied Linguistics*, 25, 189–210.

Pérez-Hernández, L. (2013). Illocutionary constructions: (multiple source)-in-target metonymies, illocutionary ICMs, and specification links. *Language and Communication*, 33, 128–149.

Pérez-Hernández, L. (2019). From research to the textbook: assessing speech acts representation in course book series for students of English as an L2. *Spanish Journal of Applied Linguistics*, 32(1), 248–276.

Pérez-Hernández, L. & Ruiz de Mendoza, F. J. (2002). Grounding, semantic motivation, and conceptual interaction in indirect directive speech acts. *Journal of Pragmatics*, 34(3), 259–284.

Pérez-Hernández, L. & Ruiz de Mendoza, F. J. (2011). A Lexical-Constructional Model account of illocution. *Vigo International Journal of Applied Linguistics*, 8, 98–137.

Petraki, E. & Bayes, S. (2013). Teaching oral requests: an evaluation of five English as second language coursebooks. *Pragmatics*, 23(3), 499–517.

Radden, G. (2014). Making sense of negated modals. *Argumentum*, 10, 519–532.

Rajabia, S., Azizifar, A. & Gowhary, H. (2015a). Investigating the explicit instruction of apology speech act on pragmatic development of Iranian EFL learners. *Advances in Language and Literary Studies*, 6(4), 53–61.

Rajabia, S., Azizifara, A. & Gowhary, H. (2015b). The effect of explicit instruction on pragmatic competence development; teaching requests to EFL learners of English. *Procedia. Social and Behavioral Sciences*, 199, 231–239.

Recanati, F. (1987). *Meaning and Force. The Pragmatics of Performative Utterances.* Cambridge: Cambridge University Press.

Recanati, F. (1994). Contextualism and anti-contextualism in the philosophy of language. In S. L. Tsohatzidis, ed., *Foundations of Speech Act Theory. Philosophical and Linguistic Perspective.* London: Routledge, pp. 156–166.

Ren, W. & Han, Z. (2016). The representation of pragmatic knowledge in recent ELT textbooks. *English Language Teaching Journal*, 70(4), 424–243.

Reza, N. & Zohreh, E. (2016). Critical perspectives on interlanguage pragmatic development: an agenda for research. *Issues in Applied Linguistics*, 20(1), 25–50.

Richards, J. C. (1985). *The Context of Language Teaching.* Cambridge: Cambridge University Press.

Rintell, E. M. (1979). Getting your speech act together: the pragmatic ability of second language learners. *Working Papers on Bilingualism*, 17, 97–106.

Rintell, E. M. & Mitchel, C. J. (1989). Studying requests and apologies: an inquiry into method. In S. Blum-Kulka, J. House & G. Kasper, eds., *Cross-Cultural Pragmatics: Requests and Apologies.* Norwood, NJ: Ablex, pp. 248–272.

Risselada, R. (1993). Imperatives and other directive expressions in Latin. A study in the pragmatics of a death language. *Amsterdam Studies in Classical Philology*, Vol. 2. Amsterdam: J. C. Gieben Publisher.

Römer, U. (2004). Comparing real and ideal language learner input: the use of an EFL textbook corpus in corpus linguistics and language teaching. In G. Aston, S. Bernardini & D. Stewart, eds., *Corpora and Language Learners.* Amsterdam: John Benjamins, pp. 151–158.

Römer, U. (2006). Looking and 'looking.' Functions and contexts of progressives in spoken English and 'school' English. In A. Renouf & A. Kehoe, eds., *The Changing Face of Corpus Linguistics: Papers from the 24th International Conference on English Language Research on Computerised Corpora (ICAME 24).* Amsterdam: Rodopi, pp. 231–242.

Römer, U., O'Donnell, M. B. & Ellis, N. C. (2014). Second language learner knowledge of verb-argument constructions: effects of language transfer and typology. *The Modern Language Journal*, 98(4), 952–975.

Rose, K. R. (2005). On the effect of instruction in second language pragmatics. *System*, 33(3), 385–399.

Rose, K. R. & Ng, C. K. (2001). Inductive and deductive teaching of compliments and compliment responses. In K. R. Rose & G. Kasper, eds., *Pragmatics in Language Teaching.* Cambridge: Cambridge University Press, pp. 145–170.

Ross, A. (2018). The pragmatics of requesting in the Canadian workplace: a comparative investigation of requests presented in workplace ESL textbooks and oral discourse completion task responses. PhD thesis. Carleton University Ottawa, Ontario.

Ross, J. R. (1970). On declarative sentences. In R. A. Jacobs & P. S. Rosenbaum, eds., *Readings in English Transformational Grammar*. Waltham, MA: Ginn, pp. 222–277.

Ruiz de Mendoza, F. J. & Agustin, P. (2016). Cognitive pedagogical grammar and meaning construction in L2. In S. De Knop & G. Gilquin, eds., *Applied Construction Grammar*. Berlin: Mouton de Gruyter, pp. 151–184.

Ruiz de Mendoza, F. J. & Baicchi, A. (2007). Illocutionary constructions: cognitive motivation and linguistic realisation. In I. Kecskes & L. Horn, eds., *Explorations in Pragmatics: Linguistic, Cognitive, and Intercultural Aspects*. Berlin: Mouton de Gruyter, pp. 95–128.

Ruiz de Mendoza, F. J. & Galera Masegosa, A. (2014). *Cognitive Modelling*. Amsterdam: John Benjamins.

Rutherford, W. E. (1987). *Second Language Grammar: Learning and Teaching*. London: Longman.

Ruytenbeek, N. (2017). The comprehension of indirect requests: previous work and future directions. In I. Depraetere & R. Salkie, eds., *Semantics and Pragmatics: Drawing a Line*. Amsterdam: Springer, pp. 293–322.

Ruytenbeek, N., Ostashchenko, E. & Kissine, M. (2017). Indirect request processing, sentence types and illocutionary forces. *Journal of Pragmatics*, 119, 46–62.

Sadock, J. M. (1974). *Toward a Linguistic Theory of Speech Acts*. London: Academic Press.

Schauer, G. (2009). *Interlanguage Pragmatics Development: The Study Abroad Context*. London: Continuum.

Schegloff, E. A. (1979). Identification and recognition in telephone conversation openings. *Psathas*, 1979, 23–78.

Schegloff, E. A. (2007). *Sequence Organisation in Interaction: A Primer in Conversation Analysis I*. Cambridge: Cambridge University Press.

Schmidt, R. W. (1990). The role of consciousness in second language learning. *Applied Linguistics*, 11(2), 129–158.

Searle, J. R. (1969). *Speech Acts. An Essay in the Philosophy of Language*. Cambridge: Cambridge University Press.

Searle, J. R. (1975). Indirect speech acts. In P. Cole & J. L. Morgan, eds., *Syntax and Semantics*. Vol. 3. New York: Academic Press, pp. 59–82.

Searle, J. R. (1976). A classification of illocutionary acts. *Language in Society*, 5(1), 1–23.

Searle, J. R. (1979). *Expression and Meaning*. Cambridge: Cambridge University Press.

Sercu, L. (2002). Implementing intercultural foreign language education. Belgian, Danish and British teachers' professional self-concepts and teaching practices. *Evaluation and Research in Education*, 16(3), 150–165.

Shaffer, D. E. (2004). Teaching particles with image schemas. *The Internet TEFL Journal*, 51, 1–16.

Sharwood Smith, M. (1981). Consciousness-raising and the second language learner. *Applied Linguistics*, 2(2), 159–68.

Shimizu, T., Fukasawa, E. & Yonekura, S. (2007). Introductions and practices of speech acts in oral communication 1 textbooks: from a viewpoint of interlanguage pragmatics. *Sophia Linguistica: Working Papers in Linguistics*, 55, 143–163.
Soozandehfar, S. M. A. & Sahragard, R. (2011). A textbook evaluation of speech acts and language functions in Top-Notch series. *Theory and Practice in Language Studies*, 1(12), 1831–1838.
Spada, N. & Tomita, Y. (2010). Interactions between type of instruction and type of language feature: a meta-analysis. *Language Learning*, 60, 263–308.
Spencer-Oatey, H. (1996). Reconsidering power and distance. *Journal of Pragmatics*, 26, 1–24.
Sperber, D. & D. Wilson. (1995). *Relevance, Communication and Cognition*, 2nd ed. Oxford: Basil Blackwell.
Stefanowitsch, A. (2003). A construction-based approach to indirect speech acts. In K. U. Panther & L. Thornburg, eds., *Metonymy and Pragmatic Inferencing*. Amsterdam: John Benjamins, pp. 105–126.
Sung, M. & Yang, H. K. (2016). Effects of construction-centred instruction on Korean students' learning of English transitive resultative constructions. In S. De Knop & G. Gilquin, eds., *Applied Construction Grammar*. Berlin: Mouton de Gruyter, pp. 89–114.
Taguchi, N. (2011). Teaching pragmatics: trends and issues. *Annual Review of Applied Linguistics*, 31, 289–310.
Taguchi, N. (2015). Instructed pragmatics at a glance: where instructional studies were, are and should be going. *Language Teaching*, 48(1), 1–50.
Takahashi, S. (2001). The role of input enhancement in developing pragmatic competence. In K. R. Rose & G. Kasper, eds., *Pragmatics in Language Teaching*. Cambridge: Cambridge University Press, pp. 171–199.
Takahashi, S. (2005). Pragmalinguistic awareness: is it related to motivation and proficiency? *Applied Linguistics*, 26, 90–120.
Takahashi, S. (2012). *A Cognitive Linguistic Analysis of the English Imperative. With Special Reference to Japanese Imperatives*. Amsterdam: John Benjamins.
Talmy, L. (1988). Force dynamics in language and cognition. *Cognitive Science*, 12, 49–100.
Tan, K. H. & Farashaiyan, A. (2016). Challenges in teaching interlanguage pragmatics at private EFL institutes in Iran. *Pertanika Journal of Social Sciences and Humanities*, 24(3): 45–54.
Tateyama, Y. (2001). Explicit and implicit teaching of pragmatics routines: Japanese 'sumimasen'. In K. R. Rose & G. Kasper, eds., *Pragmatics in Language Teaching*. Cambridge: Cambridge University Press, pp. 200–222.
Tateyama, Y., Kasper, G., Mui, L., Tay, H. M. & Thananart, O. (1997). Explicit and implicit teaching of pragmatic routines. In L. Bouton, ed., *Pragmatics and Language Learning*, 8. Urbana-Champaign, IL: University of Illinois, pp. 163–177.
Tatsuki, D. H. & Houck, N. R. (2010). *Pragmatics: Teaching Speech Acts*. Alexandria, VA: TESOL.

Taylor, J. R. (2008). Some pedagogical implications of cognitive linguistics. In S. De Knop & T. De Rycker, eds., *Cognitive Approaches to Pedagogical Grammar*. Berlin: Mouton de Gruyter, pp. 37–67.

Tello Rueda, Y. (2016). Developing pragmatic competence in a foreign language. *Colombian Applied Linguistics Journal*, 8, 169–182.

Thibault, P. J. & Van Leuween, T. (1996). Grammar, society and the speech act: renewing the connections. *Journal of Pragmatics*, 25, 561–585.

Tomlinson, B. (2013). Introduction: applied linguistics and materials development. In B. Tomlinson, ed., *Applied Linguistics and Materials Development*. London: Bloomsbury, pp. 1–8.

Tomlinson, B., Dat, B., Masuhara, H. & Rubdy, R. (2001). ELT courses for adults. *English Language Teaching Journal*, 55(1), 80–101.

Ton Nu, A. T. (2018). How EFL textbooks accommodate pragmatics: an investigation into a newly published textbook series for Vietnamese upper-secondary school students. *English Australia Journal*, 33(2), 37–43.

Tromp, J., Hagoort, P. & Meyer, A. S. (2016). Pupillometry reveals increased pupil size during indirect request comprehension. *Quarterly Journal of Experimental Psychology*, 69(6), 1093–1108.

Trosborg, J. (1995). *Interlanguage Pragmatics. Requests, Complaints and Apologies*. Berlin: Mouton de Gruyter.

Trott, S. (2016). The interpretation of indirect speech acts. Available at https://seantrott.com/2016/12/10/the-interpretation-of-indirect-requests/.

Tsui, A. B. M. (1994). *English Conversation*. Oxford: Oxford University Press.

Tyler, A. (2012). *Cognitive Linguistics and Second Language Learning: Theoretical Basics and Experimental Evidence*. London: Routledge.

Tyler, A. & Evans, V. (2004). Applying cognitive linguistics to pedagogical grammar: the case of over. In M. Achard & S. Niemeier, eds., *Cognitive Linguistics, Second Language Acquisition, and Foreign Language Teaching*. Mouton de Gruyter, pp. 257–281.

Tyler, A., Mueller, C. & Ho, V. (2011). Applying cognitive linguistics to learning the semantics of English to, for, and at: an experimental investigation. *Vigo International Journal of Applied Linguistics*, 8, 181–205.

Ulum, O. G. (2015). Pragmatic elements in EFL course books. *Western Anatolia Journal of Educational Science*, 1, 93–106.

Usó-Juan, E. (2008). The presentation and practice of the communicative act of requesting in textbooks: focusing on modifiers. In E. Alcón & M. P. Safont Jordà, eds., *Intercultural Language Use and Language Learning*. Dordrecht: Springer, pp. 223–243.

Valdman, A. (2003). The acquisition of sociostylistic and sociopragmatic variation by instructed second language learners: the elaboration of pedagogical norms. In S. Sieloff Magnan, ed., *Issues in Language Program Direction*. Boston, MA: Heinle, pp. 57–78.

Valenzuela, J. & Rojo, A. M. (2008). What can language learners tell about constructions? In S. De Knop & T. De Rycker, eds., *Cognitive Approaches to Pedagogical Grammar*. Berlin: Mouton de Gruyter, pp. 197–230.

Van Ackeren, M.J., Casasanto, D., Bekkering, H., Hagoort, P. & Rueschemeyer, S-A. (2012). Pragmatics in action: indirect requests engage theory of mind areas and the cortical motor network. *Journal of Cognitive Neuroscience*, 24(11), 2237–2247.
Vassilaki, E. (2017). Cognitive motivation in the linguistic realisation of requests in Modern Greek. In A. Athanasiadou, ed., *Studies in Figurative Thought and Language*. Amsterdam: John Benjamins, pp. 105–124.
Vellenga, H. (2004). Learning pragmatics from ESL & EFL textbooks: how likely? *The Electronic Journal for English as a Second Language*, 8(2), 1–18.
Verschueren, J. (1985). *What People Say They Do with Words. Prolegomena to an Empirical-Conceptual Approach to Linguistic Action*. Norwood, NJ: Ablex Publishing Corporation.
Wardhaugh, R. (1985). *How Conversation Works*. Cambridge, MA: Basil Blackwell.
Widdowson, H. (2003). *Defining Issues in English Language Teaching*. Oxford: Oxford University Press.
Wierzbicka, A. (1987). *English Speech Act Verbs. A Semantic Dictionary*. New York: Academic Press.
Wildner-Bassett, M. (1994). Intercultural pragmatics and proficiency: 'Polite Noises' for cultural awareness. *International Review of Applied Linguistics in Language Teaching*, 32(1), 3–17.
Wong, J. (2002). 'Applying' conversation analysis in applied linguistics: evaluating dialogue in English as a second language textbooks. *International Review of Applied Linguistics in Language Teaching*, 40, 37–60.
Wunderlich, D. (1980). Methodological remarks on speech act theory. In J. R. Seale, F. Kiefer & M. Bierwisch, eds., *Speech Act Theory and Pragmatics*. Dordrecht: Reidel Publishing Company, pp. 291–312.
Yasuda, S. (2010). Learning phrasal verbs through conceptual metaphors: a case of Japanese EFL learners. *TESOL Quarterly*, 44, 250–273.
Yin, Ch. P. & Kuo, F. Y. (2013). A study of how information system professionals comprehend indirect and direct speech acts in project communication. *IEEE Transactions on Professional Communication*, 56(3): 226–241.

Index

Abbas, L. H., 170, 177
Achard, 9
adjacency pair, 33, 71, 83
advice acts
  solicited, 152–154
  unsolicited, 152–155, 158
Agustin, P., 183, 208
Aijmer, K., 112
Alcón, E., 147, 162
Austin, J., 177, 218
authority. *See illocutionary ICM variables, knowledge power*

Bach, K., 28–29, 35
Baicchi, A., 61, 104, 209
Bardovi-Harlig, K., 82, 147, 185, 211
Bataller, R., 119
Blum-Kulka, S., 84, 104, 110, 119
Borer, B., 79
Bouton, L., 80, 84, 119
Brdar-Szabó, R., 61
Brown, P., 30, 104, 140, 155, 168, 174

Carstens, A., 169
Castro, P., 85
Cenoz, J., 84
Chomsky, N., 20, 232
Clark, H. H., 35
codification, 16, 27, 28, 29, 35, 56
cognitive linguistics, 3, 8, 11, 39, 62, 208, 228
cognitive operations, 37, 81, 111
  (multiple source)-in-target metonymy, 54, 71
  conceptual metonymy. *See metonymic operation*
  force dynamics, 71, 120, 187, 190
cognitive pedagogical grammar, 87, 88, 183, 196
  directive speech acts, of, 87, 209, 218
cognitive-constructional approaches, 35, 111
conceptual metaphor, 89

conditions of satisfaction, theory of, 24
  preparatory condition, 25, 26
confianza, 168, 181, 210, 213
construct-i-con, 62
construction, 8, 62
constructional accounts of illocution, 61
contrastive approach. *See cross-cultural approach*
convention, 17
  of language, 26
  of usage, 26
conventionalisation, 27, 29, 35, 64, 110
  degree of, 27
conversational approaches, 32–34, 36, 82, 112
conversational presumption, 28
co-operation, principle of, 24
Coulson, S., 36, 46
cross-cultural approach, 72, 84, 85
cross-cultural studies of illocution.
  See cross-cultural approach
cross-linguistic approach, 72, 84
Crystal, D., 173

De Knop, 9, 208
De Rycker, T., 208
Del Campo, N., 61, 91, 104, 111
Derwing, T., 79
Diepenbroek, L. G., 79
Dik, S. C., 4, 23, 60, 61, 233
direct access approaches, 29, 36
directives, 69, 73, 75, *See also* speech acts, directive
  advice acts, 70, 73, 83, 152, 159
  beggings, 70, 73, 81, 120
  negotiable, 173
  non-negotiable, 173
  orders, 53, 57, 69, 73
  requests, 53, 61, 73, 81, 104
  suggestions, 69, 73, 83, 136
  threats, 57
  warnings, 70, 73, 81, 169, 191

246

directives, know-how of
  advice acts, 159–168
  beggings, 130–136
  orders, 96–102
  requests, 110–120
  suggestions, 143–151
  warnings, 177–182
directives, know-what of
  advice acts, 152–160
  beggings, 123–129
  orders, 90–96
  requests, 103–110
  suggestions, 137–143
  warnings, 170–176
directness, 110, 136
Dirven, R., 183

EFL textbooks, 69–87, 119, 120, 143, 168, 177, 184
  qualitative treatment, 71, 72, 77–87
  quantitative representation, 71, 73–77
Ervin-Tripp, S., 36
expert power. See illocutionary ICM variables, knowledge power
explicit approach, 86
explicit instruction, 10, 60, 79, 83, 183, 209
explicit performative, 17
explicitness, 32, 44, 54, 63, 65, 119, 199, 200

face, 30, 133, 174, 214
  face-threatening acts, 155, 168, 186, 193, 202, 209, 214
force schema, 89
  advice acts, 152
  beggings, 120–123, 188
  compulsion, 89, 187
  iterative, 120
  orders, 89
  removal of restraint, 103
  requests, 102–103
  suggestions, 137, 189
  warnings, 169
Fraser, B., 136, 139
Fukushima, S., 104

Geis, M., 25, 28, 32, 35
general principles of cooperative conversation.
  See cooperation, principle of
Gerrig, R., 36
Gibbs, R. W., 36, 49
Givon, T., 59
Goldberg, A. E., 62

Halliday, M. A. K., 20–23, 25, 27, 35
Harnish, R. M., 28–29, 35
Hartford, B. S., 147

Haverkate, H., 140, 155
Havertake, H., 138
Hayakawa, S. L., 123
Hernández Flores, N., 168
Hinkel, E., 136, 145, 156, 157, 165
Holme, R., 209
Holmes, J., 139
House, J., 84, 104, 110, 119, 142
Huddleston, R., 50

IFIDs. *See* illocutionary force indicating devices
illocutionary construction, 4, 60–68, 69,
  See also directives, Know-How of
  base construction, 8, 63, 71, 81, 87, 88
  family of constructions, 66
  fluid illocutionary construction, 63, 196, 200
  inventory of base constructions for requests, 66
  realisation procedure, 8, 59, 63, 71, 77, 81, 87, 88
  request construction, 61
illocutionary conversors, 23, 60
illocutionary force
  direct, 35
  indirect, 23, 28
  literal, 19, 23, 26
  secondary. *See* illocutionary force, indirect
illocutionary force indicating devices, 60
illocutionary ICM, 7, 50–60, 69, 77, 88, 111
  directive, 87, *See also* directives, Know-What of
  ontology, 50–52, 78
  requesting ICM, ontology, 51
  requesting ICM, structure, 59
  structure, 50, 59–60, 78
illocutionary ICM attributes, 51–52, 71, 77, 88
  addressee's willingness, 51
  agent, 51
  agent's capability, 51
  beneficiary, 51
  cost–benefit, 51
  interactional attributes, 71, 78
  mitigation, 51
  optionality, 51, 53
  politeness, 51, 56, 78, 84
  possession of the requested object, 51
  scalar, 58
  speaker's need, 51
  speaker's willingness, 51
  transactional attributes, 71, 77
illocutionary ICM variables, 59–60, 71, 77, 88
  formality, 59, 78
  institutional power, 158, 164, 175

illocutionary ICM variables (*cont.*)
   knowledge authority. *See* illocutionary ICM variables, knowledge power
   knowledge power, 157
   physical power, 175
   social distance, 59, 78
   social power, 59, 78, 175
illocutionary idealised cognitive model.
   See illocutionary ICM
illocutionary metonymy, 111
illocutionary scenario, 49, 52, 53, 56
   after component, 49, 54
   before component, 49, 53, 56
   core component, 49, 52, 54
   inferential schemata, 49
   request scenario, 49, 52
illocutionary scenario of requesting. *See* illocutionary scenario, request scenario
image schema. *See* force schema
implicitness, 44
indirectness, 44, 46, 84, 119
inference, 27, 29, 32, 35, 37
inference trigger, 24
interlanguage pragmatics, 84
interpersonal rhetoric, 29

Jiang, X., 82, 143, 146
Johnson, M., 89, 103
Judd, E. L., 185

Kasper, G., 84, 104, 110, 119, 142
Kissine, M., 64
Koike, D., 145, 147, 185

Lakoff, G., 50
Leech, G., 21, 28, 29–32, 34, 35, 36, 91, 104, 108, 110, 117, 123, 133, 169
Levinson, S. C., 20, 28, 30, 33, 35, 104, 140, 155, 168, 174
linguistic underspecification, 45
literal force. *See* illocutionary force, literal
Literal Force Hypothesis, 17, 18–29, 32, 35, 60
   compatibility, 41
   weak version, 18, 34, 39–43, 145
Literal Force Hypothesis, revised version of. *See* Literal Force Hypothesis, weak version
Locher, M. A., 168
Lovett, C., 36, 46
Lucy, P., 35
Luomala, P., 85

Márquez-Reiter, R., 119
Martínez-Flor, A., 138, 143, 145, 162, 185
Matsumura, S., 136, 184

Mauri, C., 50
Merin, A., 157
metapragmatic declarative knowledge, 86–87
metapragmatic procedural knowledge, 87
metonymic operation, 54
Morgan, J. L., 26–27, 35

Neddar, B. A., 85
Nguyen, Th. Th., 80, 82, 119, 219

optionality, 32, 186
over-grammaticalisation, 22
over-pragmaticalisation, 27–34

Panther, K. U., 3, 21, 49, 53, 61, 231, 240, 243
pedagogical grammar, 10–11
Pérez-Hernández, L., 3, 4, 7, 22, 34, 50, 51, 53, 54, 56, 61, 70, 75, 79, 83, 89, 91, 104, 111, 123, 125, 126, 128, 133, 138, 158, 174, 184, 219
performative hypothesis, 19
politeness, 32, 38, 47, 119, 141, 156, 158, 174, 186, 187, 192, 194, 196, 198, 201, 204
Politeness Principle, 30, 47, 126, 133
   tact maxim, 30, 133
practice activities, 185
   comprehension tasks, 185
   consciousness-raising tasks, 185, 196, 211, 212
   discourse-completion tasks, 215
   knowledge-development tasks, 185, 191, 196, 200
   production-development tasks, 185, 205, 213, 216
   productive-skills tasks. *See* practice activities, production-development tasks
   repairing activities. *See practice activities, production-development tasks*
pragmalinguistics, 32, 34
pragmatic approach, 110
pragmatic scales
   scale of cost–benefit, 31
   scale of horizontal distance. *See* scale of social distance
   scale of indirectness, 31
   scale of optionality, 31
   scale of social distance, 47
   scale of vertical distance, 31
pragmaticalisation, 34
preference organisation, 33, 71
preferred/dispreferred response, 33, 71, 83
pre-sequence, 33, 83
Pullum, G. K., 50

rational power. See illocutionary ICM variables, knowledge power
relevance, principle of, 29

requests, 69
Richards, J. C., 139
Rintell, E. M., 141
Risselada, R., 40–41, 145
Ross, J. R., 19
Ruiz de Mendoza, F. J., 61, 89, 104, 183, 208
Ruytenbeek, N., 37, 64

Saad, Q. K., 170, 177
Sadock, J. M., 19
Safont, P., 147, 162
Sansò, A., 50
scenario approach. *See* illocutionary scenario
Schauer, G., 104
Schegloff, E. A., 35
Schmidt, R. W., 183
Searle, J. R., 23–26, 27, 35, 60, 104, 136, 153, 169, 177
short-circuiting implicature, 26
social variables. *See* illocutionary ICM variables
speech act construction. *See* illocutionary construction
speech act schemas, 28
speech acts, 17
 assertive, 74
 codified, 27
 commissive, 41
 conventional, 25, 26, 27, 34, 36, 39
 direct, 43–47
 directive, 1, 10, 53, 62, 69, 75, 80, 82, 86, 88, 98, 136
 explicit, 44, 48
 expressive, 74
 implicit, 44
 indirect, 19, 24, 25, 30, 35, 37, 39, 43–47
 ISA. *See* speech acts, indirect
 literal, 30, 35
 non-conventional, 13, 36, 37, 38, 39, 47, 232
 prototypical, 57, 195
 representative, 41
 social constructs, 21, 25, 35, 38
Spencer-Oatey, H., 157
Sperber, D., 28
standard pragmatics approach, 28–29, 36
standardised. *See* speech acts, conventional
Stefanowitsch, A., 61, 104
Suttle, L., 62
systemic-functional grammar, 20–23

Taguchi, N., 212
Takahashi, S., 50
Taylor, J. R., 183
Tello Rueda, Y., 86
Thornburg, L., 3, 21, 49, 53, 61, 231, 240, 243
Ton Nu, A. T., 79
Tyler, 9, 82, 226

Ulum, O. G., 74–75, 219

Valencia, J. F., 84
Vassilaki, E., 111
Vellenga, H., 2, 12, 70, 79, 82, 185, 211, 230, 245
Verschueren, J., 124, 136, 139, 157

Wardhaugh, R., 147
Wierzbicka, A., 123, 136, 139, 147, 152
Wilson, D., 28
Wunderlich, D., 162